ENTERING ARCHITECTURAL PRACTICE

//////////////////////////////

I0881583

Entering Architectural Practice is a practical and honest guide for architecture students, entering the world of architectural practice.

There is often a disconnection between what you are taught in architecture school and the actual practice of architecture in the workplace. As both a practising architect and architecture school tutor, the author has first-hand experience of this disconnection and so helps students bridge this divide between academia and practice.

Focused on providing industry insight, dispelling myths, and above all providing a combination of reality and hope to students of architecture entering the workplace, the book is beautifully and richly illustrated, providing a compelling visual story alongside the invaluable information it imparts.

Serious but enjoyable, thoroughly researched but highly approachable, this book is simply essential reading for every individual about to embark on a career in practice.

James Tait is an Architect, Author and Educator. James has led a range of high-profile projects at some of the best architectural practices in the UK. He is also author of *The Architecture Concept Book*; a contributing writer to the *Architects' Journal*; and a Studio Tutor at the Mackintosh School of Architecture, The Glasgow School of Art.

ENTERING ARCHITECTURAL PRACTICE

JAMES TAIT

Routledge
Taylor & Francis Group
LONDON AND NEW YORK

First published 2021
by Routledge
2 Park Square, Milton Park, Abingdon, Oxon OX14 4RN

and by Routledge
52 Vanderbilt Avenue, New York, NY 10017

Routledge is an imprint of the Taylor & Francis Group,
an informa business

British Library Cataloguing-in-Publication Data
A catalogue record for this book is available from the British Library

Library of Congress Cataloging-in-Publication Data
Names: Tait, James (Architect) author.
Title: Entering architectural practice / James Tait.
Description: Abingdon, Oxon ; New York : Routledge, 2021. | Includes bibliographical references and index.
Identifiers: LCCN 2020031969 (print) | LCCN 2020031970 (ebook) | ISBN 9780367365134 (hardback) | ISBN 9780367365141 (paperback) | ISBN 9780429346569 (ebook)
Subjects: LCSH: Architecture–Vocational guidance.
Classification: LCC NA1995 .T35 2021 (print) | LCC NA1995 (ebook) | DDC 720.23–dc23
LC record available at https://lccn.loc.gov/2020031969
LC ebook record available at https://lccn.loc.gov/2020031970

ISBN: 978-0-367-36513-4 (hbk)
ISBN: 978-0-367-36514-1 (pbk)
ISBN: 978-0-429-34656-9 (ebk)

Designed and typeset by Alex Lazarou

CONTENTS

0.1 BETWEEN ANTICIPATION AND REALITY

“WHAT YOU DO HERE IS NOTHING compared to designing *real* buildings in practice”, uttered my studio tutor toward the end of a design tutorial.

↓

This comment lingered and grew. I wanted to know about the realities of being a *real* architect in practice – a question which evaded me throughout architecture school. Obfuscated in professional practice lectures referencing dry contracts, text-heavy codes of conduct, and outmoded methods of working. Hinted at from pieced-together anecdotes or overheard conversations from those in practice we engaged with once, maybe twice a week. Or collected from the few skewed representations of architects in popular culture. I had no experience of it. No reference point that wasn't too dry, anecdotal, or idealised.

I did have *Content*. Rem Koolhaas' 2004 book displayed architecture intertwined with the technological limitations, global politics, office dynamics, local regulations, economic concerns, popular culture, societal shifts, and environmental conditions that influence it. *Content* also hinted at the production of architecture. *How* it was practised. Tensions with clients, long working hours, wasted projects, calamitous events, rampant egos, and bureaucratic interventions. This was invaluable insight, but I was sure it wouldn't be *my* reality. This was 1% architecture, atypical projects by globetrotting architects at the peak of mid-2000s 'starchitecture'. What about the 99%, everyday buildings by everyday architects? Me? Koolhaas had left the door ajar but I still couldn't open it.

My final year thesis project won multiple student awards.

WHEN BUILDINGS ATTACK

In *Content*, an irreverent glimpse of the realities of architectural practice. Hyperbuilding, Thailand. 2004. OMA and &&&.

Content (Taschen Publishers), 2004 by OMA/AMO, Rem Koolhaas and &&& / Simon Brown and Jon Link (graphic designers).

THE UNTESTED IDEAL

Loved by architects. Hated by the local community.

Time and Tide for Seaweed (RIBA Silver Medal Winner). Arisaig, Scotland. 2008. J. Tait.

THE ADAPTED REALITY

Accepted by the local community. Hated by architects.

Time and Tide for Seaweed (Master's project). Arisaig, Scotland. 2008. J. Tait.

The earlier question still growing in my head, I used this project as a case study. To make it a *real* building. I tailored the design to local planning and building regulations, canvassed the opinion of community groups and residents, took advice from governmental bodies on regulatory and technical concerns, and researched the exact environmental conditions of the site. The project changed so much to meet these influences that two distinct projects emerged. One accepted by the architectural profession – expressive, expansive, progressive, new, if naïve. One accepted by wider society – constrained, reduced, unambitious, traditional, if realistic. This was a rude awakening. How could the untested ideal be so different from the adapted reality? Was it inevitable that my architectural dreams would become sullied and neutered at the first sight of reality?

The fear of career compromise and the discrepancy between conceived dreams and built reality are reflective of a gap between the anticipation of the role and the reality of it. These issues are not limited to architecture. Ask any teacher, lawyer, engineer, or doctor and they will raise the same general problems. The gap between the anticipation of what the profession will be and the reality of what it entails, is, however, more acute in architecture.

It is primarily accentuated by a discrepancy of process. Architecture schools "highlight the importance of pure design"[1]. A framework of methods and approaches to establish an appreciation of, and an ability to create, space, form, and order as well as site responsive and environmentally aware designs centred around human functions and needs. These fundamentals of architectural design are typically cultivated in isolation from the aspects that influence professional practice. This embryonic period is crucial to the development of any emerging architect, allowing these fundamentals to blossom and form without external disruption. This incubation period is also the primary source of discrepancy between "anticipation and reality"[2] upon entering the profession. In practice, design is impure. Space, form, and order are sullied and tested by multiple forces. Site responsiveness and ecological awareness can be marginalised and limited too. Even human functions and needs risk being compromised. The design process often feels more like a battle than the sequential journey it did in architecture school.

Further, there is a discrepancy between the anticipation of the role and the experience of it. Are we true designers and coordinators of buildings, "creative artists and leaders"[3]? Or those who follow orders from others, who never meet clients, who spend most of their time producing basic drawings and mundane documents? The reality is that we are both. The concept of the architect as an omnipotent polymath was jettisoned long ago. Most architects are specialist monomaths who produce the information that allows buildings to be constructed.

THE ARCHITECT AS POLYMATH
Michelangelo: artist, designer, sculptor, poet, architect.

THE ARCHITECT AS MONOMATH

Producers of the information for buildings.

This book is for those who will become, or already are, engaged in the production of architecture. To introduce you to the truths of the profession. To prepare you for the long hours, limited opportunities for creativity, economic precariousness, confrontations, and often the sheer mundanity and repetition that will likely await you. Simultaneously, to introduce you to the moments of joy and wonder that the practice of architecture affords. The sense of self progression, the perpetual discovery, the culture and camaraderie, the impact of your work on society, and the quiet satisfaction of doing good work for its own sake.

This is an initiation. To limit the surprise or shock. To guide you in dealing with the realities of practice with confidence and acuity. A response to the self-interested and amnestic complaints of the majority of employers[4] that they are often burdened with "woefully unprepared recent graduates",[5] and to the idealist academic architects removed from practice only "committed to pushing the boundaries of current thinking".[6] Both practice and theory exist in fragile symbiosis. Boundaries of thinking can still be pushed without succumbing to the myopia which can often characterise professional practice. The successful realisation of architecture depends on the successful practice of it.

15 CLERKENWELL CLOSE
TYPICAL DETAILS

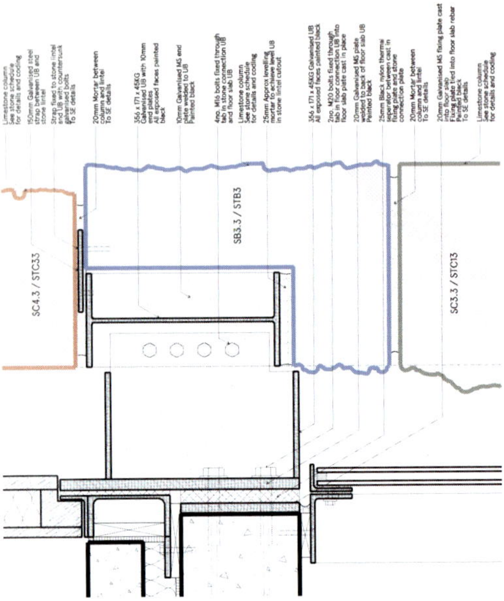

STONE CONNECTION DETAIL
SECTION THROUGH SLAB AND COLUMN

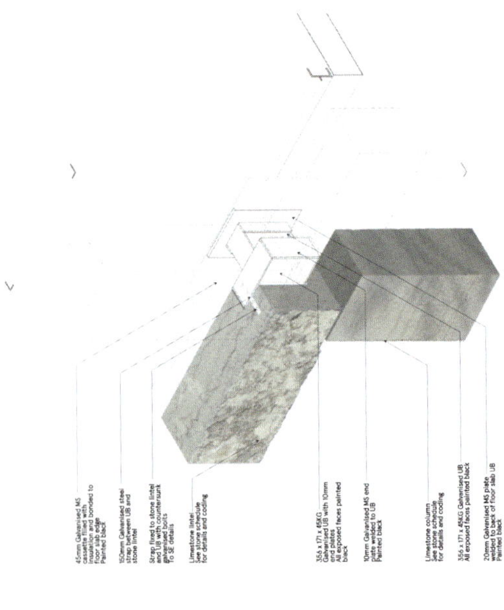

STONE CONNECTION DETAIL
ISOMETRIC CUTAWAY

THE SUCCESSFUL REALISATION OF ARCHITECTURAL AMBITION

"You might have fantastic ambitions for a building – its appearance, its finish, its story. But one of the things you learn very quickly is that unless those drawings and that information is tightly bound into a legal contract ... you won't get that result."[7]

15 Clerkenwell Close, London. 2017. Groupwork + Amin Taha.

The primary interest of this book is in the quality of the built environment. How the practice of architecture, and the complex negotiations and compromises it entails, impacts the quality of it. To propose ways in which young graduates and professionals can realise their own architectural ambitions in practice, but more importantly improve the buildings, spaces, and interventions that have the capacity to enrich human existence. This is both an indictment and a celebration. An exposé and a blueprint. By exposing what needs to be changed in the practice of architecture to improve the consequences of it.

Notes

1 Cuff, D., 1991. *Architecture: The Story of Practice*. Cambridge, MA: The MIT Press. p. 45.

2 Hughes, E.C., 1958. *Men and Their Work*. Glencoe, IL: The Free Press. p. 126.

3 Jenkins, F., 1961. *Architect and Patron*. Oxford: Oxford University Press. p. 231.

4 Marrs, C., 2015. *Report: Universities not equipping architecture students for real world*. [Online] Available at: https://www.architectsjournal.co.uk/home/report-universities-not-equipping-architecture-students-for-real-world/8677848.article [Accessed 17 March 2020].

5 Cuff, *Architecture*, p. 262.

6 Ibid., p. 262.

7 Taha, A., 2019. Q&A: Amin Taha. *Icon Magazine*, 196(October), pp. 104–110.

0.2 THE REALITY

6.45am. MY HEAD FILLS UP with all the things I tried to empty it with around four hours ago. It's still dark.

↓

I stumble to the shower and let it heat up, staring back at two bloodshot eyes, the right one reminding me of its myokmia – a pulsing twitch caused by not enough sleep and too much caffeine. Precious calm. I finally decide to disturb myself and let the shower fade to silence. *"Daddy!"... "Morning girls"*. I shuffle to the end of the hall, pick up my two daughters carrying them down the stairs with false energy. Cereal, toast, juice. Not for me. Coffee, not for them. My head already a swirl of things to do. I stare out of the window as my wife enters the room. *"Morning"* as we pass, and I kiss the two miniature heads in front of me. I make my first promise of the day. *"See you tonight girls!"*

The door closes and my phone opens. 8.05am. I check my emails and decide whether to take the subway or walk. The darkening sky makes the decision for me. I fidget for my ticket, a fine-line marker falls to the floor followed by a paperclip – the remnants of a previous day's work. Ticket now between my pursed lips, I pick up the pen and rush through the barrier. Steel screeches on steel. I spill down the stairs and pour into the carriage, its doors closing behind me. I squeeze in and zone out. My empty mind punctuated only by the rhythm of jolts and judders. Steel on steel again. I squeeze out and up the stairs, not quite as quickly as I came down them and pass the coffee place. There's a queue and I don't have time.

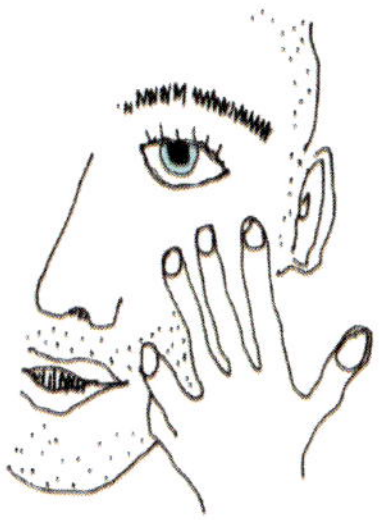

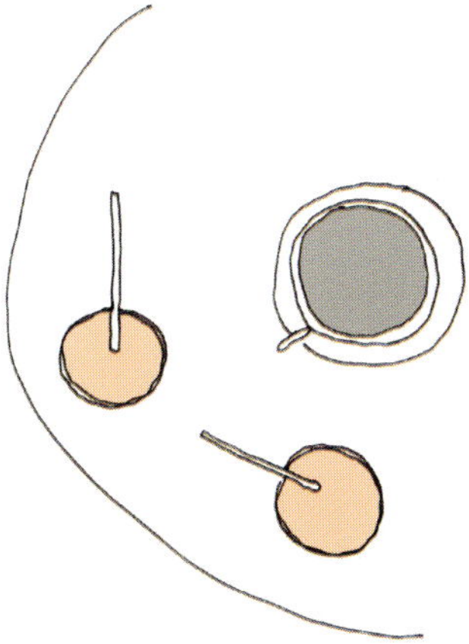

Through the office door, squeeze past the bikes, past reception, mutter a "morning", and ascend the stairs with purpose to my desk. It's 1.5 metres wide by 0.75 metres deep and next to the window. Two black screens stutter to life. I survey my desk, an organised mess of paperclips, various pens (thick black pen for sketching ideas; two thin black pens for sketching details; thick red pen for reviewing drawings; and a discarded empty biro for scribbling notes); a 24-foot measuring tape; folded A1 plots, single A3 drawings, stacked A4 documents – some stained, some dog-eared, some freshly printed; an empty white coffee cup on a glazed tile; a brushed aluminium door handle; a scale ruler with some forgotten supplier's name emblazoned across it; and a shelf on which sits a white site helmet and lightly stained fluorescent yellow vest. I'm looking for my notebook and realise it is underneath the coat I placed on my desk. The notebook contains my 'list' – a folded sheet of paper of things I need to get done this week.

I open my emails. There is one from Alex at the building site (Project 965 – an education building currently being constructed) requesting I call him. He sent it two hours ago – site always starts before us. Another from a client about the small residential project (1261) asking if we have any ideas yet for the house. He's copied in my director this time too. I mentally shift this up the list of priorities – we've neglected this project for too long now because there is little fee. I type my second promise of the day … *"Morning. We are working on this at present. We will get something through to you by close of business today."* When is close of business anyway? 5pm? 8pm? Tomorrow morning? Suitably vague.

TO DO

Urgent (Today)

Relatively Urgent (By End of Week)

Later

Project 965

1 - ~~Complete outstanding RFIs~~
- Update window schedule to accommodate glazing specification change
- Check balustrade manufacturers' shop drawings
- Re-issue updated specification to QS
- Arrange for stone panel samples

3 - ~~Do site observations report~~

Project 1113

- Update flat plans to reflect VE updates
- Check and incorporate acoustics consultants' details.

2 - ~~Check draft bill of quantities~~
- Complete final co-ordination exercise with Structural and Services Engineers
- Update foundation detail
- Prepare stage 2 building warrant information
- Elevation updates (check with Felicia)

Project 1261

- Check conservation area guidelines and planning policy
- Arrange pre-application meeting
- Gather together interiors precedents board
- Model initial sketch options
- Speak to visuals about doing a rendered image.

General

- Do Timesheets
- Speak to JD re: holiday

The office is now starting to fill up. New girl shuffles in, quiet and flustered. I say good morning, think I get a reply. Joe, the document controller, comes in like a cloud in trousers after his two-hour commute. His canvas rucksack thuds on the desk opposite me. Still others arrive, the office now a chorus of start-up chimes, rustling coats and clicking bags, underpinned by the background hum of grinding coffee beans. Soon everyone is working. 9.20am. The office manager, all brusque bluster, reminds us we have an office meeting in less than two hours. Each Wednesday the office gathers downstairs in the meeting room to briefly discuss the progress of each project. I need to rehearse my story – Project 965 is *"progressing well on-site to completion, but we still have the usual mountain of RFIs – it's controllable."* Project 1113 (a large 140-unit residential block) is *"going to tender next week, we are finalising the coordination exercise and making some final adjustments to the plans and elevations."* Project 1261 … *"I'm aiming to get something to the client today."* Third promise of the day. I scribble this down and recite it.

Now *I* start wanting things. I email Teddy, the architectural visualiser to ask if he can do a 3D visual for project 1261. I'll get the 3D model finished before the office meeting, giving the visualiser the rest of the day to do it. Next, I email the Structural Engineer and the Services Engineer on project 1113 inviting them to a coordination meeting. I check Felicia knows what she is doing with the elevation updates for the same project. She will have them complete by the end of the week. Teddy has emailed me to say he can get the images rendered – provided I send him the model by lunchtime. I tell him I'll get it to him in the next hour or so. Promise number four.

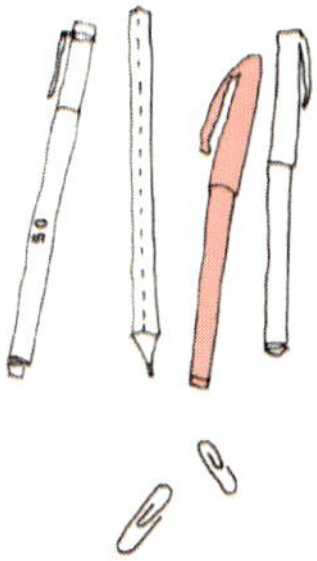

The office is in full gear now. Footsteps continue back and forth – some rushed, some relaxed. The printer clatters out sheet after sheet and a cloud of tones and voices hangs in the air – some animated, some laconic, some monosyllabic. The background hum of the coffee grinder now intermittent. The office chatter wakens from an early morning silence. An indistinguishable babble of architectural critique, amateur political commentary, football results, film reviews, recipe sharing, second-hand weather predictions, and weekend plans.

10.55am. I head for the team meeting. It goes as expected. On return to my desk I notice two notes on my screen. The second one tightens my chest. If Bryce (the project manager on project 965) calls, it is never for some light chit-chat, or a pat on the back. There is always something wrong. He has emailed too, demanding I visit site today and whether I have called Alex. I call Alex. There's an issue with the brickwork. They've started setting it out and none of the sizes or dimensions reflect those noted on our drawings. *"I'm down tomorrow for the progress meeting, can we sort it then?"*, he tells me no. They have a squad of brick-workers about to walk off the site. They need an answer now. *"I'll be down in an hour"*. Site is a half-hour walk from the office. I hang up, take a deep breath, find the project drawing file, and try to figure out what has happened before I go down.

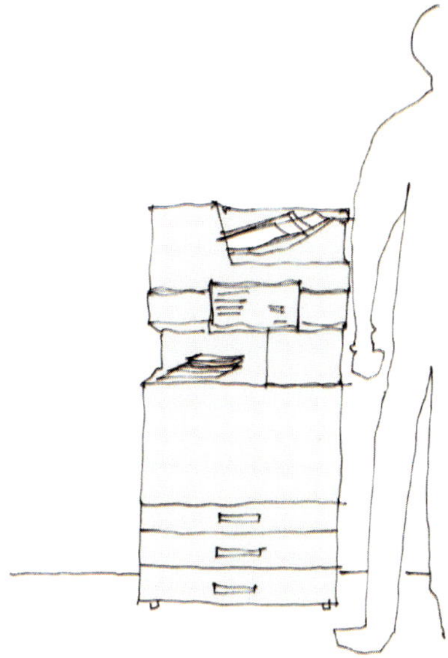

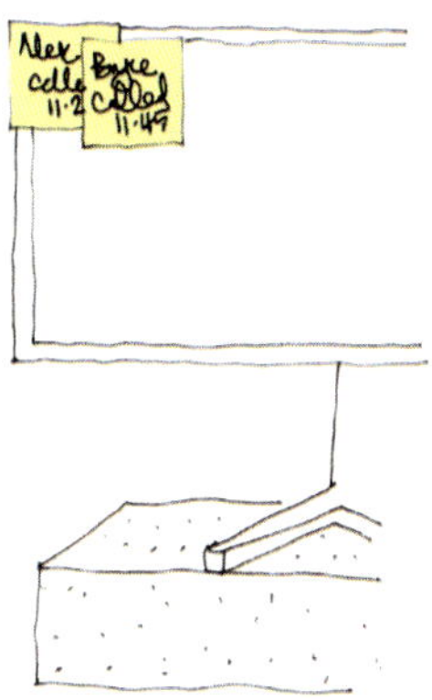

I barely pick the drawings up and the phone rings again. Bryce. He asks if I have spoken with Alex. I tell him yes. He asks what the issue is. I tell him it's to do with the brickwork. He asks what specifically. I tell him I'm not sure yet but that whatever it is we, the project team, will sort it out. Fifth promise of the day. He says we need to. It is 12.30pm. I grab my site gear on the shelf and a pair of mud-caked black steel-toe-capped boots, stuffing them in my bag as I take out the pair of sneakers packed in the hope of a lunchtime gym session. Climbing the site scaffold will have to do. I gather my thoughts in the half-hour walk to site. I get a creeping feeling this is going to be a long day.

Can't say I don't enjoy this though. The pressure of finding a solution, quickly and efficiently – removed from the relative calm of the office. I can hear the site office before I see it. Cliff is banging the table as I walk in. Three pairs of eyes fix on me. Alex the site agent; Sean the contractor's quantity surveyor; and Cliff the contracts manager, Alex's boss. I only see him when there is a problem. I take a deep breath, then a seat.

I see a copy of our elevation drawings scrawled over in red pen; and another pile of paper similarly scrawled. My heart sinks and stomach tightens. I recognise it as our specification document from the font. Contractors don't use Helvetica. *"We got to the bottom of the issue"* boasts Sean. *"Your drawings are dimensioned to standard brick sizes but your specification is for reclaimed brick, which is the older imperial size. They're 10mm bigger per brick in height and width ... so every opening size and brick level on your drawings is wrong."* This is a disaster. We pushed for this brick for sustainability reasons and its weathered aesthetic properties. I check the evidence. They are right, and I acknowledge that monosyllabically. We discuss two options. We agree on the second, meaning updating the drawings to show the correct dimensions for the bricks now sitting on palettes on-site. The one-million brick question – *"When?"*. I say a week. They say no – they need it now. They needed it three months ago. I say we'll review internally once I am back in the office. Never discuss internal resourcing externally. I am reminded that this is a 'design team' problem. It's our fault, and I have been tasked to fix it, even though I only took this project on from a previous incumbent now departed two months ago. No excuses, no qualifications. I assure them we'll sort it. Sixth promise of the day. I leave the site office and wander onto the construction site.

There are two stages of any project where most architects get their moments of joy. Firstly, when an idea begins to formulate into a design, ideas materialising onto paper. Secondly, when those paper intentions come off the page and into reality. I'm having one of those moments now as I look up through a nascent atrium. Steel columns vanish to infinity, intersected by planes of raw concrete, illuminated by dust-flecked shafts of light. It is the first time that I can begin to see the project come together. I pause for a moment to appreciate it. This makes it all worthwhile – being involved in 'good work'.

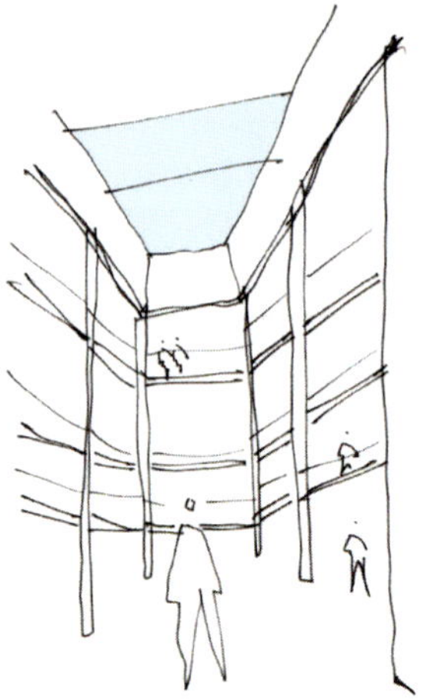

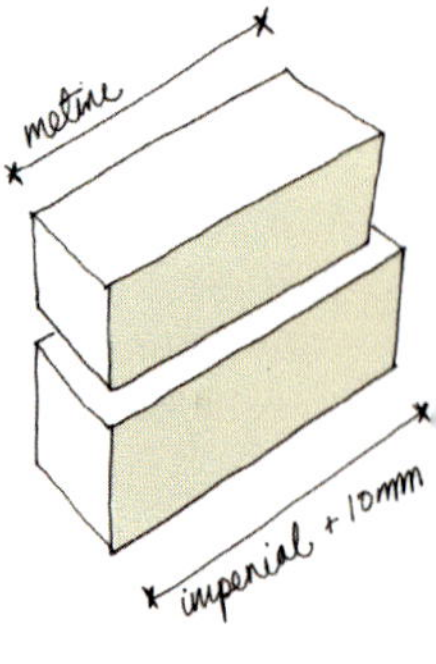
metric
imperial + 10mm

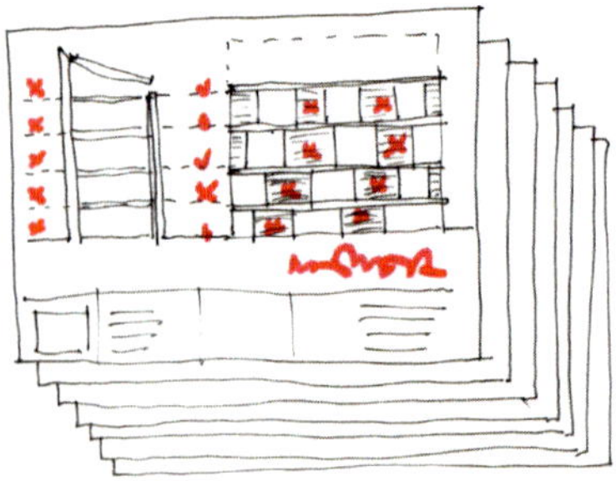

I call my director, Kamal, and leave a message. 3pm. I'm back in the office and nothing on my list has been scored out. It *is* going to be a long day. I remember I didn't finish the model for the visualiser and call in the hope he can still turn it around today if I get it to him in 15 minutes. He says no. I then start to take stock of the brick problem, marking the extent of changes required. I check my emails and notice the brick issue has now been formalised in writing by the contractor.

The office is quiet, the clatter of the printer has tailed off and the footsteps less frequent. All I can hear is the clicks of multiple mice and the intermittent pressing of keys. I'm now zoned in and have been for a while, only realising it's 5pm when the non-architectural staff start to leave. My phone lights up. *"Hi Kamal"* ... he's at the airport. I explain the issue and that I'll need some help with this. He says we'll talk in the morning when he gets back.

6.15pm. The model is taking longer than expected. Most things in architecture take longer than expected, especially if you want to do them right. I notice Felicia has her coat on and is approaching me with a stack of drawings. She apologises for having to leave 'early' – she has something else on. I remind her she has already worked 45 minutes past her contracted hours. Most architects feel guilty about leaving before 7pm – they shouldn't. I shouldn't. *"Thanks, we'll go through them tomorrow."*

I save my file and an error message pops up ... the network is down again. News starts to ripple through the dozen architects, architectural assistants, and technicians left in the office. Sighs, exclamations, slumps. We break. Some pull out magazines, pontificating on the latest published buildings, others eat what should be dinner but is probably lunch, two or three take the opportunity for a cigarette, and some take the opportunity to leave early. This lull lasts 15 minutes. *"Servers back!"*. I open the 3D model and reflect on it. Panning and zooming, I get the other moment of joy as the first realisations of the initial sketches that have lain dormant on my desk for two weeks start to appear. I'm surprised, it looks good, really good.

Two portents of potentially disappointed children. The cleaners have arrived; and there is no light left in the sky except the streetlamp outside my window. I drag the file I'm working on to a memory stick, need to take it home to finish it. It's the only way I'll keep my promise to the two little faces I left at 8am this morning *and* get done what I need to. 25 minutes until they go to bed. I'll run home. 22 minutes if I go at a good pace. Running against an imaginary clock of broken promises, my phone is bleeping. I check it as I stop at the traffic lights *"where r we meeting tomorrow?"*, from a friend. Forgot about that, I'll have to cancel our lunch. Tomorrow is not going to work. I need to meet Kamal, then talk things through with Felicia, as well as sort out this image and the brick issue. Not to mention all the other things left on my list. *"Sorry ... snowed under ... sort something next week ..."*

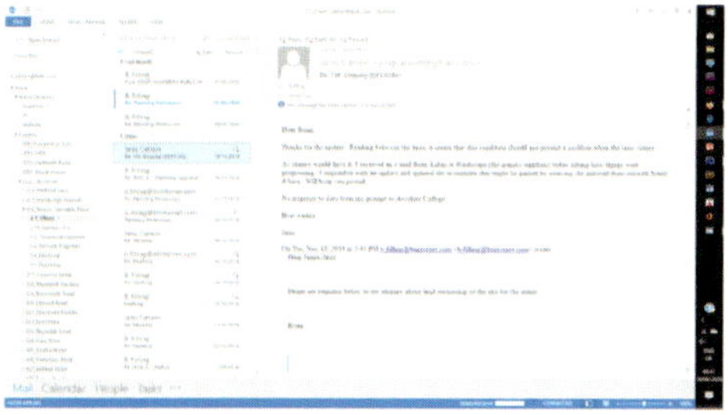

7.55pm. Sprint upstairs to two little tired faces. I read them a book and kiss them on the head. I go down to make dinner and open the fridge. I ask myself a familiar question – wine or work? I choose work. We have dinner. My wife tells me about her day and asks about mine ... *"the usual, manic ..."*. It's 9pm. I get my laptop and finish off the model then set up the render (the screen tells me it will take 53 minutes) and sit down again, switching on the TV ... I wake up in a ball and realise the TV is off and someone has put a thin blanket over me. I shuffle to the laptop screen, now the room's primary source of light, and check the image. It looks OK, not as good as I thought it was earlier. I admit it's time for bed and save it onto the same memory stick. 2.05am. I crawl up to bed and try to empty my head with all the things it will fill up with four and a half hours from now.

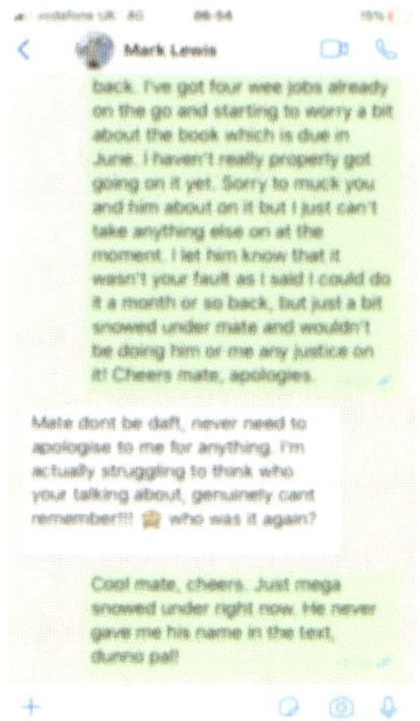
Mark Lewis

back. I've got four wee jobs already on the go and starting to worry a bit about the book which is due in June. I haven't really properly got going on it yet. Sorry to muck you and him about on it but I just can't take anything else on at the moment. I let him know that it wasn't your fault as I said I could do it a month or so back, but just a bit snowed under mate and wouldn't be doing him or me any justice on it! Cheers mate, apologies

Mate dont be daft, never need to apologise to me for anything. I'm actually struggling to think who your talking about, genuinely cant remember!!! 🙈 who was it again?

Cool mate, cheers. Just mega snowed under right now. He never gave me his name in the text, dunno pal!

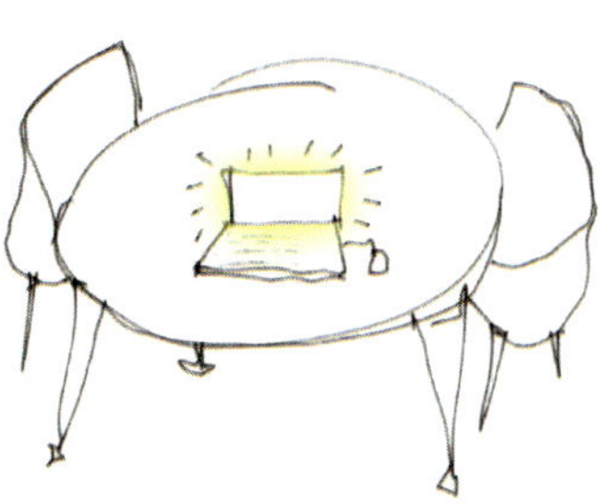

0.3 THE WRITER

IF YOU ARE NOT AN ARCHITECT, the previous chapter will give you a taste of what an architect really does. What a typical day designing *real* buildings entails. To give you a window to the realities of architectural practice. If you are already an architect, you will know it's the truth. The truth of a varied and chequered career in architectural practice so far.

↓

I've worked for multinational corporations of over one thousand employees; and collaborated with a loose collective of three people led by a friend. I've squeezed into leaking, draughty, makeshift offices in discarded shipping containers; and spread out in glass-walled corporate meeting rooms. I've designed palatial residences surrounded by lush grounds – no expense spared; and laboured over tiny house extensions squeezed into suburban gardens – every expense spared. I've drawn up plans for essential facilities helping poverty-stricken communities; and facilitated vanity projects for ruthless property developers. I've spent thousands of hours tabulating spreadsheets and churning out repeat details; and moments of discovery and joy sketching, discussing, modelling, and thinking. I've been involved in projects from the sandy beaches of the Middle East, to the rocky shores of rural Scotland. I've made embellishments to the streets of some of Europe's most exclusive addresses; and made interventions in the derelict high streets of its most deprived regions. I've basked in the afterglow of successful projects; and distanced myself from those I'm embarrassed by. I've seen the excesses of the boom years of unfettered construction; and the desperation of the bust years of stagnant growth. I've had some disagreements and conflicts along the way; and experienced many instances of successful cooperation and consensus. I've been inspired and motivated by the talent, knowledge, and drive of those around me; and sometimes been dismayed and frustrated by them too. I've won multiple international design awards in one year; then been laid off and out of work the next. I've been so disillusioned and fatigued with my work that I've considered leaving the profession for something else, anything else; and been so obsessed and committed to my work that I've forgotten to eat, sleep, or even think about anything else.

I've experienced the highs and lows that each one of the estimated 2–3 million architects globally will identify with. A career in architecture is unique and varied, it offers some incredibly rewarding experiences and opportunities as well as challenges and dilemmas. I hope to prepare you for them. To guide you towards dealing with them with confidence and acuity.

1.0
THE TRANSITION: THE CHOICE IS YOURS

'PRACTICE' IS DEFINED AS THE "customary performance of professional activities",[1] as "action rather than thought or ideas",[2] or used to describe "what actually happens, as opposed to what you think will happen".[3]

↓

These three definitions of practice – custom, action, and discrepancy – accurately describe the practice of architecture. An ancient custom whose norms and standards have been shaped over millennia. A realm where thought and exploration are often usurped by necessity and action. And where original intentions evolve and adapt daily, to the multiple forces of reality acting upon them.

The core of architecture school is the design studio,[4] led by 'units' of architect-teachers who set hypothetical themes for students to explore, developing architectural design projects with an emphasis on artistry rather than practicality.[5] Methods of working are often frantic and intense, culminating in an endurance test called a 'charrette'[6] of extended working through the night. The work is then exhibited and presented in a "trial by jury",[7] where more experienced tutors and professionals critique the work on display. A system with an emphasis on competition, intensity, and individual expression.[8] If you recognise these aspects of architecture school, as I do, you recognise the hallmarks of an 'Atelier'-type education modelled on the École des Beaux-Arts in Paris at the turn of the 20th century.[9] The main objective of the Beaux-Arts system is in the "development of the artists' personality".[10]

THE ENVIRONMENT YOU ARE USED TO

Crowded desks in the Yale Art and Architecture Building, littered with food, models, draft designs, and instruments of architectural design.

Photographer: Sage Ross.

EXPLORATION IN EDUCATION

RIBA Silver Medal Winning Project, 2019.

Surface Tension: Blueprints for Observing Contamination in the Sydney Harbour Estuary. 2019. Victoria King.

Practice instead is primarily concerned with the collective *production* of architecture. Personal development is a side-effect. In architecture school design problems are often static and unambiguous,[11] in practice they are fluid and equivocal. In architecture school design projects are largely executed individually. In practice they are always carried out collectively with other architects and professionals. In architecture school projects are ideal – unsullied by the budgets, banality, and bureaucracy that can define them in practice. There are alternative systems of architectural education where the focus is less on nurturing the 'genius' of the individual,[12] and where real-life scenarios, live-builds, and more practical concerns are part of the curriculum,[13] but they remain alternative not convention.

Yet, architectural education should not mimic practice, as some would have it.[14] It should retain the ability to challenge and question the "hegemonic paradigm"[15] of practice. Concurrently, it is possible to learn the realities of practice on the job,[16] within the current post-university frameworks that are already established. What is critical, is that you are fully lucid and responsive to the discrepancy between the means and ends of the environment you are leaving, and the one you are entering.

This discrepancy is linked to the eternal distinction between thought and action. To manifest his or her thoughts the thinker must acquire practical skills;[17] the idea for a painting, is not a painting.[18] Unlike the artist, however, the architect does not directly manifest what he or she conceives. The distinction becomes sharper and more acute in architecture, when this task is outsourced to multiple different hands, many of whom are completely disconnected from the original thought process. Architectural practice then is the intermediary process between thought and action.

Converting thought into action presents a series of "dialectical dualities"[19] – between the instantaneity of thought against the protracted process of multiple actions; the needs of the individual and the collective; the competing aims of those creating architecture and those realising it; and the challenges of designing in a commercial context. It is within this commercial context that architectural practice needs to prove its worth to society.[20] Architecture expands beyond its basic role of providing shelter and space for human activity to become a productive construct. Evident in the fact that architecture is legally defined as a facet of the "creative economy".[21] [22] Through their creativity, or sometimes lack of it, architects add economic value.

In this commercial context architects have never cornered their market,[23] like other professionals. If an unregistered person assumed the role of a medical professional and performed surgery, a crime would have been committed.[24] When an unregistered person assumes the role of an architect and designs a building, it is entirely normal. It is estimated that around 75% of all buildings erected today[25] are done so without an architect's involvement. The built environment in its totality is a "landscape almost entirely uninformed by the critical agendas or ideas of the discipline".[26] The involvement of an architect can even seem as an impediment to the "blunt expediency"[27] of many buildings required to satisfy purely commercial needs. In many spheres of building today, design is dead.[28]

CREATIVE ECONOMY

Architects are often restricted to finding "new expression to existing problems".[29]

The Shed, New York. 2019. Diller Scofidio + Renfro / Rockwell Group. Photographer: Ajay Suresh.

DESIGN IS DEAD

"A landscape almost entirely uninformed by the critical agendas or ideas of the discipline of architecture."

Urban sprawl. Las Vegas, Nevada. USA.
Photographer: Lynn Betts.

Architects have always been required to sell their dispensable wares,[30] forcing them into an "ever-renewed bargain with society".[31] The practice of architecture becomes focused on the need to maintain and obtain commissions, each characterised by compromise and the acceptance of multiple realities. This societal bargain requires an organisational framework – architectural practice. Whether simple or complex, small or large, each practice is arranged to find a route to the optimum conditions for producing architecture. An arrangement typically formed around, then evolving according to, the commissions an office is engaged in designing. A framework created in pursuit of the elegant ideal, that "excellence produces beautiful deeds".[32]

Of course, this *is* the ideal. The optimistic diagram scribbled out by the founding partners of your current or future place of employment. Not the reality of this diagram, in practice. The framework of architectural practice is tested on a daily basis by "much more instrumental demands, in which action is determined in reaction to the short term priorities of clients and the market".[33] This imbalanced relationship can take its toll, not only on the ideal office structure and the employees that constitute it, but on what is created and produced too.

It is within this context that you embark on your journey from student to architect. Architecture school teaches you what architecture is. The first years in practice – how to produce the information required to create it. The progression to fully fledged architect – how to gain responsibility through the command and coordination of what architecture is and how it is produced. The sequential process of gaining knowledge, experience, and authority. The almost endless list of challenges and complexities that you will face on this journey – not encountered yet in architecture school – can appear overwhelming at the beginning of your professional career. You now need to understand these vicissitudes, to engage and grapple with them, even control them. This is for the sake of the integrity and quality of the built environment, of the architecture that you will be involved in creating, and the realisation of your own architectural ambition. Will your career be defined by "the daily realities of drudgery, impotence and insecurity"?[34] Or will it be defined by discovery, personal growth, and autonomy while working in close cooperation to further a common cause?[35] The choice is yours.

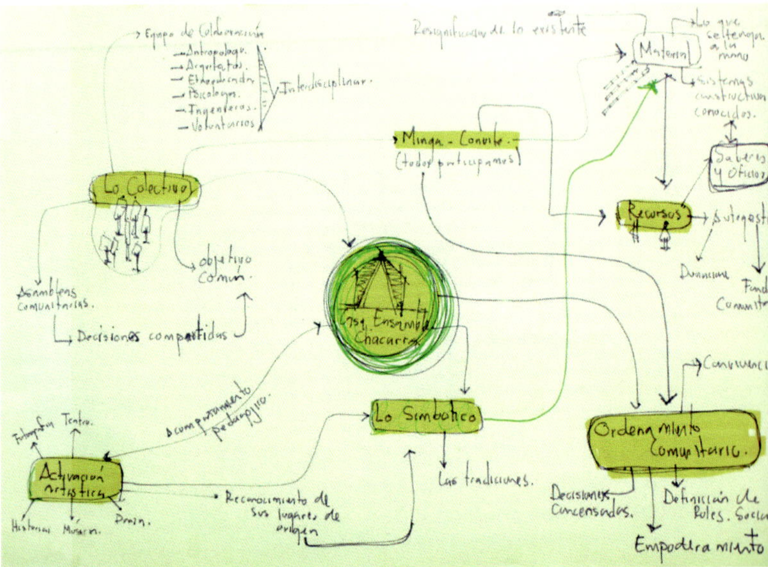

UNDERSTANDING THE COMPLEXITIES

The Collective / Artistic Activation / Community Engagement / Resources / Symbiosis.

Casa Ensamble chacarrá, Pereira, Colombia. 2015. Ruta 4 Arquitectura.

Notes

1 Cuff, D., 1991. *Architecture: The Story of Practice*. Cambridge, MA: The MIT Press. p. 4.

2 Anon., n.d. Meaning of practice in English. [Online]. Available at: https://dictionary.cambridge.org/dictionary/english/practice [Accessed 3 April 2020].

3 Ibid.

4 Cuff, *Architecture*, p. 28.

5 Saint, A., 1983. *The Image of an Architect*. New Haven, CT: Yale University. p. 80.

6 Lewis, R., 2013. *Architect? A Candid Guide to the Profession*. Cambridge, MA: MIT. p. 73.

7 Warren, L., 1916. The Atelier System. *American Magazine of Art*, 7(3), pp. 112–114.

8 Ibid.

9 Ibid.

10 Cuff, *Architecture*, p. 31.

11 Ibid., p. 90.

12 Griffiths, S., 2019. *"It is emphatically not the job of architecture education to mimic practice"*. [Online] Available at: https://www.dezeen.com/2019/08/02/architecture-education-opinion/ [Accessed 16 April 2020].

13 Ibid.

14 Marrs, C., 2015. *Report: Universities not equipping architecture students for real world*. [Online] Available at: https://www.architectsjournal.co.uk/home/report-universities-not-equipping-architecture-students-for-real-world/8677848.article [Accessed 17 March 2020].

15 Ravenscroft, T., 2019. "*Architecture education is in crisis and detached from the profession, says Schumacher.*" [Online] Available at: https://www.dezeen.com/2019/07/09/patrik-schumacher-crisis-architectural-education/ [Accessed 16 April 2020].

16 Metzstein, I., 2008. Gillespie, Kidd & Coia: 1956–1987 Learning, Building, Teaching. *Paperspace*, pp. 74–87.

17 Arendt, H. 1998. *The Human Condition* (2nd ed.). Chicago: University of Chicago Press. p. 90.

18 Sennett, R., 2009. *The Craftsman*. London: Penguin Books. p. 65.

19 Cuff, *Architecture*, p. 11.

20 Arendt, *The Human Condition*, p. 92.
21 Olcayto, R., 2013. *How did the architecture profession get lumped in with the 'creative industries'?*. [Online] Available at: https://www.architectsjournal.co.uk/opinion/how-did-the-architecture-profession-get-lumped-in-with-the-creative-industries/8644811.article [Accessed 17 April 2020].
22 Florida, R., 2016. *Comparing the Creative Economies of Canada, the U.K., and the U.S.* [Online] Available at: https://www.citylab.com/life/2016/04/how-do-the-worlds-top-creative-economies-stack-up/479022/ [Accessed 17 April 2020].
23 Saint, *The Image of an Architect*, p.160.
24 General Medical Council, n.d. *Unregistered medical practice*. [Online] Available at: https://www.gmc-uk.org/registration-and-licensing/the-medical-register/a-guide-to-the-medical-register/unregistered-medical-practice [Accessed 17 April 2020].
25 Smith, L., 2016. *Builders of 'banal' modern homes urged to hire architects to design their housing*. [Online] Available at: https://www.independent.co.uk/arts-entertainment/architecture/builders-of-banal-modern-homes-urged-to-hire-architects-to-design-their-housing-a6926656.html [Accessed 06 April 2020].
26 Dunham-Jones, E., 2000. Seventy-Five Percent. *Harvard Design Magazine*. [Online] September. [Cited: 6 April 2020.] www.harvarddesignmagazine.org/issues/12/seventy-five-percent.
27 Kwinter, S. 2001. Generica. In: R. Koolhaas, et al. *Mutations*. 1st. Barcelona: Actar. p. 526.
28 Ibid., p. 526.
29 Diller, L., 2019. Q&A: Liz Diller. Icon Magazine, 190(April), pp. 106–116.
30 Saint, *The Image of an Architect*, p. 160.
31 Spector, T., 2001. *The Ethical Architect: The Dilemma of Contemporary Practice*. New York: Princeton Architectural Press, p. 12.
32 Arendt, *The Human Condition*, p. 13.
33 Awan, N., Schneider, T., & Till, J., 2012. *Spatial Agency: Other Ways of Doing Architecture*. Abingdon: Routledge. pp. 28–29.
34 Saint, *The Image of an Architect*, pp. 60–61.
35 Gropius, W., 1965. *The New Architecture and the Bauhaus*. Paperback ed. Cambridge, MA: MIT. p. 51.

TECHNICAL ADVICE NOTE

01

TERMINOLOGY

project team

the multiple stakeholders, sponsors, clients, advisers, designers, cost consultants, project managers, contractors, suppliers, and construction workers involved in any one project.

spec.

a specification - a set of written instructions prepared by designers to describe the materials, products, methods, and standards required in any project. They are usually cross referenced with drawings, models, schedules and bills of quantities.

tender

where invited or selected parties submit prices for the supply of material and services. The architects' information is crucial in defining the outcome of this process - describing the scale, complexity, layout, detail, materials and standards required in any project. Tenders are usually provided based on the bill of quantities, specification, and drawings.

V.E.

'value engineering' proposes ways in which a design can be streamlined, made more efficient, or employ more economical materials in order to represent the best value for money for the client. Sometimes, it can also be used as a smokescreen to cheapen the building and maximise profit.

design team

a group of organisations or individuals who prepare designs for a construction project. Including architects, landscape architects, structural and services engineers, interior designers and a myriad of consultants (ecologists, acousticians, lighting designers, energy assessors, fire engineers, inclusivity designers etc.)

setting out

The process of transferring architectural proposals and information into accurate locations, dimensions, and levels on-site.

R.F.I.

a 'request for information' is used in a project to formally request that gaps in information are filled in, or any uncertainties clarified in order for the construction works to proceed correctly and timeously.

bill of quantities

an itemised pricing document prepared by the Quantity Surveyor, itemising and pricing, the quality and quantity of material, works and standards of workmanship required for any construction project. Usually closely cross-referenced with the architects' drawings, specifications and schedules.

co-ordination

the act of a design team checking for and rectifying clashes or conflicts between their respective information - architectural, structural, services etc. Usually carried out in the form of 'workshops' at each stage of a project to resolve any inconsistencies before construction.

'shop' drawing

a detailed fabrication drawing - prepared by the contractor, their sub-contractors, or suppliers - based on design team information. They provide detail on how the components of a building will be fabricated, assembled, and installed on-site, such as steelwork, staircases or windows. The design team typically review these drawings prior to manufacture.

1.1

CHOOSING A PRACTICE

"WHAT IS A 'DESIGN-LED' Architect?!" I thought as I embarked on a career in architectural practice, looking through job adverts and practice websites.

↙

Why do so many architecture practices need to reveal they are led or oriented by design? Would you expect a medical practice to proclaim they were 'medicine-oriented' doctors? Lawyers to specifically state they were a 'justice-led' law firm? A restaurant to confirm it was run by 'cuisine-based' chefs? What are other architects doing if not designing?! I discovered many architects are instead 'client-focused' or 'commercially based' – turned so far toward blind service that designing architecture was a by-product of enabling it. Many architects were simply facilitators of buildings. Not all creators, as we had been led to believe at architecture school.

I also discovered many architects in practice were not like architecture students, or the architects I had encountered in education. They had different priorities, inculcated in a new practice-based ethos of service and delivery. Their natural habitat was usually larger commercial firms defined by a production-line system, producing standardised replicas requiring little thought or creative input along the way.[1]

Antithetical to this corporate image is the small 'atelier' or design studio dominated by one or two resolutely design-oriented leaders. These types of practices, most like the architecture school design studio, are usually also embedded in architectural education. Their habitats, less hierarchically structured than the corporate office, are typified by a more discursive and exploratory ethos.

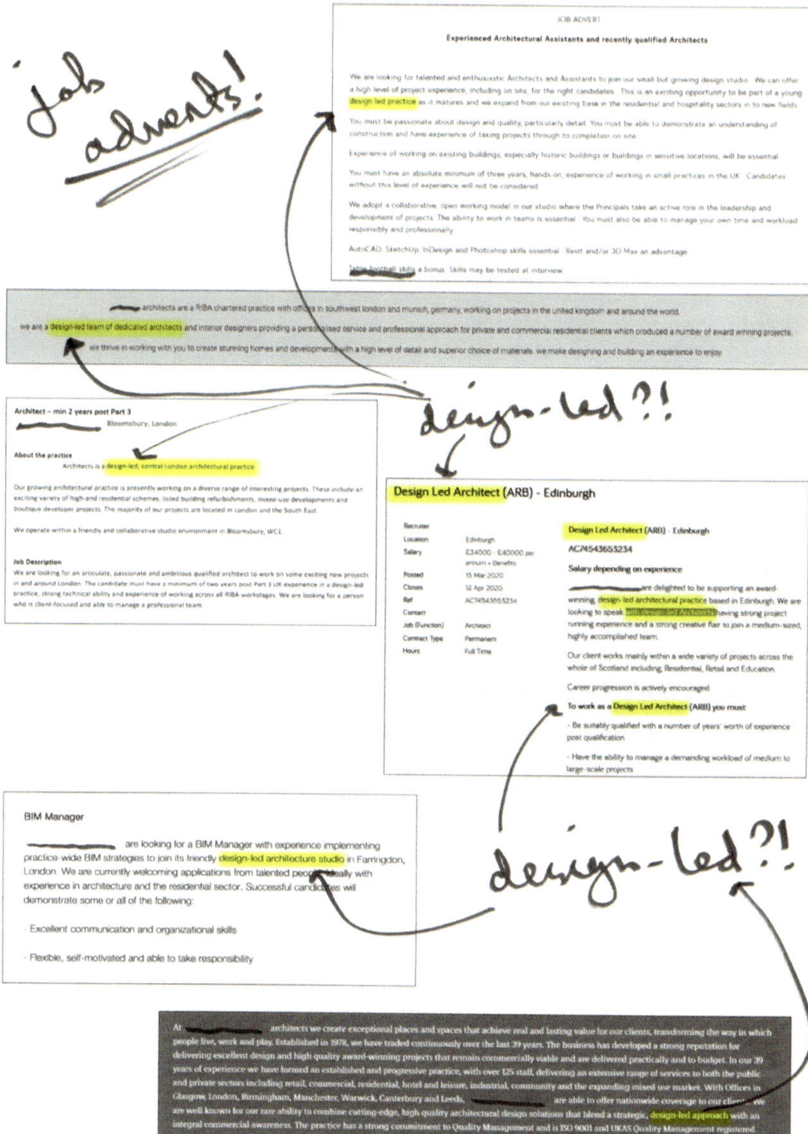

A 'DESIGN-LED' PRACTICE?!

Real job adverts for roles at 'design-led' practices in the UK.

SERVICE AND DELIVERY

A busy architect at Perkins + Will, Chicago.

Photographer: Jaysin Trevino.

A DESIGN STUDIO

Moreau Kusunoki, Paris.
Photographer: Moreau Kusunoki Architectes.

As Peter Zumthor describes: "They have to be willing to help me. They enjoy helping me. I listen to them. I ask them what do you think? They are not just 'pencils'."[2]

Architects are acutely aware of where they want to be on this spectrum of practice. An ex-colleague once experienced a mild panic attack at the prospect of teaching at architecture school directly following a client meeting in practice where wearing a suit, shirt, and tie was mandatory. Worried he would be exposed as a corporate enemy of the students, he concocted an elaborate plan to have a change of (less formal) clothes delivered to the architecture school by another colleague to then change Superman style in the restroom cubicles. Architects orchestrate their actions and image according to how they want to be perceived. There are many bands of this spectrum, and practices can easily maintain aspects of the corporation and of the design studio. Yet commercial success doesn't necessarily breed critical acclaim and vice versa. Some practices, a small and elite group, can even filter this spectrum into the white light of combined creativity and commerciality.

CREATIVITY AND COMMERCIALITY

Only three of the world's 100 largest architectural practices (in terms of fees earned) could justifiably argue to be included as one of the 'best' in terms of critical acclaim and awards – Foster+Partners, MVRDV and Bjarke Ingels Group.

Danish architect Bjarke Ingels at a press conference in front of his design of a mixed-use tower in Frankfurt am Main (June 2015).

Architects typically characterise offices first by size.[3] Size gives an indicator to the type of clients and therefore projects a practice can attract. Large corporations will rarely take on a private house renovation, just as a small practice will struggle to meet the demands of a city-wide masterplan. The larger office is more hierarchical, responding to increased volume and complexity of work and requiring an increasingly sophisticated system of delegation, division of labour, and chains of command. Smaller practices rarely need to divide themselves up in this manner. Size can give a good indicator to the uninitiated as to the nature of the practice – what you will be involved in producing, and how it will be produced.

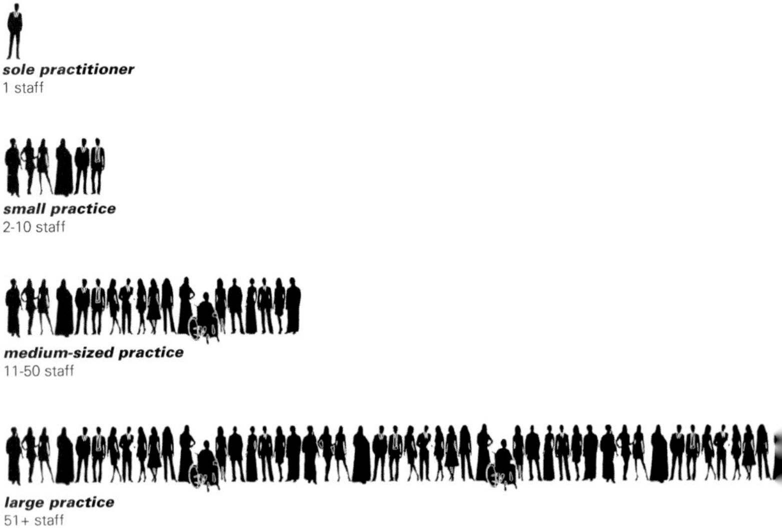

XS / S / M / L / XL

The spectrum of size: from the sole practitioner to the international conglomerate.

Before entering this new world, ask yourself: What is it you want from your experience in practice? Is your focus on gaining experience at the most critically acclaimed architecture practices? Are you focused on swift career progression and hands-on experience? Are you motivated by money, looking for the highest pay and best benefits? The answer may be all of these, but that would be optimistic, if not naïve. Think about what your *main* goal is first. I say this from the experience of working at two small practices, four medium-sized practices, and two large practices over the past 15 years or so.

My experience of small practice varies between one of swift career progression and close mentorship; to another of uninspiring projects and fractious relations. In large practice, an experience of inordinate responsibility working in close contact with company directors and clients; to another of being trapped in a hierarchical system doing laborious repeat tasks for little recognition beyond decent pay. Medium-sized practices can offer a variety between the extremes of large and small practices,[4] tending to be less hierarchical, yet able to gain and maintain a reasonable profile and quality of work. They can have their downsides too – often dominated by a culture of egos and cliques, less prevalent in the intimacy of small or the organisation of large practices, creating obstacles to career development. There is also the question of 'depth'.[5] You may have been given more responsibility and worked on a greater number of projects in a small practice, but if that responsibility was limited to simple projects of minimal complexity and little impact then this responsibility becomes Janus-faced. Conversely, you may experience project depth – complex high-impact projects, composed of complex relationships – in a large practice but only by second-hand observation.

Once you have passed the stage of initial courtship and engaged in a mutual exchange, the interview gives you a chance to assess the environment and the culture of an architecture practice. The working environment can provide clues to what your experience there will be. Where is the office located? In an arts hub, corporate office block, or shopfront? This is an indicator of how integrated within a community a practice is or what type of work it is set up to attract. Is it arranged like any other office[6] with rows

A TYPICAL SCENE

The main production space in practice with computers on desks arranged in rows.

Killa Design, Dubai.

of computers on desks? Or is the set-up more anarchic, and free, like a studio? Do all staff share the same space, or are they portioned off into separate teams and private offices? These aspects can give you clues as to how a practice produces architecture. There is also the secondary question of convenience and amenity – the quality of equipment provided, access to fresh air and daylight, lunch space, and social events. These physical aspects give clues to how a practice promotes the second aspect, its culture.[7]

STUDIO CULTURE

Bare concrete, models rest on suspended cable trays, and stools await impromptu chats.

6a Architects, London.

The 'culture' of a practice is less apparent, a complex organic set of codes requiring interpretation. Most practices develop an "internalised ethos"[8] of appropriate behaviour and standards. I have worked in offices where everything sent out (from an email to a working drawing) was checked and scrutinised; and others where nothing was. I have worked in offices that had strict guidelines on how each piece of information produced followed the same standards and processes; and others with only ad hoc and informal guidelines. I have worked in offices where bad language and loud music were omnipresent; and others where silence and obedience were demanded. Whether planned or unplanned, each practice has its own culture of appropriate behaviour and standards.

A good culture will foster the continuation of education and create a human-focused environment not solely based on output. If architecture schools have an obligation to develop you as a student, architecture practices have an obligation to develop you as an architect.[9] This is not always the case. Some see staff merely as "numbers to get the work done",[10] to be hired or let go as work increases or subsides. A good culture will retain the spirit of progression and discovery which you found in architecture school: fairly delegating tasks and responsibilities; providing an appropriate framework for freedom of expression; welcoming a 'bottom-up' approach to office discourse and engagement; and allowing for practice members to engage in relevant extraneous research activities. With education not merely to comply with regulatory standards, but as a fundamental mode of practice embedded in everything they do.

Further, "a well-crafted organisation will focus on whole human beings in time. It will encourage mentoring, and it will demand standards framed in language that anyone in the office might understand."[11] This type of practice would be driven by the concept of "sociable expertise",[12] underpinned by transparency of process and active mentorship, designed to stretch the capabilities of its constituent members towards collective excellence. This human-focused approach also recognises you first as a human being. A valued embodiment of a practice's culture and ethos, who can develop and grow with them.

One of the dichotomies for the ambitious architecture student however is none of this might matter. Working for a critically acclaimed practice involved in exciting projects you can be proud of may be your primary focus above anything else. I know I have endured poor working conditions and stunted professional development simply because I was involved in high-profile projects at practices who had a reputation for good work. This can be a powerful draw. Will that couple of years spent in a commercial practice hamper you when applying for the practice you really want to work for? Will they think you have 'sold out' before you have even begun?

However, you may be surprised by the benefits of working at practices initially dismissed. Frustrated by the 'second-rate' architecture he was involved in during his apprenticeship, Victorian architect Sir George Gilbert Scott realised he had learned a great deal about the "common routine of building" and was allowed a "good deal of time for reading and drawing on my own account", both of which he noted "might have been missed" in a better practice.[13] The decisions you make now can affect the rest of your career.

SOCIABLE EXPERTISE

The office canteen: a space for informal engagement.

Baumschlager Eberle Architekten, 2226 Lustenau.
Photographer: Eduard Hueber.

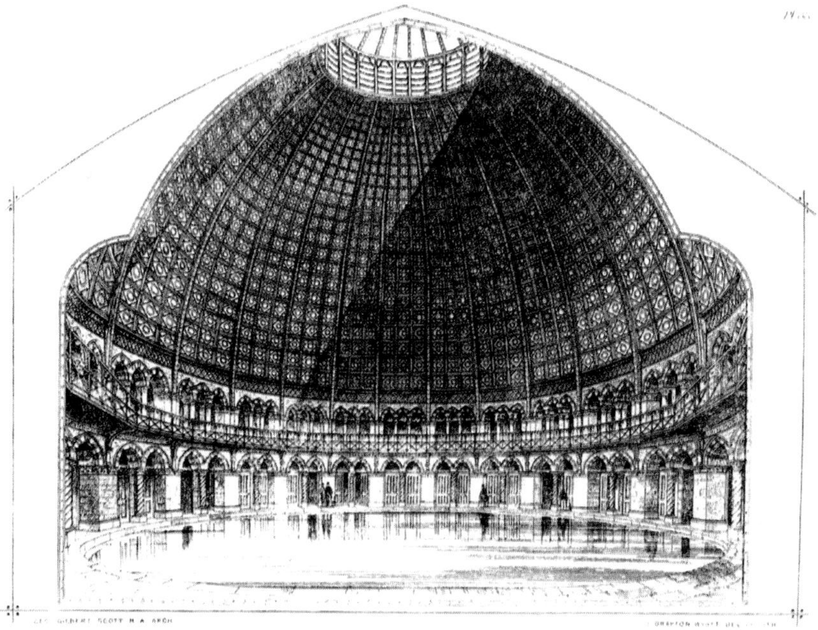

BRILL'S BATHS, BRIGHTON: INTERIOR OF SWIMMING BATH.

PUTTING YOUR EXPERIENCE TO USE

Panoramic view of Brill's swimming bath, Brighton.

Lithograph by J. Drayton Wyatt himself after Sir George Gilbert Scott.

Ask yourself what you want from your experience in practice. Prestige, experience, progression, money? Choose wisely. If you don't like the office environment or culture, your professional development is stagnating, or simply aren't excited by what you are designing – there will be future opportunities to rectify that. Your first practice will not be your last.[14] There are multiple trade-offs to be made before even entering practice; ensure your ambition is not one of them.

Notes

1 Boyle, B.M., 1977. Architectural practice in America, 1865–1965. In: *The Architect: Chapters in the History of the Profession*. New York: Oxford University Press. p.329.
2 Zumthor, P., 2008. Atmospheres, authorship and autonomy. *Paperspace*, pp. 48–51.
3 Cuff, D., 1991. *Architecture: The Story of Practice*. Cambridge, MA: The MIT Press. p. 45.
4 Ibid., p. 45.
5 Lewis, R., 2013. *Architect? A Candid Guide to the Profession*. Cambridge, MA: MIT. p. 174.
6 Cuff, *Architecture*, p. 253.
7 Ibid., p. 113.
8 Ibid., p. 159.
9 MacMillan, A., 2008. Gillespie, Kidd & Coia: 1956–1987 Learning, Building, Teaching. *Paperspace*, pp. 74–87.
10 Ibid.
11 Sennett, R., 2009. *The Craftsman*. London: Penguin Books. p. 249.
12 Ibid., p. 249.
13 Scott, G.G., 1879. *Personal and Professional Recollections by the Late Sir George Gilbert Scott*. London: Sampson Low, Marston, Searle & Rivington. pp. 55–56.
14 Cuff, *Architecture*, p. 164.

INTERVIEW A

↘ Fernanda Canales

Describe your studio. How is it organised?

My practice is based on the notion of a non-studio: I work from my home, at universities, libraries and, most importantly, at the site. That is where it is extremely important to test ideas and show the clients the issues that are impossible to communicate in a phone call or a meeting. It is precisely there where the importance of views, orientation and topography make sense.

Do you think architecture school prepares students for architecture practice?

Architecture schools prepare students to be frustrated architects – usually there is little connection to real problems and everyday matters. In the United States just 2% of new homes are designed by architects and in Mexico around 70% of houses are built informally, illegally, usually with no support of a specialist of any kind. We should no longer consider the main building process of a country as marginal. Rather we should change our definitions, laws, education programs, and the way architects engage with society. In that sense, often architecture schools are disconnected from the actual needs of cities and citizens.

Reading Rooms. Throughout Mexico. 2015. Fernanda Canales.

Photographer: Jaime Navarro.

Much of your work involves active participation with communities …

Architecture is frequently considered in an abstract way. It is hard to grasp its many complexities during the design process. Many important issues only arise during or after construction. The only way to anchor a building in a place is to engage deeply with the context and the users – to consider the users in a wider sense. Not only design according to the needs of the client and the people who will occupy the building, but neighbours and construction workers too. Community participation means understanding everyone involved or affected by the building. It is not about negotiating or convincing them but instead learning their customs, fears, and desires. Trying to make everyone part of the building.

Can you tell me about your design process?

Ideas don´t stop or begin with a specific project. Research informs and appears in different ways when you are developing a project. That is why I consider it so important to develop utopian proposals, to teach and do research or curatorial projects. Sometimes memories or references take a lead, or something you are doing in another project suddenly makes sense in another context. I consider projects to be a continuation of interests, and they take their specific shape not just because of the site, and the client´s brief, but because you carry dreams, experiences, and past projects with you. In that sense, I never consider a project a finished work, instead, I believe each project is just part of an ongoing process that sometimes develops in the shape of a book, other times in a syllabus or in a model done with no clear purpose.

Casa Bruma. Valle de Bravo, Mexico. 2017. Fernanda Canales + Claudia Rodríguez.

Photographer: Rafael Gamo.

Your work displays a strong connection with materials …

The material of each project is not something that can be decided independently from the shape and the structure of the building. It is never something that can be applied or changed. Material becomes the idea of the building itself – that decision is what defines the building in every sense. This connection with materials is because they are understood not as materials but as the structure of a building. The decision is made based on the soil, the topography, the weather, the program, budget, and especially the future maintenance of the building.

You often collaborate with other architects. Is collaboration a smooth process or a difficult one?

Collaboration is always difficult because it makes you change your plans and desires but it makes you learn from others. It is easier not to have to make any compromises but it is better to have ideas tested and put into play. I am not used to having much feedback since I work mainly alone, so collaborations force me to interact more and discuss ideas with someone else other than my own kids. Actually I believe children are the best critics for architecture. I always try to involve collaborations with people from other backgrounds, especially landscape designers, but the best collaborations are always with the clients, the future users of the spaces.

Casa Terreno. Valle de Bravo, Mexico. 2018. Fernanda Canales.

Photographer: Rafael Gamo.

You achieve extremely high consistency of quality regardless of budget, typology, location ...

I am used to working simultaneously on a low-income house that can fit entirely in the space of the kitchen or the closet of a large residential home for the weekends. The huge contrasts that exist in a country like Mexico, characterized by its social and economic inequalities, have forced me to design with the same attitude to luxury, regardless of program or budget. I always try to design according to the same price per square meter and with the same materials (concrete, wood, brick). Everyone should have a great view, natural light and ventilation, and sun entering their home in wonderful ways. My effort in providing a sense of luxury is placed in the most basic elements that are affordable to anyone. Sun, wind, and shade are not expensive.

Your projects are often located in extreme climatic conditions. How do you respond to these conditions?

Designing my own house completely made me change my understanding of climate conditions. Things that can be common for an architect, such as designing a parking space that is disconnected from the main house or cladding that can become too hot, too cold or too old due to weathering, are unthinkable if you are considering spending your life in that place. Working in places where you go from almost freezing to completely melting (having changes of almost 30° Celsius in one day) has made me reconsider everything I learned in school or have built before. My main concerns now are the rain and the sun. Making the most of those experiences instead of considering them as problems is the first change I made.

Portales Housing Development. Mexico City, Mexico. 2015. Fernanda Canales.

Photographer: Rafael Gamo.

What advice would you give to graduates entering architectural practice?

Never expect somebody to teach you. Don't understand education as something given to you by someone else, but rather something that is taken from anywhere and anyone. My most important education has come from books, from visiting buildings and measuring them with my body and slowly discovering their surroundings before approaching the building, and also from the construction workers and the experience on the building site. Architecture without the knowledge found in books would be for me just a daytime job.

Centro Cultural Elena Garro. Coyoacan, Mexico. 2013. Fernanda Canales + Arquitectura911sc.

Photographer: Sandra Pereznieto.

1.2 LABOUR, AUTHORSHIP, AND YOU

ONCE YOU ARE IN PRACTICE, no one really cares how good you were at architecture school.

↓

Your colleague just wants you to take your turn in the coffee rounds; your teammates working on the same project as you only want you to keep the BIM (Building Information Modelling) model or CAD (Computer-aided Design) files organised and clear; your job captain just wants you to deliver the required information accurately and timeously; your directors don't care unless they are boasting to their competitors they have snapped up all the 'good talent' this year. Not to mention the many external consultants and contractors you will collaborate with – they care even less. Your academic achievements validate your skill and ability, distinguishing you in a competitive environment. Once you find that job and are thrust into the realities of practice, they don't *really* matter anymore. Academic achievements "neither destroy nor ensure your future career".[1] This is indicative of the different role, and tasks, you will carry out in practice.

The core of architects' role in practice is 'work' – the production of drawings, images, models, sketches, specifications. Specialist teams of workers who produce them – architects, architectural assistants, modelmakers, students, draughtspersons – are organised according to the design process and agreed outputs at key stages. The core of architectural activity concerns the "specialisation of work",[2] different teams working in concert to a unified and identified goal.

TAKE OFF THE MEDAL

Academic achievements "neither destroy nor ensure your future career. Once you are out of architecture school, probably no one will ever again see or care about your grades as a student."[3]

ARCHITECTS AT 'WORK'

Drawing, modelling, typing, measuring, adapting, checking, thinking.

There are also many tasks which only support this work. Tasks you will not have been introduced to, trained, or prepared for in architecture school (see image on page 84 for details). I know I wasn't. This ancillary labour is dependent on practice size. Larger firms will hire more non-architectural staff – document controllers, CAD/BIM managers, receptionists, office managers, etc. – to carry out these tasks. Smaller firms tend to lack the required structure and volume of work to employ non-architectural staff, so ancillary tasks ultimately fall to least experienced, and least remunerated, employees. Probably you. You will likely have little sympathy or confidence[4] for these tasks. They will not satisfy the creative impulses cultivated in architecture school.

Secondly, as in any industry when the natural fate of its products is mass consumption, work becomes labour.[5] This applies to architecture produced solely for the property market. Characterless apartment blocks and office towers cluttering our skylines; generic retail and industrial sheds clustered along our roads. Reproductions for repeat clients, characterised by repeat forms and floor plans regardless of location; composed of repeat materials and construction methods. They require only large pools of labour concerned solely with reproduction of an original prototype, more akin to a factory floor. This labour force constitutes "everyone else"[6] below principals, directors, and associates. Students, interns, architectural assistants, draughtspersons, and registered architects producing hundreds if not thousands of replica construction documentation. Some firms even exploitatively outsource this labour-intensive work to overseas CAD workshops in less affluent countries.[7]

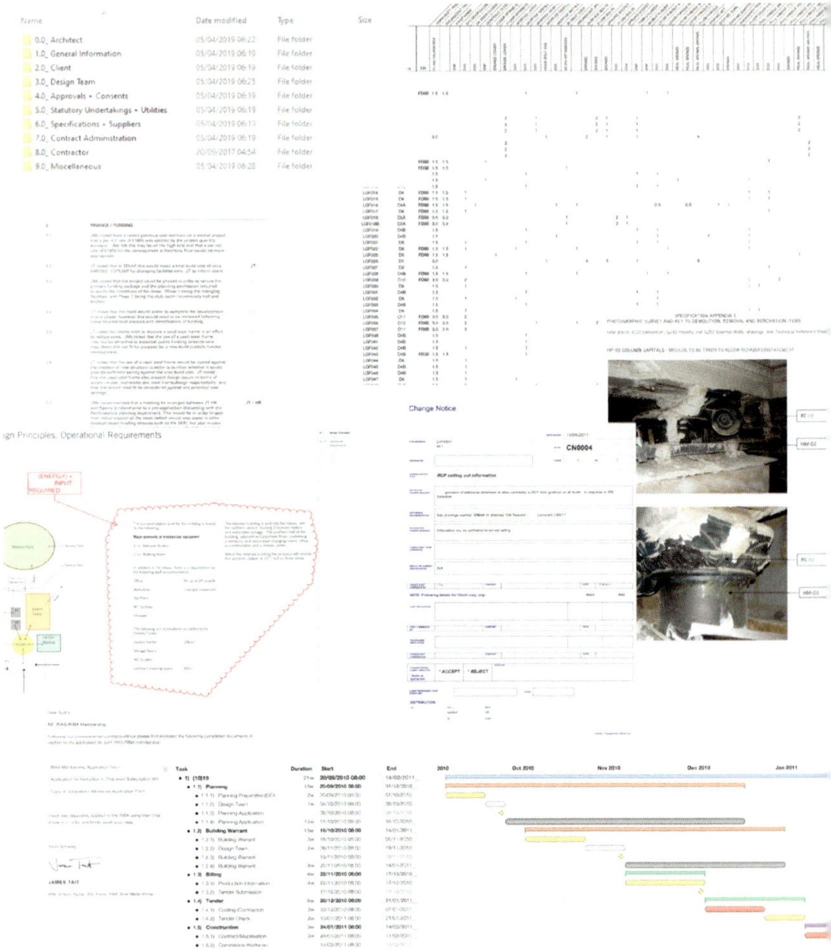
Name
Date modified
Type
Size
0.0_Architect
1.0_General Information
2.0_Client
3.0_Design Team
4.0_Approvals + Consents
5.0_Statutory Undertakings + Utilities
6.0_Specifications + Suppliers
7.0_Contract Administration
8.0_Contractor
9.0_Miscellaneous
File folder
Change Notice
CN0004
Task
Duration
Start
End
Oct 2010
Nov 2010
Dec 2010
Jan 2011
JAMES TAIT

THE PRODUCTS OF REPETITIVE LABOUR
Generic office blocks and residential towers – repeat buildings for repeat clients.

Downtown. Toronto, Canada. 2017.

facing page

ANCILLARY LABOUR
Ancillary tasks include: keeping detailed records of all information issued out and received in; the filing of all project documents both digital and physical; the copying and scanning of drawings; the creation of reports and records; the review of programmes and schedules produced by others; the answering of phone calls and emails; the typing of dictated documents; the creation of office templates; the development of office drawing and modelling standards; the ordering of office supplies; folding drawings; the preparation of speculative bids and accompanying CVs; the taking of minutes. An almost endless list of tasks, wholly incidental to the quality of the design.

Ancillary labour could be addressed by its appropriate organisation. Secretarial staff would be better placed to carry out administrative tasks than an unexperienced architecture student. Dedicated document controllers more suited to documenting and scheduling the flow of information than those trained to design. Why hire the best young architectural talent if they are only involved in tasks unrecognisable to their training and abilities? Appropriate organisation of ancillary tasks would open up spaces of incremental action, allowing young creatives to "reveal their unique personal identities ... qualities, gifts, talents and short-comings".[8] It could be manifest in an approach similar to OMA, where everybody gets the opportunity to test their ideas;[9] a well-structured and managed employee-ownership system which gives all employees a sense of shared direction; or a clear mentorship system which encourages responsibility and career progression.

Detachment from the design process can be confusing and frustrating for architecture students entering practice,[10] when they have been trained to think independently and work autonomously. The scope for these cultivated habits is diminished in practice. The entry-level architect is "caught in a schism"[11] between anticipation and reality, as the initial role rarely offers much design responsibility.[12] When responsibility is meted out, it is often only at first on small, minor projects or less significant parts of larger ones – *"Do you fancy taking ownership of the washroom designs?" "Eh, yeah, thanks."* Seize these opportunities, you will get more responsibility next time.

In larger offices, a handful of senior design partners are usually responsible for generating design ideas then passed down through the office structure. This separates many producers of these designs from the decision-making process. A good office will recognise architectural staff crave design responsibility and a degree of authorship.

Diminishment of authorship can cultivate new habits in practice where design excellence becomes dependent on participatory engagement.[13] Like regular group design reviews where the decision makers engage directly with those producing the work as a way for staff to present and discuss their work, encouraging collaborative and objective evaluation. This also helps identify hidden potential and unseen flaws in a design. Careful and considered apportioning of design responsibility within a project also allows employees to take ownership of certain aspects of a project, under the guidance of more experienced colleagues. With careful tutelage these elements can be enriched by less entrenched and pessimistic young minds while engaging and exciting staff. Architects need a sense of authorship, to have some input in the decision-making process and an ability to effect positive change. If their roles do not provide it, they will move on.

AN INTERNAL DESIGN REVIEW

A chance to present, debate, and decide as a team.

Killa Design, Dubai.

Your influence in any project is also impacted by the length of time an architectural idea takes to come to fruition. You will likely be employed, as and when required, at various stages of different projects. This makes collaboration and agency even more pertinent. You may have been involved for a period of six months on early design stages of a project, then moved on to a more demanding or resource-hungry project. You may not have been involved in earlier or development stages of a project, then drafted in to assist during the construction phase. Regardless, you will be expected to collaborate effectively by carrying out the tasks required. Critical to your own sense of agency and career contentment, is to also demonstrate your capacity to effect positive change. Unlocking potential or overcoming design challenges through creativity at each stage.

In 15 years of practice I have not been involved in a project in its entirety – from it arriving as a client's statement of need to an inhabited edifice. Set yourself periodic milestones of development. Never submitted a competition proposal? Never gained a building permit? Never worked on a building site? Use your involvement at each stage of any project to identify and attain new skills essential in your development as an architect. This can work in two ways. By keeping up your momentum on a project with a steady stream of goals, and by giving you a sense of closure and achievement should you move on, or be moved on, before the project is complete. To ensure the manic labour of each project does not give way to disillusioned abandonment.[14]

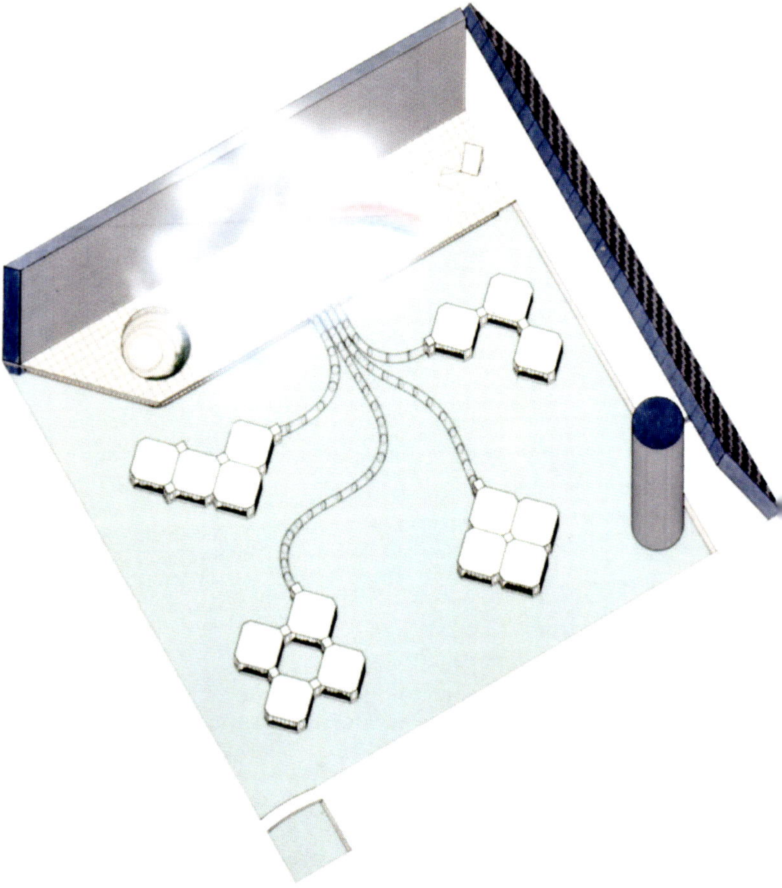

ONE THAT GOT AWAY (ONE FOR OUR TIMES)

"Behind the design of this environment is the premise that nobody should have to work. At worst, one would work at home and not need a large building but rather a small one to simply house a computer and receive messages. The building has been conceived, therefore, as a set of elements that can be progressively reconfigured and recombined as the needs of the office vary over time. Ultimately, barges can be removed as the need for on-site space diminishes."

Center for Applied Computer Research. Mexico City, Mexico. 1975. Emilio Ambasz.

Many projects also never get built. This surprised me upon entering practice, naively assuming this only happened in architecture school. Every architecture practice has overflowing drawing files and terabytes of data created in the pursuit of unbuilt buildings. Funding problems, changes of heart, bureaucracy, personal disagreements, legal issues, recessions, even pandemics have all derailed or extinguished projects in which I have been involved. The product of architecture's reliance on a multifarious and precarious framework of external needs and demands for its realisation. Learn from this inevitability. That beautiful staircase or well-proportioned room you designed may not be built, but you will know how to design the next one which does. Learn, move on, grow.

Notes

1 Lewis, R., 2013. *Architect? A Candid Guide to the Profession.* Cambridge, MA: MIT. p. 85.
2 Arendt, H., 1998. *The Human Condition* (2nd ed.). Chicago: University of Chicago Press. p. 123.
3 Lewis, *Architect?.* p. 85.
4 Cuff, D., 1991. *Architecture: The Story of Practice.* Cambridge, MA: The MIT Press. p. 170.
5 Arendt, *The Human Condition,* p. 124.
6 Cuff,*Architecture.* p. 129.
7 Silberman, S., 2008. Offshore Drawing. *Dwell,* 8(5), pp. 172–176.
8 Arendt, *The Human Condition,* p. 179.
9 Wiles, W., 2011. Inside OMA. *Icon Magazine,* October(100), pp. 144–153.
10 Cuff, *Architecture,* p. 51.
11 Ibid., p. 135.
12 Ibid., p. 134.
13 Ibid., p. 51.
14 Firket, N. & Schaefer, M., 2004. Out of fashion. In: R. Koolhaas, ed. *Content.* Koln: Taschen, p. 326.

TECHNICAL ADVICE NOTE

02

TYPICAL DAY

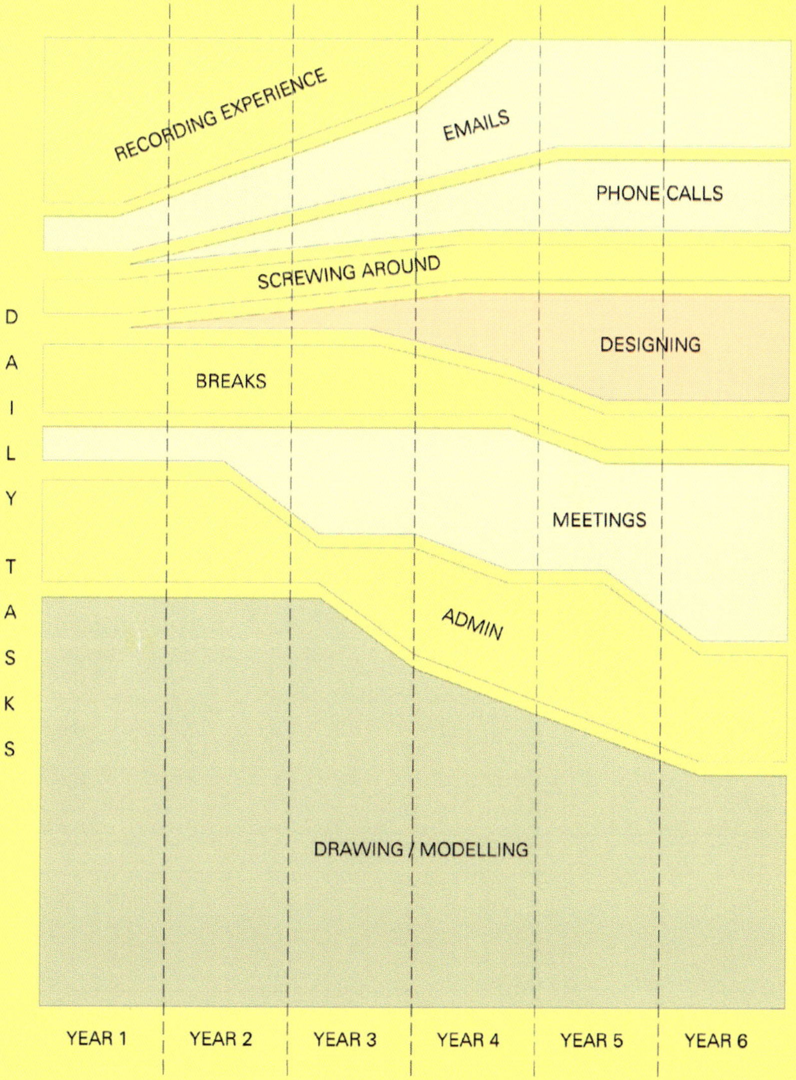
RECORDING EXPERIENCE
EMAILS
PHONE CALLS
SCREWING AROUND
DESIGNING
BREAKS
MEETINGS
ADMIN
DRAWING / MODELLING
DAILY TASKS
YEAR 1
YEAR 2
YEAR 3
YEAR 4
YEAR 5
YEAR 6

1.3 WORKING CONDITIONS

ARCHITECTURE OPERATES outside of standard working practices.

↓

At every practice I have worked I have taken less holidays than legally obliged; regularly gone 12–14-hour shifts without a rest break; worked through the night with a few hours rest between shifts; and in one practice worked on average around 65–70 hours per week – 30 hours of unpaid overtime, 20 over the legal limit. This is a widely corroborated reality. Many feel the reality of working in architectural practice is a "bleak prospect",[1] characterised by unpaid overtime, precarious contracts, and antisocial working hours.[2] These conditions can lead to frustration and anxiety,[3] while those who do not keep up with this culture are shown little mercy.[4]

ANOTHER LATE NIGHT

City of Glasgow College Campus Site Office.
Glasgow, United Kingdom. 2015.

This bleak outlook needs context. The current situation has existed at least since the 1960s,[5] accelerating in the 1980s–1990s.[6] Further, we do not have it as bad as the medieval architect who on completion of a job well done was 'complimented' by having his hands severed, so as not to replicate the design elsewhere.[7] The same architect faced prison and dispossession if the job was not completed well or within a reasonable time frame.[8] Spare a thought for the Ancient Greek architect who, if he accepted a design commission, was required to put up his home and possessions as a guarantee should the project exceed his own price estimates by a quarter.[9] If that rule were still in place most architectural practices would not exist.

We are also not alone. Marx and Engels stated the economic system precipitated by the Industrial Revolution had stripped every occupation of its halo,[10] the physician, the lawyer, the scientist were all paid wage labourers.[11] A contemporary example being junior doctors, similarly overworked and underpaid,[12] but crucially playing a more important role in society. Architects do not save lives. This historical and comparative context is important to avoid omphaloskeptic over-inflation. We will not, however, avoid honesty.

THE ARCHITECT: BEHEADED

Hestia: Goddess of Architecture (far left), Dione and Aphrodite, from Parthenon east pediment.

Parthenon Galleries. British Museum, London, United Kingdom. Photographer: Marie-Lan Nguyen.

The root of the current situation is a belief the 'art of making money' is unconnected with the art of making buildings.[13] Making money is rightly secondary to the impulse to do a thing well, for its own sake.[14] There is, however, a dark side to this belief in practice.

This belief is linked to architects pricing their services on outdated and arbitrary fee scales rather than the performance or quality of what they provide.[15] Not reflective of the inordinate number of hours that the production of architecture entails. Nor the abortive or modified work carried out in the process of each project, deemed un-chargeable to a client and seen as inevitable collateral in the creative process.[16] If your employer is not paid for this work, it is unlikely you will be. A situation exasperated by the practice of 'undercutting' each other to gain work, then allowing overworked and underpaid employees to bear the brunt of these tactics.[17] Low fee culture becomes low pay culture. Low pay is the primary source of frustration for those entering the profession.[18]

What we do becomes entangled with our sense of identity – long hours and hard work seen as an inevitability of the role. I have been interrupted by midnight revellers dancing outside the office window to the music I was playing. I have sat in amazed fury when told by a director that my previous night's 1am finish "wasn't too late then" as I stumbled in at 9am the following morning. I have walked home at 4am on a Monday morning after a 20-hour Sunday shift trying to meet an impossible deadline.

VITRUVIUS

"The architect should cherish a good reputation without thought of monetary rewards."[19]

A 1684 depiction of Vitruvius (right) presenting De architectura to Augustus.

Employees become valued for their endurance and dedication rather than what they produce. In the current system within which architecture operates, the noble ethic of doing a good job for its own sake can be exploited. The view that architecture must be laboriously sacrificed for, is evident in the paradox that the better regarded a practice is, generally the worse the employment conditions. Some of these practices overtly advertise for candidates without a 9–5 work ethic, are staffed by scores of interns only covering their expenses,[20] and openly admit to operating computerised sweatshops.[21] A practice ratified by previous employees who regularly worked from 10am to 2am seven days a week for little to no pay.[22] Some enjoy this high-powered, high-profile environment. It can be alluring to the ambitious young professional, but it is not sustainable. Most employees last a maximum of three years, burned out by the breakneck pace of daily work.[23]

facing page

CAD MONKEY

Students, interns, architectural assistants, draughtspersons, and registered architects too. A group often disparagingly referred to as 'CAD Monkeys' – producing hundreds if not thousands of replica construction documentation, images, and models. A CAD Monkey can be defined as: "Somebody who has gone through years of difficult and strenuous education in engineering, architecture, or a similar field only to wind up with a mindless and repetitive job where they do one task on a computer drafting program over and over again."

"Laugh now, but one day we'll be in charge". 2003. Banksy.

Photographer: Benjamin A. Melville.

now,
but one day
we'll be
in charge

Not all internationally acclaimed practices operate in this way. Herzog and de Meuron foster a working environment of "long weekends, lunches, coffee breaks and short workdays".[24] A picture corroborated by a former colleague who describes a demanding environment, but one of relatively short hours, paid overtime, above average remuneration, and a generally healthy working environment. Many offices are good employers. Some discourage long hours or weekend working believing that the decisions that guide good architecture cannot be made by tired or frustrated employees.[25] Your working conditions can also vary within an office depending on what projects you are involved in, with some more demanding and under-resourced than others. Something I have benefited from and been encumbered by.

There is also the question of unpaid internships. Most interns work on speculative projects for clients who pit architects against one another with the enticement of a commission. This happens in open and invited competitions, and framework agreements. Offices should have enough 'float' to carry this workload without exploiting staff, but many do not. To compete, they hire willing graduates for free. Only financially comfortable graduates can afford to do this, narrowing the already limited diversity of the field. These interns then use the reputation of the practice to enhance their future job prospects. If architecture remains a competitive and elite course of study, it is unlikely that students will stop accepting internships. Further, clients must stop expecting work for free. This requires action from our own professional bodies – who perversely often organise unpaid competitions – to take a stand against this practice. Only a combination of clients, professional bodies, practices, and students themselves can put an end to it.

H&deM AFTER HOURS

Herzog & de Meuron, Basel.

EGG @ NIGHT

Tencent Campus Competition Proposal. Shenzen, China. 2019. MVRDV.

There are pathways to a more rewarding and sustainable working environment. Firstly, choose a practice wisely. There is an infinite range of practices each with varying attitudes to the value of their employees.[26] If you do want a high-octane experience and are willing to do the time, please remember that there is a big difference between being dedicated and being exploited.

I have been guilty of working an unhealthy number of unpaid hours and putting up with more stress and strain than I should have. I did so largely through choice. Firstly, because I have a passion for architecture and most of what practising it entails. Secondly, I didn't want to let anyone down. To meet the standards and deadlines required, I felt

I had to put in the extra hours. Sometimes it was enforced. This is when dedication becomes exploited – when it is no longer a choice.

One example of this is the practice of undermanning – deliberate under-resourcing to induce employees to assume more responsibility while working harder and longer[27] for no extra pay. Aged 27, I ran two high-profile projects at a large international practice. Both projects were demanding of time and energy, meaning I regularly worked 15–16-hour shifts for over a year – double my contracted hours. The prestige and responsibility seemed an acceptable trade-off for the long hours and modest pay. Yet I was not being paid a project architect salary. Worse, my director had told both clients that I was solely dedicated to their project, charging them on that basis. I only discovered this when I answered a phone call from one client while on the construction site of the other project. Hearing the clatter of steel and hammers he asked what site I was on, because I wasn't on his one – he was there. My dedication, and naivety, was exploited. Hopefully you can spot it happening to you before I did.

Architecture demands dedication. Sometimes you will need to work late to put in the extra hours that excellence requires, or to meet an unavoidable deadline. However, when this culture becomes ingrained and used to compensate for low fees, speculative work, or to maximise profit – it becomes exploitation. Poor working conditions are not a rite of passage to becoming an architect as some may have you believe.[28]The final step to bettering the working situation of the young architect is unionisation, either by collectively joining existing ones or organising new ones – as has recently happened in the UK.[29] A new generation of young architects, saddled with more debt than ever,[30] are collectively organising around the value of their labour.[31] This action is reinforced by others. From architect and educator Peggy Deamer who advocates the creation of architects' unions as an alternative to organisations like the RIBA (Royal Institute of British Architects) and AIA (American Institute of Architects),[32] to Pier Vittorio Aureli of Dogma who promotes the creation of a union or similar social organisation to prevent architects from exploitation.[33] As architect Kate Macintosh notes of her time working in unionised local government: "Terms and conditions of employment were problems we simply did not have ... you could just get on with your job."[34]

The unhealthy relationship architecture has with money, time, and the welfare of those that produce it needs

ARCHITECTURAL WORKERS ARE UNIONISING!

London, United Kingdom. 2019. Section of Architectural Workers.

fundamental industry-wide change. There are immediate things you and your colleagues can do through recognition, prevention, and organisation. If enough of you recognise exploitation when it happens, refuse to habitually work long hours for little or no pay, and become organised collectively then the industry will be forced to notice. Not purely to change your own situation, but to improve the conditions and lives of all of those involved in creating architecture. As 92-year-old architect Ben Stephenson told a colleague of mine: "if you enjoy it, the better you will become at it and the more other people will enjoy what you create as a result."[35] Improving our working conditions, will improve the quality of what we produce.

MUNICIPAL MODERNISM

Dawson's Heights. London, United Kingdom. 1972.
London Borough of Southwark Architects' Department.

Notes

1 Wainwright, O., 2019. *"It's in complete crisis" – architects form trade union amid fury and despair over exploitation.* [Online] Available at: https://www.theguardian.com/artanddesign/2019/oct/30/architects-form-trade-union-uvw-saw [Accessed 3 May 2020].

2 Ibid.

3 Aureli, P., 2013. *Less is Enough: On Architecture and Asceticism.* Moscow: Strelka Press. pp. 56–57.

4 Ibid., pp. 56–57.

5 Saint, A., 1983. *The Image of an Architect.* New Haven, CT: Yale University. p. 147.

6 Hobsbawm, E.J., 1999. *Industry and Empire: From 1750 to the Present Day.* London: Penguin Books. p. 315.

7 Kostof, S., 1977. The Architect in the Middle Ages, East and West. In: *The Architect: Chapters in the History of the Profession.* New York: Oxford University Press. p. 65.

8 Ibid., p. 84.

9 Oleson, J., 2008. *The Oxford Handbook of Engineering and Technology in the Classical World.* Oxford: Oxford University Press. p. 228.

10 Marx, K. & Engels, F., 1888. *The Communist Manifesto.* Penguin Classics ed. London: Penguin Random House. p. 5.

11 Ibid., p. 5.

12 Kay, A., 2018. *This is Going to Hurt: Secret Diaries of a Junior Doctor.* London: Picador. p. 110.

13 Arendt, H., 1998. *The Human Condition* (2nd ed.). Chicago: University of Chicago Press. p. 128.

14 Saint, *The Image of an Architect,* p. 103.

15 Baker, K., 2019. *Can Technology Solve Architects' Productivity Challenge?* [Online] Available at: https://www.architectmagazine.com/aia-architect/aiafeature/can-technology-solve-architects-productivity-challenge_o [Accessed 1 May 2020].

16 Townley, B. & Beech, N., 2010. *Managing Creativity: Exploring the Paradox.* Cambridge: Cambridge University Press. p. 249.

17 Wainwright, *"It's in complete crisis"* [Online].

18 Waite, R. & Jessel, E., 2019. *AJ student survey 2019: the harsh realities of life in practice.* [Online] Available at: https://www.architectsjournal.co.uk/news/aj-student-survey-2019-the-harsh-realities-of-life-in-practice/10043685.article [Accessed 29 April 2020].

19 Vitruvius, 1960. *The Ten Books on Architecture*. New York: Dover Publications. p. 6.
20 Office for Metropolitan Architecture, 2020. *Jobs Listings*. [Online] Available at: https://oma.eu/jobs [Accessed 4 May 2020].
21 Koolhaas, R., 2004. CCTV. In: *Content*. Koln: Taschen. p. 485.
22 Wainwright, *"It's in complete crisis"* [Online].
23 Wiles, W., 2011. Inside OMA. *Icon Magazine*, October(100), pp. 144–153.
24 Wagenaar, F.H., 2004. Astrology: protect us from what we want. In: R. Koolhaas, ed. *Content*. Koln: Taschen. p. 204.
25 Matthewson, G., 2013. *Architecture and the Goldilocks syndrome*. [Online] Available at: https://archiparlour.org/architecture-and-the-goldilocks-syndrome/ [Accessed 4 May 2020].
26 Ibid.
27 Ledbetter, C.B., 1974. *Undermanning and Architectural Accessibility*. Hanover: Corps of Engineers, U.S. Army. p. 2.
28 Lewis, R., 2013. *Architect? A Candid Guide to the Profession*. Cambridge, MA: MIT. p. 75.
29 Wainwright, *"It's in complete crisis"* [Online].
30 Ibid.
31 Ibid.
32 Deamer, P., 2019. Prove our worth. *Architecture Today*, 303(November), p. 16.
33 Aureli, *Less is Enough*, pp. 56–57.
34 Macintosh, K., 2020. *Interview with J.Tait* [Interview] (3 June 2020).
35 _baxendale, 2018. *Instagram*. [Online] Available at: www.instagram.com/_baxendale/ [Accessed 4 May 2020].

INTERVIEW B

↘ Jonathan Sergison (SERGISON BATES)

What was your first experience of architecture in practice, as a student?

Before I started my studies, I worked in a drawing office. I wanted to know what awaited me when I finished my studies. I could compare what we were being asked to do as students to how the profession organised itself. A really important time was between degree and diploma studies. I worked with David Chipperfield which was a very important education. There was a creative ambition that I found really inspiring. At architecture school, I learned many things but none as relevant to life in practice as working with David Chipperfield, and later Tony Fretton, was. When I finished my studies there was still a lot that I did not know about being an architect.

Did your experience with Chipperfield and Fretton influence the culture in your own studio?

What I learned most from David Chipperfield was the highest demand on building. His work is consistently well constructed. Everything we did was well organised and built well. There were also many conceptual aspects there that I benefited from, being able to talk to him over many years. Tony is more of an artist. He would always say "what relationship does this detail have to the overall understanding of the project?". Tony also taught me to look at normal things and learn from them. Walking though London with Tony was an education. He was always pointing out things that excited him about the city. With both these figures, the culture of architecture is very high in their minds – there is a lot of ambition. The closeness to that discourse was a huge education.

Can you describe your design process?

It has changed over the years. When we first started it was just the two of us sitting over a table – a project would develop through a first proposal and then a reaction it. A collaborative way of working is at the core of architecture. As the office has grown and the tasks have become more complex and demanding, different structures have emerged. Some projects require bigger teams structured with a partner in charge then an associate or project architect closely involved in the project. Their role is to ensure that things are well coordinated. The right level of experience is applied to a project at the right moment. There are different intensities so it's not always seamless.

How do you deal with commercial demands and constraints, particularly in housing?

It is a discreet form of negotiation. We want to make the best version of housing we can and if that task is framed by economic circumstances, it's part of the discipline. We quickly learned the space standards and the opportunities were more promising for social housing than private developments because they had a set of reasonable standards. A developer is often only thinking about profit ratio – particularly in London. What has been built in the last 30 years there is shocking because the market is so strong for whatever

Prototype for suburban housing. Stevenage, United Kingdom. 2000. Sergison Bates.

Photographer: Hélène Binet.

is built. The standard and quality of building is so poor and the space standards so mean. To some extent it's why I have self-exiled to the centre of Europe. Culturally it is seen, by all of those who contribute to the building process, as one of the greatest responsibilities to build to the highest reasonable standard because it's what you leave behind for future generations.

How does time impact your work?

Our relationship to the process of building has changed from our early projects. Then, we had a lot of influence over the appointment of the builders and scrutiny of their building standards. Now you are lucky to even be on a building site. To me this is a big change which I think is not going to be reversed but to complain about it wouldn't do me any good. The current situation makes me reflect on our earlier projects which were made with incredible intensity and the pleasure of working on site with good people with a lot of knowledge. The big difference between me and of any of my students, is for three or four months they work on one thing intensely and continuously. At any moment in time I am working on many projects simultaneously. I often encourage students to do projects collaboratively. Unlike other creative practices, architecture is always dependent on different versions of collaboration. The structure of the studio or other consultants and the whole complex structure of the building industry. It always amuses me when students talk about 'my' project.

Urban Villas. London, United Kingdom. 2008. Sergison Bates.

Photographer: Stefan Müller.

Inner city housing and crèche. Geneva, Switzerland. 2011. Sergison Bates.

Photographer: David Grandorge.

Suburban housing. Zürich, Switzerland. 2019. Sergison Bates.

Photographer: David Grandorge.

What future challenges does architecture face and how will we deal with them?

The danger being created through man's activity, and building plays a big part, has been a question in my mind since we set up in practice. It is so sharply in focus now. Every single decision has a responsibility. The first question we must ask ourselves is, "is it necessary to build this building?". Could we not extend the life of an existing building before we build a new one? Next, what do we use to build things from? Every decision in the specification of a building needs to be assessed in terms of its impact on the environment. For me this is more important than anything else. I think students now understand it without needing to make any argument for it. I passionately believe as a teacher I have a responsibility to share things which are useful for the students. I am not sure if that is true of architectural education in the UK generally. A lot of schools teach things which are at best esoteric and not always useful for what architecture can be. The worst version of that is when a student needs to unlearn what they have learned. Especially now when they are paying so much money for their education, I have a big problem with this.

1.4

PLAY YOUR POSITION

THE STRUCTURE OF AN architecture practice can be complex, if not confusing to the uninitiated.

↓

Multiple layers of hierarchy stacked on top of one another, with no clear definition where each layer starts or ends. The image opposite gives a breakdown of the seven tiers indicative of the typical structure of practice, which are:

1. Partners / Directors (18–20+ years)

The founding partners or directors of a company who own all or a share of the company. Their role involves getting work and keeping it. Ensuring there is a steady stream of projects and fees coming through the office, as well as shouldering the responsibility for the smooth running of the projects the practice is currently engaged in.

2. Associate Directors (15–18 years)

This second tier typically own a smaller share of the practice taking on many of the roles of a director, such as developing client relationships and ensuring the smooth running of projects. This is essentially an audition for the step up to director level.

3. Associates (12–15 years)

Associates don't typically own a share of the company, but carry out many of the roles of an Associate Director with more of a focus on the internal management of the practice and closer contact with the day-to-day running of the projects that they oversee.

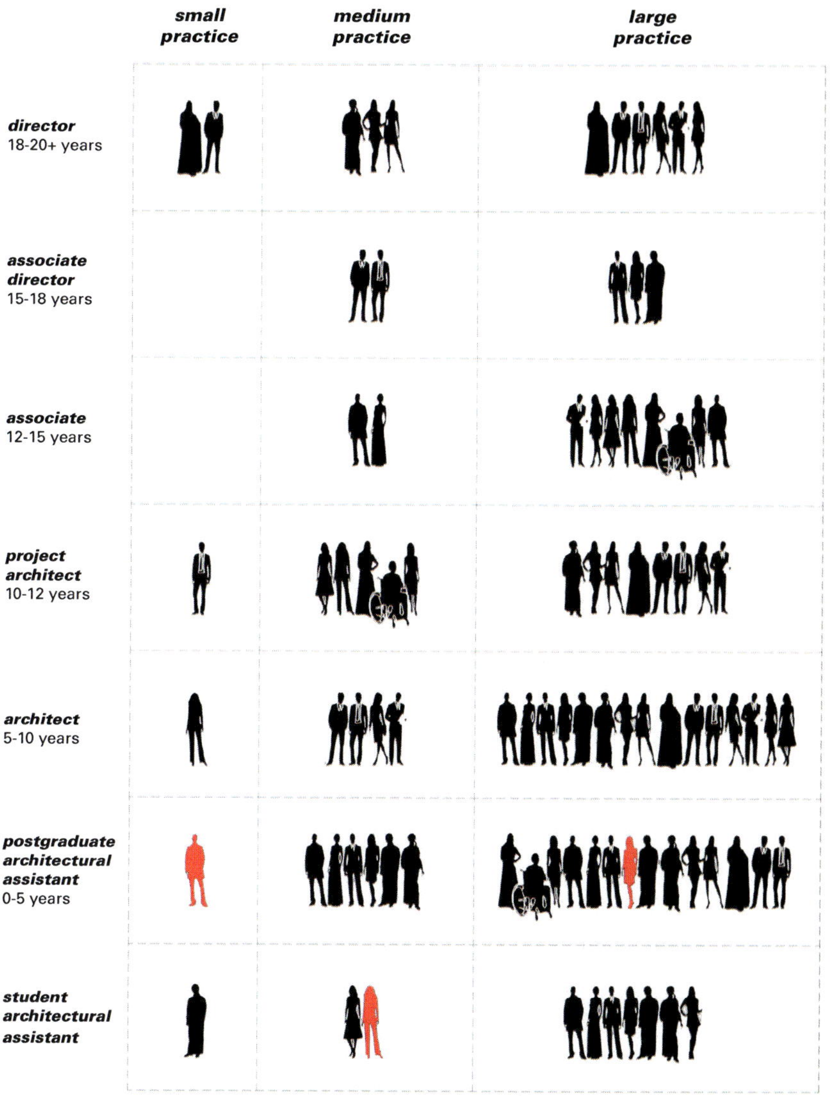

TYPICAL PRACTICE STRUCTURES

4. Project Architects / Project Managers (10–12 years)

This group tend to focus on the delivery of one or two projects – delegating tasks, dealing with other consultants and clients and generally coordinating the smooth running of them. Project Architects differ from Associates in that they have a much more specific role and are largely not expected to participate in office management or gaining new work.

5. Architects (Licensed) (5–10 years)

In most offices this is probably the largest cohort. In larger practices, often taking direction from the Project Architect or Associates with a degree of delegation of production tasks to those further down the office structure. In small to medium practices Architects can act more like Project Architects. The core of the architects' role involves both organisation and production, perhaps with some authorship and management of smaller projects or sections of larger projects with less direct engagement with other consultants and clients.

6. Postgraduate Architectural Assistants (0–5 years)

This group have typically completed five years of architectural education, taking their first steps fully into architectural practice. This role is characterised by the need to gain knowledge and experience of the construction industry, and to practise the production of architecture (drawings, details, schedules, specifications). This can mean that the Postgraduate Architectural Assistant can either be given a large degree of responsibility or none – dependent on the practice. They will also spend a lot of their time liaising with the Architects or Projects Architects.

7. Graduate Architectural Assistants / Interns

This role is typically temporary, usually for a year in the UK or in between semesters in the US – a taster of practice. Owing to lack of experience, this group tend to be less involved in technical or critical tasks, often more likely to be engaged in tasks suited to their existing skill base honed at architecture schools such as visualisation, modelmaking, presentation drawings, etc.

Most medium to large firms also carry large numbers of non-architectural staff varying from secretarial, financial, marketing, as well as dedicated modelmakers, interior designers, and landscape architects.

Not all offices, particularly smaller ones, have staff inhabiting each of these tiers. Employee ownership and cooperative practice[1] have also increased, offering less hierarchy and more transparency.[2] Presently these only constitute around an estimated 5% of practices in the UK[3] and the USA.[4] There are also many multidisciplinary collaboratives of creatives, pooling their knowledge and skill set such as Assemble or Operadora – this is to be encouraged. A hierarchical and layered practice structure, however, remains the orthodoxy across the profession.

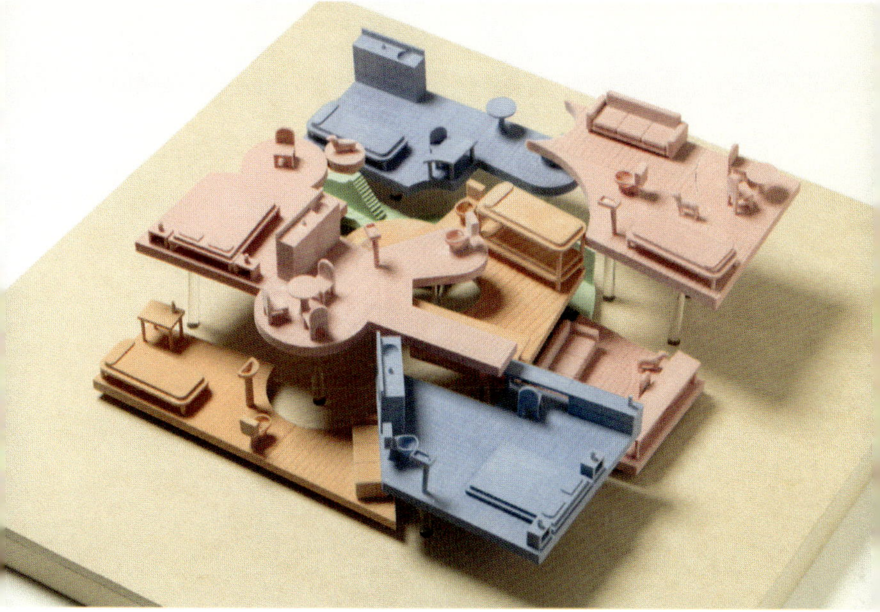

ALTERNATIVE PRACTICE: MULTIDISCIPLINARY

"We have designed houses, buildings, stores, apartments, toys, pavilions, helmets, books, logos, t-shirts, websites, and cultural events."
WŏWū – Future Living Space. 2018. Operadora.

Photographer: Estudio C129.

facing page

ALTERNATIVE PRACTICE: EMPLOYEE-OWNED

Groupwork + Amin Taha.
Photographer: Tim Soar.

You will likely enter practice at layer 6 or 7. Those inhabiting the tiers above you will have entered at this level too. Nepotism aside, most graduates or interns enter practice as equals. The route for progression in this system can be unclear. Loyalty and hard work alone are not enough. Talent and skill do not guarantee advancement either. The practice of architecture encompasses many different roles – designer, technician, businessperson, market analyst, contractor, negotiator, arbitrator, counsellor – requiring different characters with varying skill sets. More technical-minded architects may be better suited to the later detailed design and construction phases of projects; more creative and expressive architects to the concept design stages. An architect with a gift for organisation and delivery will be more suited to managing work within the office, than an architect with a natural ability to charm and convince clients. Architecture is a broad field requiring a broad range of talents.

You may not even know what your talents in practice are yet. This process usually happens organically, as individuals distinguish themselves (or not) in certain situations, developing aptitudes and reputations for certain aspects of practice. Before entering practice, you will probably have some idea of where your natural tendencies lie. Honestly appraise your strengths and weaknesses. Will you reinforce your strengths and lean towards a distinct facet of practice? Or balance them out by improving on your weaknesses? Appraise them but don't be bound by them. Sometimes hidden passions or talents can arise in the process of practice that surprise you.

Every aspiring architect has to 'earn their stripes', to gain advancement through the ranks by their deeds. This is primarily a question of time. If around 10,000 hours is required for one to develop and master a trade or skill,[5] an entrant has around six to eight years within which to earn

LOOKING FORWARD TO ANOTHER 10,000 HOURS OF PRACTICE
Violinist Yehudi Menuhin, age 12.

their stripes. To cope well with whatever is tasked of them and show certain aptitudes or areas within which their talents can develop. By which time you should be able to accept more responsibility, delegative powers, and autonomy.

This is a period of self-discovery. Testing your capabilities, limits, and strengths. Establishing how you respond to situations or events through intuition, reason, or both. Learning from your inevitable mistakes. Absorbing and growing from the working environments you inhabit. The quality of the environment you are learning in and what you are producing will determine what type of architect you will become. If you are enveloped by a supportive culture which demands high standards set by patient mentors, and engaged in meaningful tasks designing buildings that you are passionate about – you are more likely to become the architect you want to be at the end of this period. The reverse would be true in an unsupportive environment, with low standards set by uninterested colleagues, carrying out repetitive tasks for buildings you have no passion for. Demand, or seek elsewhere, the right type of environment and experience.

This period also means dealing with whatever comes your way. No matter how alien, menial, or valueless a task may seem, you will always learn from it. How can you delegate tasks in the future if you don't know what they entail? How will you explain a certain process to a client or other consultant if you haven't experienced it? I have spent months scheduling out thousands of doors for a large project, detailing their size, colour, frame thickness, wood type, hinge type, etc. An arduous and repetitive task, but I now know enough to be able to discuss them confidently and instinctively with the carpenters who make them. I spent weeks producing a tenants' guidance

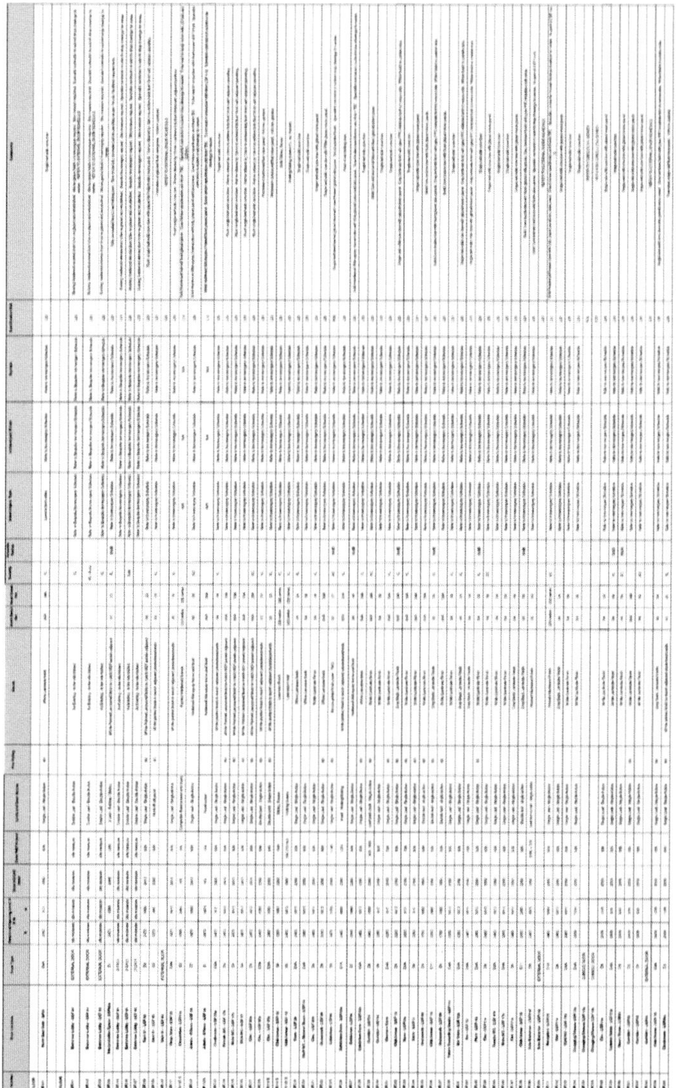

THE DREADED DOOR SCHEDULE

Size, colour, frame thickness, wood type, hinge type, fire rating, finish, signage, ironmongery …

document describing how the boiler worked, what type of curtains they had installed, the specification of the tiles used in the kitchens, the capacity of the bins, even where the local transport connections were. I saw these tasks as unconnected to what I was trained to do, yet I now know what is important to the daily existence of people who inhabit the homes we design, and ensure I consider these aspects more carefully. Even when you feel your efforts are leaving little trace or value, the information contained in them is stored subconsciously to become useful in the future.

This is also a buffer period, allowing your employer to assess your strengths and weakness before granting you responsibility to liaise directly with clients and other professionals, or command others internally. In the litigious environment of the construction industry, this is crucial. A 'buffer period' protects them as much as it allows you to develop.

It is also crucial to recognise when your talents or reputation are being taken advantage of at the expense of your own development. Practices sometimes use staff only to their 'best economic advantage'.[6] An individual expert at Building Information Modelling, visualisations, or negotiating with contractors can be regularly, if not exclusively, assigned these specialist tasks to improve efficiency and standards. This happens often in practice. I have known many committed young graduates being hampered by their talent in visualisation or modelmaking from gaining the necessary breadth and experience required to gain registration. One colleague even admitted to deliberately not performing tasks 'too well' so that he would not become typecast. This is a dangerous tactic. Instead have a frank and open discussion with

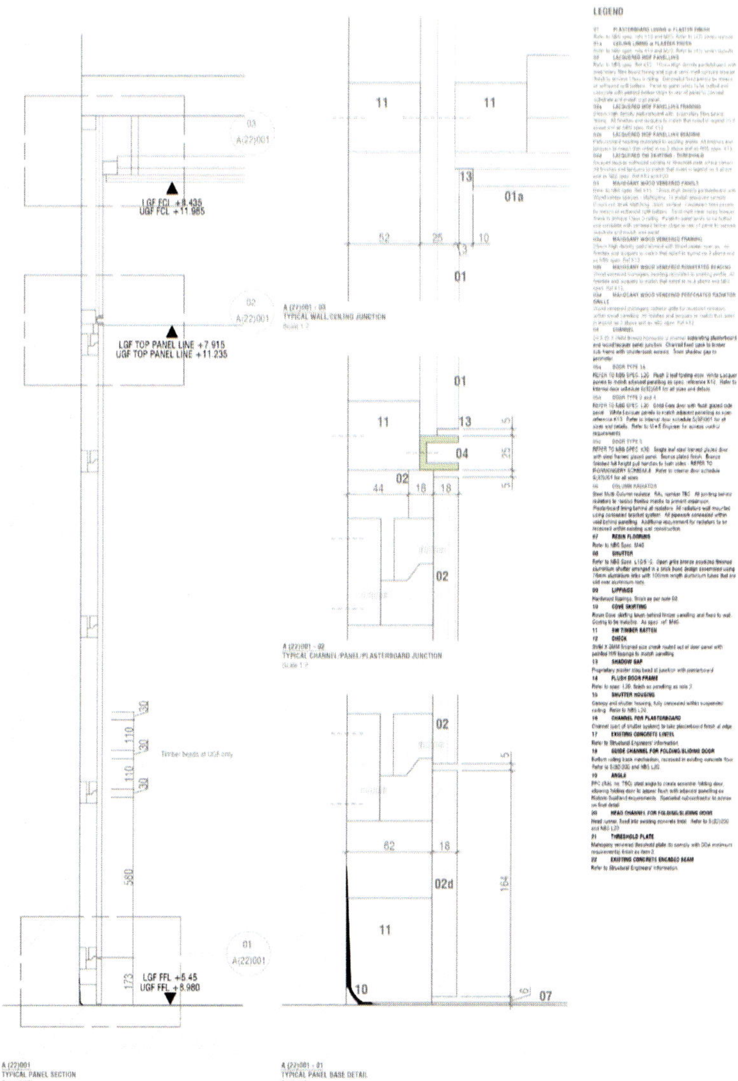

JOINERY AND DOOR DETAILING

Developing an understanding through practice.

your employer about your ambitions and interests. If the situation does not improve, you may need to seek an experience more suited to your needs – elsewhere.

This is a period of perpetual discovery, not specialisation and repetition. Nor is it a period for you to get comfortable if you have ambitions of being a well-rounded professional. You cannot afford to be used for the same task repeatedly. However, if you have real esoteric expertise in something you enjoy then specialisation can be a good career move. Many of those who set out to become architects instead become experts in BIM, modelmaking, or visualisation, able to carve themselves a niche within an organisation which allows them to progress outwith the typical layer system. It is a question of regularly assessing your current trajectory against your future aims.

You will first learn your position through practise. This then allows you to "play your position"[7] by using this foundation to step up and prove your attitude, ability, and versatility. You may have been engaged in detailed design work for weeks or toiling on repetitive room layouts for months. When the opportunity arises – for example to assist on an exciting new project more attuned to your passions or step in for a more senior colleague – be prepared to prove you can carry out the tasks asked of you, and can exceed them when required too. Only by proving your worth by your deeds will you deserve the responsibility and progression you presumably want.

Hard work, ability, and playing your position can all be diluted or concentrated by your ability to make meaningful personal connections. There is no predetermined route to progression in practice, it is a slow and uneven metamorphosis.[8] It is vital that you connect with people who define your working environment. Do you inspire confidence in those who take your lead? Do you signal promise to those who lead you?

There is no formal guidance on advancement within practice. The entrant only has visions of others who have successfully navigated the journey.[9] This is where mentorship is key. A mentor can provide an idealised future self. Reciprocally, an older incumbent sees the aspirant as an idealised former self. Both recognise qualities in each other. The aspirant gains essential inside knowledge in harnessing their unpolished talents in a professional environment. The incumbent is inspired by the energy of youth and more eager to ensure their instructions are matched by their deeds. This type of relationship is invaluable not only for your professional and personal development but also for your career progression. Gaining the trust of more senior members by your actions becomes equally as important as your attitude and skill set. The willingness of experienced members of staff to embrace discussion, explanation, demonstration of design issues, as well as providing exposure to clients and external consultants, displays a willingness to pass on responsibility.[10]

MENTORS

"unlike some of my colleagues I was unwilling to work in just any office … I learned much about the real issues of architecture leaning over Lucio's drafts."[11]

Oscar Niemeyer and his mentor Lucio Costa.

What defines the graduate in practice is character. Character can have a greater influence on one's professional life than technical skill, talent, and knowledge.[12] Through strength of character, the averagely talented graduate can often find an easier route to career progression in practice. This again comes down to a different balance of priorities. In architecture school, characteristics associated with thought tend to be more prized – ambitiousness, broadmindedness, creativity, curiosity, and spontaneity. In practice, characteristics more associated with action – adaptability, reliability, punctiliousness, and resourcefulness. These attributes are valued in both academia and the professional realm but their balance differs, meaning less talented designers can often become more important to an organisation than more talented ones.

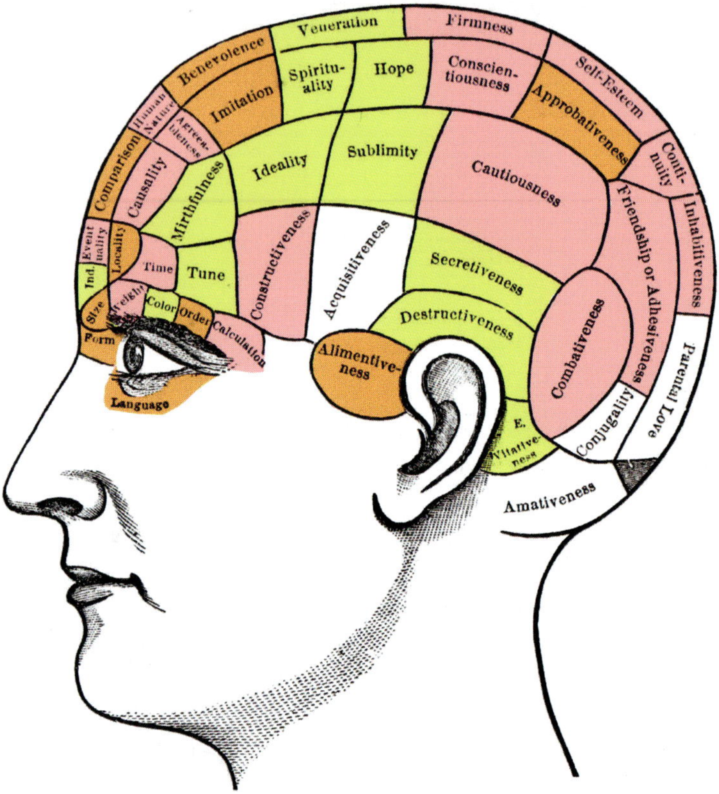

NUMBERING AND DEFINITION OF THE ORGANS.

1. Amativeness, Love between the sexes.
A. Conjugality, Matrimony—love of one. [etc.
2. Parental Love, Regard for offspring, pets,
3. Friendship, Adhesiveness—sociability.
4 Inhabitiveness, Love of home.
5. Continuity, One thing at a time.
E. Vitativeness, Love of life.
6. Combativeness, Resistance—defense.
7. Destructiveness, Executiveness—force.
8. Alimentiveness, Appetite—hunger.
9. Acquisitivene-s, Accumulation.
10. Secretiveness, Policy—management.
11. Cautiousness, Prudence—provision.
12. Approbativeness, Ambition—display.
13. Self-Esteem, Self-respect—dignity.
14. Firmness, Decision—perseverance.
15. Conscientiousness, Justice equity.
16. Hope, Expectation—enterprise.
17. Spirituality, Intuition—faith—credulity.
18. Veneration, Devotion—respect.
19. Benevolence, Kindness—goodness.
20. Constructiveness, Mechanical ingenuity.
21. Ideality, Refinement—taste—purity.
B. Sublimity, Love of grandeur—infinitude.
22. Imitation, Copying—patterning.
23. Mirthfulness, Jocoseness—wit—fun.
24. Individuality, Observation.
25. Form, Recollection of shape.
26. Size, Measuring by the eye.
27. Weight, Balancing—climbing.
28. Color, Judgment of colors.
29. Order, Method—system—arrangement.
30. Calculation, Mental arithmetic.
31. Locality, Recollection of places.
32. Eventuality, Memory of facts.
33. Time, Cognizance of duration.
34. Tune, Sense of harmony and melody.
35. Language, Expression of ideas.
36. Causality, Applying causes to effect. [tion.
37. Comparison, Inductive reasoning—illustra-
C. Human Nature, Perception of motives.
D. Agreeableness, Pleasantness—suavity.

Character in practice could be defined by an ability to take the initiative in difficult situations while others sit back and watch them unfold. A desire to assist wherever and whenever required, confident enough to overreach yourself and humble enough not to think that any task is beneath you. An ability to develop a 'tough skin', more resistant to the stresses and strains of daily practice. A disposition towards congeniality which breeds influence. In my experience, those at the very top of an organisation may not necessarily be the best designers but they are consistently characterised by a dynamism underpinned by confidence, directness, and decisiveness. Career progression is about reinforcing the skills you already have, developing additional skills relevant to your new environment, then applying those skills and acting them out through character.

The modes of advancement through the profession are unclear and uneven, but they can be navigated. This requires effort on your employers' part to ensure they set systems in place where each apprentice can become a master.[13] On your part, first recognise the office structure and your role within it. Then, through application of attitude, demonstration of skill, avoiding being typecast, knowing how and when to exceed your capabilities, as well as creating meaningful personal connections, your advancement can be smoother and clearer.

facing page

CHARACTER

Character becomes more important in practice, with a different balance of values and priorities.
Yellow: characteristics most valued in architecture school.
Pink: in practice. Orange: both.

Original public domain image amended by author.

Notes

1 Marrs, C., 2018. *Power to the people: the rise of the employee-owned practice.* [Online] Available at: https://www.architectsjournal.co.uk/news/power-to-the-people-the-rise-of-the-employee-owned-practice/10026872.article [Accessed 8 May 2020].
2 Chadha, S., 2019. *Co-operative by design.* [Online] Available at: https://www.ribaj.com/intelligence/employee-ownership-cooperative-architecture-practices-cullinan-studio-sahiba-chadha-rising-star-growing-interest [Accessed 20 May 2020].
3 Taylor, J., 2017. *Employee ownership is on the rise.* [Online] Available at: https://www.building.co.uk/employee-ownership-is-on-the-rise/5088542.article [Accessed 8 May 2020].
4 Butterfield, E., 2009. *The pros and cons of employee-owned companies.* [Online] Available at: https://www.architectmagazine.com/practice/the-pros-and-cons-of-employee-owned-companies_o [Accessed 8 May 2020].
5 Sennett, R., 2008. *Labours of love.* [Online] Available at: https://www.theguardian.com/books/2008/feb/02/featuresreviews.guardianreview14 [Accessed 8 May 2020].
6 Lewis, R., 2013. *Architect? A Candid Guide to the Profession* (3rd ed.). Cambridge, MA: MIT. p. 175.
7 Flippa, S.D., 2016. *Play your position.* [Sound Recording] (Quality Control Music).
8 Cuff, D., 1991. *Architecture: The Story of Practice.* Cambridge, MA: The MIT Press. p. 137.
9 Ibid. p. 138.
10 Lewis, *Architect?* p. 174.
11 Niemeyer, O., 2000. *The Curves of Time: the memoirs of Oscar Niemeyer.* London: Phaidon. p. 140.
12 Lewis, *Architect?* p. 17.
13 Saint, A., 1983. *The Image of an Architect.* New Haven, CT: Yale University. p. 38.

1.5 DESIGNING YOUR CAREER

YOU WILL EXPERIENCE
multiple global economic recessions in your working life.

↓

In the intervening years it is easy to carry on as normal, oblivious to what is looming over the horizon.
I graduated in 2008, entering the profession fully at the onset of the great recession. I write this now as we enter another, far worse, recession initiated by the global pandemic.[1] What can we learn from the past, to help us navigate this future?

Architecture firms suffer in a recession,[2] projects get postponed and new ones stop coming in. Employees eventually become redundant. In 2011, the number of architectural employees in the US and UK declined by 25% from a peak of three years earlier.[3] [4] The nature of the current recession may surprise us, but its occurrence should not. In the past 50 years, there have been seven global recessions.[5] You are statistically likely to experience four to five recessions in your career. Some ignore this inevitability when times are good, surprised[6] and unprepared when it happens. While the current economic system prevails, the threat of recession is omnipresent.

We can prepare firstly by recognition. The period before the last recession was driven by the "irrational exuberance"[7] of a property market which demanded increasingly redundant objects.[8] Is it enough to complain about the profession's pact with a boom-and-bust economic model only after the money has run out and the fantasy takes a wrong turn?[9] That the employees essential to propping up the fantasy are then viewed as potential liabilities in financial crises?[10] That the modes of practice which accentuated the negative impact of the last recession, chiefly reliance on the market for our employment, are impatiently returned to[11] as soon as things 'go back to normal'?

BEFORE THE MONEY RUNS OUT: Part 1

(left) Chelsea 100 11th Avenue. New York, United States. 2005–2010. Ateliers Jean Nouvel.
(right) The IAC Building. 2004–2007. Frank Gehry + Adamson Associates.
Photographer: Dan DeLuca.

BEFORE THE MONEY RUNS OUT: Part 2

Vessel: Hudson Yards. New York, United States. 2013–2019. Heatherwick Studio. Photographer: Stefan Kemmerling.

Recessions can remind the profession it does not solely exist to provide architectural statements or more sellable floor space for the rich and powerful[12] – but social housing, hospitals, schools, and public infrastructure too.[13] Recessions provide space for examining alternative modes of practice less wedded to economic boom-and-bust cycles.[14]

Recessions can also provide space for personal growth and opportunity. Made redundant (laid off) in the last recession, I experienced the worry and dented pride of being out of work – claiming unemployment benefits less than two years after graduation – and the upheaval of relocating 400 miles to find available work in the profession I had spent the previous seven years preparing for. Yet the recession gave me perspective too. I realised what I enjoyed most in architecture, writing much of my first book while unemployed. Relocating out of necessity also forced me out of my comfort zone to a bigger city, with bigger projects and greater responsibility. Recessions are not easy, but they can provide opportunities for reflection and growth.[15]

Many of my colleagues experienced the positive side of the recession, with a lack of employment opportunities forcing them to create their own – by establishing architectural practices now flourishing a decade later. Some started exciting new lives in other countries where the effects of the recession were less severe, or non-existent. There were also many who had a negative experience, leaving the profession altogether in a cloud of unfulfilled promise.

Employment depends on and follows projects. This is an inescapable fact of current practice.[16] It does not need to be the only way in which we gain work. There is a trend for architects to find new ways of subverting and appropriating existing modes of practice, while networking and engaging to find new ones. Practices such as Rural Urban Framework who assist local communities to develop new cooperative enterprises and facilities using traditional techniques and contemporary technology; or Kéré Architecture who have established non-profit organisations to design and build schools in Burkina Faso.

ARCHITECTURE IN THE COMMUNITY

"Serving also as a center for women's handicraft, the Shijia House bridges the individual and collective identity of the village. Construction of the house has initiated a new phase for the local economy, developing a new cooperative business in traditional straw weaving. Overall, the project represents an architectural attempt to consciously evolve rural house dynamics in China."

A House For All Seasons. Shijia, China. 2009–2012. Rural Urban Framework.

COMMUNITY ENGAGEMENT

"The library's ceiling is an innovative feature that makes good use of local technology. Clay pots, traditionally made by the women of the village, were brought to the site and cut, so as to be open at both the top and bottom. The pots were then cast into the concrete ceiling to create holes for light and ventilation."

Bibliothèque scolaire Gando. Gando, Burkina Faso. 2010. Kéré Architecture

COMMUNITY ASSET

Bibliothèque scolaire Gando. Gando, Burkina Faso. 2010. Kéré Architecture

This attitude can be adopted on a personal level too. The first strategy is resilience. Find ways in which you can protect yourself from the vicissitudes of the economy by doing the same things, but in a different way. Learn new skills which make you a more versatile and valuable employee. Learn a new language which might ensure a smoother passage to a country not affected by recession. Search for alternative streams of work for your practice through research grants, competitions, or crowdsourcing. This should be done in good times in preparation for the bad. Hard work and talent alone will not save you, but resilience and adaptability might.

You also need to diversify. What facets of architecture excite and interest you the most? How can you involve yourself in them, outside of your typical employment in practice? Find ways to protect yourself by doing different things. By diversifying into different sub-fields, you can broaden your knowledge base and skill set. By inhabiting different spheres of influence, you can provide an alternative stream of income to rely on when the economy stumbles. Write or teach part-time as I do; pursue construction law and become an arbitrator in legal disputes as some of my colleagues do; apply your detailing skills to help artists realise their work as some of my friends do; become involved in community activism to realise small construction projects as some of my peers do; or become an expert in a particular field of practice, advising other bodies and organisations as some of my bosses do. These examples can run in-stream with your role as a practising architect.

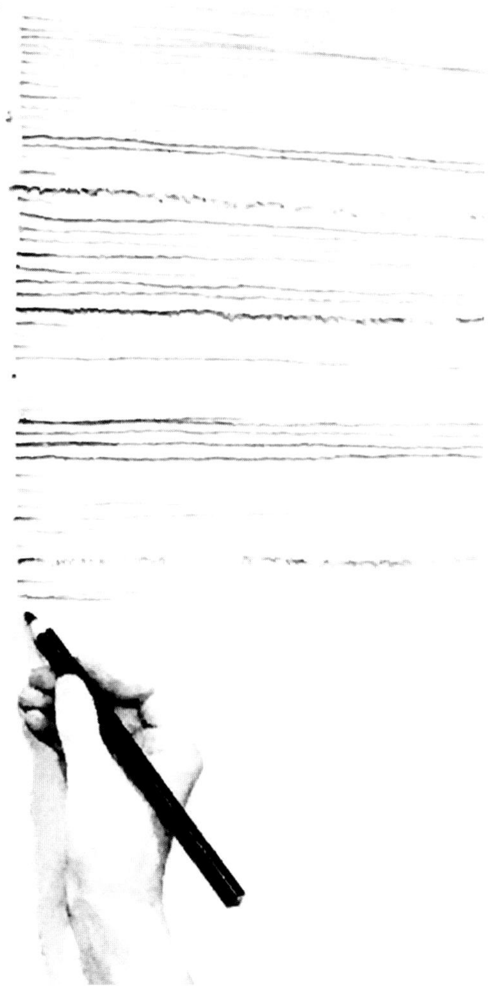

TEACHING

Line drawing exercise. Stage 1.

Mackintosh School of Architecture, Glasgow School of Art.

ACTIVISM

"In a project of this size, with a short timeframe of three months, logistics will present itself as one of the major challenges. With seventy workers taking part, eight water buffaloes hauling trees from the forest and an on-site sawmill, project management becomes essential. The entire project is made up of ten simple details. Basic and pragmatic approach to design made it possible to realize this project with an untrained workforce."

Cassia Co-op Training facility. Kerinchi, Indonesia. 2011. TYIN tegnestue Architects

Strategies of resilience and diversification are not solely crisis measures. They also allow you to take control of your career. A route to contentment within a precarious industry.[17] Plan this route out. What stages of development will mark the route to your goal? What skills or knowledge do you need to attain by each stage? This plan may be derailed by circumstances or events along the way, but if you have a varied and adaptable skill set and a diverse range of roles and streams of income, it will be easier to get back on track or find an equally fruitful new route.

Many who embark on the journey to becoming an architect do not complete it.[18] Statistically, only one in three architecture students will go on to become a licensed architect.[19] Maybe you won't become an architect either. No one tells you this when you start architecture school. You may lose interest before you complete your studies; struggle with the discrepancy between the anticipation and reality; transfer your skills elsewhere in the creative or construction industries; or be forced through economic hardship to enter another more secure profession.[20] Countless peers and friends of mine have.

Before you do … Could resilience and adaptability of your knowledge and skills strengthen your position in practice? Could you diversify alongside your role as a practising architect? Can you take control of your career rather than reset it? Do you still have a passion for creating architecture? If you answer yes to any of these questions – stay with us. We need more people like you.

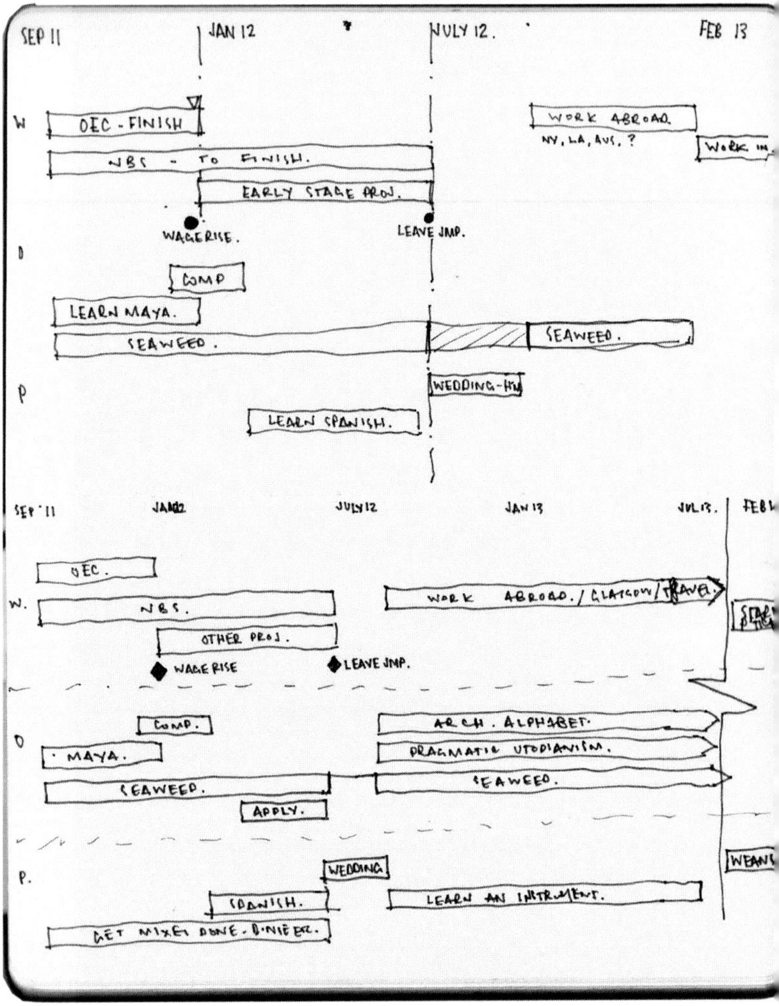

SOME WINS / SOME LOSSES

Personal Sketch Development Plan. 2011–2014. J. Tait

Notes

1 Gopinath, G., 2020. *The Great Lockdown: worst economic downturn since the Great Depression.* [Online] Available at: https://blogs.imf.org/2020/04/14/the-great-lockdown-worst-economic-downturn-since-the-great-depression/ [Accessed 11 May 2020].

2 Ouroussoff, N., 2008. *It was fun till the money ran out.* [Online] Available at: https://www.nytimes.com/2008/12/21/arts/design/21ouro.html [Accessed 11 May 2020].

3 Ibid., p. 11.

4 Construction Industry Council, 2009. *The Impact of the Recession on Construction Professional Services.* London: Construction Industry Council.

5 International Monetary Fund, 2009. *Global Economic Slump Challenges Policies.* Washington, DC: International Monetary Fund.

6 Ouroussoff, *It was fun till the money ran out,* [Online].

7 Aureli, P., 2013. *Less is Enough: On Architecture and Asceticism.* Moscow: Strelka Press. p. 7.

8 Ibid., p. 7.

9 Ouroussoff, *It was fun till the money ran out,* [Online].

10 Cuff, D., 1991. *Architecture: The Story of Practice.* Cambridge, MA: The MIT Press. p. 132.

11 Moser, C., 2014. *Architecture 3.0: The Disruptive Design Practice Handbook.* Abingdon: Routledge. p. ix.

12 Ouroussoff, *It was fun till the money ran out,* [Online].

13 Ibid.

14 Awan, N., Schneider, T,. & Till, J., 2012. *Spatial Agency: Other Ways of Doing Architecture.* Abingdon: Routledge. p. 28.

15 Moser, *Architecture 3.0,* p. 214.

16 Lewis, R., 2013. *Architect? A Candid Guide to the Profession* (3rd ed.). Cambridge, MA: MIT. p. 25.

17 Aureli, *Less is enough,* pp. 56–57.

18 Cuff, *Architecture,* p. 117.

19 Mirza & Nacey Research, 2019. *RIBA Education Statistics 2017/18.* London: RIBA.

20 Ouroussoff, *It was fun till the money ran out,* [Online].

2.0
DESIGNING IN PRACTICE

THE PROPERTIES AND VALUES of architecture remain the same in practice as they do in architecture school.

↓

You know why and what is created, but you have yet to experience *how* it is created. In practice, this process can obscure and overwhelm. What is created and why, becomes secondary to the day-to-day process of creating it. *Why* we create what we do, and *what* that can be, must always be at the forefront of our minds.

Buildings can be permanent or temporary. Designed for one simple need, or multiple competing ones. Buildings can have roofs, walls, and floors; or only some of these things. They can be static or movable. Erected carefully or carelessly. Buildings can agglomerate and huddle to form districts, villages, towns, and cities; or separate and isolate to stand alone in a landscape. Buildings can work with nature or against it. A building can be light or heavy, solid or unstable. It can be opaque or transparent, or both simultaneously. Buildings can create imprints in our memory, and they can be instantly forgettable too. Buildings can be gilded or sparse; pompous or humble. They can communicate absolute power or absolutely nothing at all. Buildings can stand resolute in the face of conflict or forces of nature, and they can crumble and fall at the first sign of attack. They can symbolise the apex of cultural endeavour and artistry, or the nadir. Buildings can be vital public assets or vacant private commodities. Buildings have the capacity to excite and delight as often as they can bore and depress. Buildings can be anything.

SHELTER AND ACTION

"We have proven, as humanity, that caves are not enough for us. We need a space that is not only a refuge but that is able to allow for and inspire our lives. This is what architecture should be, but I think we have forgotten that."[1]

Ways of Life. Conceptual Collage. 2019. Tatiana Bilbao ESTUDIO

What is definable of all buildings is that they provide for the second most important human need, shelter, after sustenance, and for the environments within which society performs its most essential functions and urges. Architecture provides secured and delineated space for human beings to act. The foundation of any civilisation lies in its walls, roofs, and floors. Architecture provides the framework, just as laws do in a non-material sense, around which human life and action can take place. As Hannah Arendt explains of Ancient Greece: "Before men[2] began to act, a definite space had to be secured and a structure built where all subsequent actions could take place, the space being the public realm of the polis[3] and its structure the law; legislator and architect belonged in the same category."[4]

Architecture is also one of the few remaining "public arts".[5] It is all around us. Architecture has the capacity to "correspond to the three states of human existence: facing oneself; facing the other people; and facing the unimpeachable natural world".[6] To engender visceral emotional reactions; contribute to our understanding of society; and engage with the natural world which sustains us.

This capacity needs to be squared with the other role of architecture – for private provision. Buildings can also be pieces of a privately owned world,[7] inextricably linked to the fortunes and principles of those who own and occupy them. We see parallels in the practice of destroying the dwellings of those expelled from society in medieval France;[8] and the propagandistic[9] destruction of the ancient city of Palmyra by Islamic militants in recent years. By erasing the edifice, the characteristics and memory of its owners and occupants are erased too.

Providing for both public art and private provision exposes a duality. Is architecture practised for the sake of individuals and the needs of the market, or a communal undertaking dedicated to the service of society?[10] The reality is both. Whether conceived for public good or private gain, the role of architecture remains as it always has: to provide shelter, and for the spaces and structures which allow human beings to act.

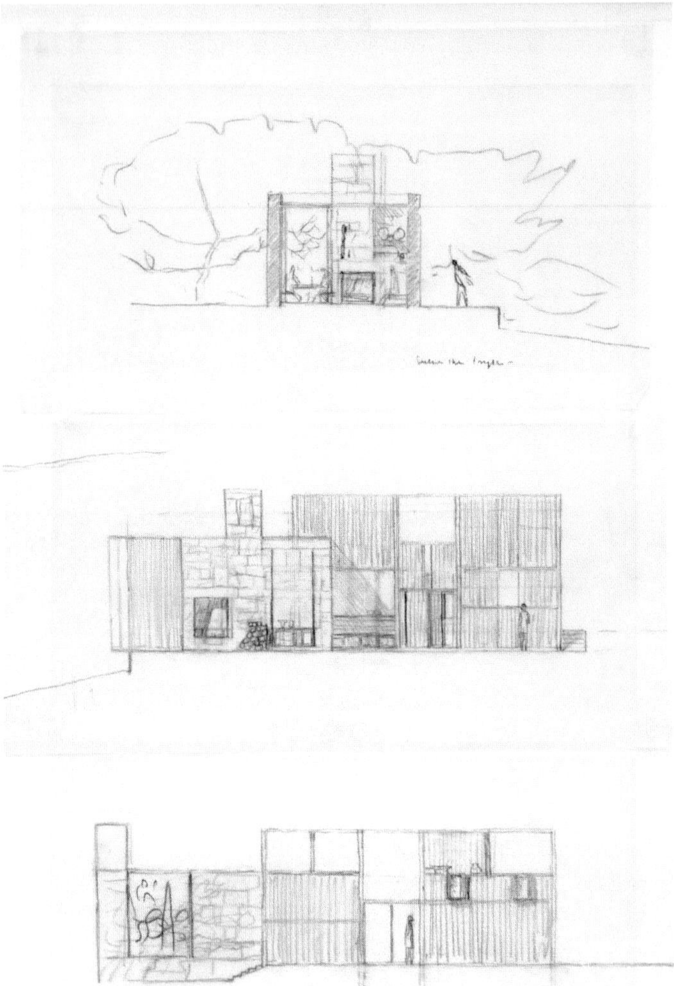

FROM A HOUSE TO A CITY

"The realm of the architect is as expansive as that of human life itself. As Louis I Kahn has said, 'the Architect can build a house, and build a city in the same breath'."[11]

Fisher House. Pennsylvania, USA. 1967. Louis I. Kahn. © Fisher Family Collection, The Architectural Archives, University of Pennsylvania.
Civic Center Studies. Philadelphia, USA. 1956–1957. Louis I. Kahn. © Louis I. Kahn Collection, University of Pennsylvania and Pennsylvania Historical and Museum Commission.

This becomes the hidden value of the architect. The capacity to connect with and enrich the human experience. Architecture which "reaches the soul".[12] A capacity often placed under daily strain in the process of creating architecture. Why and what we create becomes at risk from *how* we create it. Understanding this process in practice, then, becomes even more critical. Not only for your ability to realise your architectural ambitions, but for the future quality of the built environment itself.

Notes

1 Frearson, A., 2019. *"We banned renders' from the design process says Tatiana Bilbao."* [Online] Available at: https://www.dezeen.com/2019/12/04/tatiana-bilbao-banned-renderings-architecture-interview/ [Accessed 1 April 2020].

2 Arendt's gendered distinction.

3 *Polis* is the Ancient Greek word for the 'city'.

4 Arendt, H., 1998. *The Human Condition* (2nd ed.). Chicago: University of Chicago Press. pp. 194–195.

5 Ibid., p. 39.

6 Shepheard, P., 1994. *What is Architecture?* Cambridge, MA: MIT Press. p. 24.

7 Kostof, S., 1977. The Architect in the Middle Ages, East and West. In: *The Architect: Chapters in the History of the Profession.* New York: Oxford University Press. pp. 61–62.

8 Ibid., pp. 61–62.

9 Curry, A., 2017. *Ancient sites damaged and destroyed by ISIS.* [Online] Available at: https://www.nationalgeographic.co.uk/history-and-civilisation/2017/11/ancient-sites-damaged-and-destroyed-isis [Accessed 14 May 2020].

10 Saint, A., 1983. *The Image of an Architect.* New Haven, CT: Yale University. p. 6.

11 International Design Conference of Aspen (IDCA). Kahn, L. Aspen: Sci-Arc, 1972.

12 Markli, P., 2018. *My Profession, The Art of Building.* Cambridge, MA: Harvard Graduate Design School.

ARCHITECTURE WHICH REACHES THE SOUL

Casa de Retiro Espiritual. Seville, Spain. 1978. Emilio Ambasz

2.1 FUTURE

ARCHITECTURE IS A MIX OF eternal principles and contemporary responses.

↓

The architect is required to handle convention and history as much as create new solutions for unique challenges.[1] The next step of your journey is both daunting and exciting. You are entering a realm where architecture is real. What you are involved in creating will have a material impact on society. This is the most rewarding and challenging aspect of being an architect in practice – to apply your creative mindset and toolset in practice. What will your contribution be? How will you respond to the future challenges facing society?

Climate change, the destruction of nature,[2] and inequality are the most complex and important challenges facing society in the twenty-first century.[3] Architecture regularly interfaces with each of these crises. It produces vast amounts of carbon dioxide in its production and use; the extraction of materials used to create it often cause irreversible damage to nature; and many of the projects architects are engaged in create new or entrench existing inequalities.[4]

These crises should not surprise us, we have been given at least 150 years forewarning. Marx and Engels highlighted the inequalities precipitated by an "epidemic of over-production"[5] needed to satiate the overconsumption which is the root cause of climate change.[6] Alerting us, too, to the destruction of nature in the pursuit of short-term profit.[7] The climate crisis, destruction of nature, and inequality should not surprise a society now hastily attempting to rectify them.

A PANDEMIC OF OVER-PRODUCTION

Construction site. Ulaanbaatar, Mongolia.

Equilibrium, stability, and durability[8] has been surrendered to super-abundance.[9] Architecture, responding to societal and political demands, is no different. Architects have aided and abetted this situation. If society wishes to overconsume, destroy nature, and promote inequality, architecture has been only too willing to oblige.

The construction industry is responsible for nearly 40% of all global energy use and carbon dioxide emissions.[10] There is a moral dilemma[11] central to the profession you are entering. How does the creation of new buildings, using new materials extracted to then be eventually discarded, contribute positively to the health of the planet? How can we square this urgent demand with the innate desire of each generation to contribute to the concomitant experience of the ever-renewing human artifice?[12]

This begins with a fundamental shift in our approach to reuse. We could do worse than adopt the rallying cry of Lacaton & Vassal to "Never demolish, never remove or replace, always add, transform and reuse."[13] This approach dramatically reduces the amount of new material employed, but has a deeper principle of rejecting the tabula rasa approach favoured by much modern development which sees demolition and building anew as economically and politically preferable. This philosophy is manifest in the transformation of the modernist Grand Parc housing project in the outskirts of Bordeaux where the original façades were opened up to offer an "intoxicating rush of light, air and views"[14] as well as the addition of semi-outdoor space with the careful creation of glazed balconies. Challenging clients, fellow professionals, and your colleagues perhaps less attuned to these issues about their dependency on building anew will become a more important feature of your future in practice.

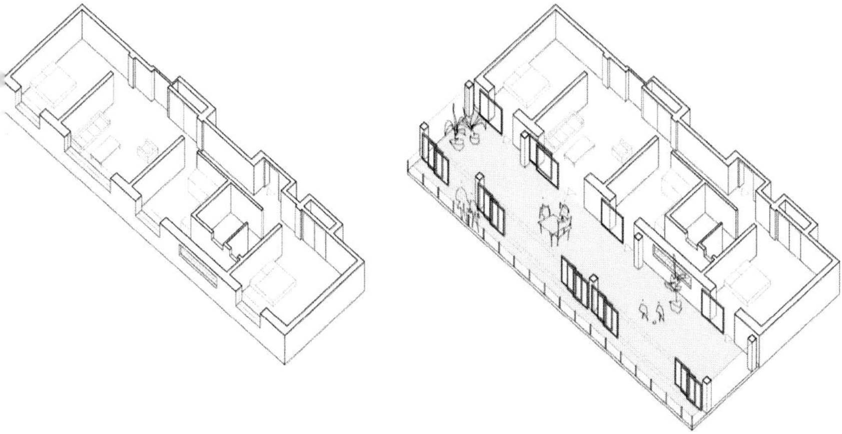

NEVER DEMOLISH

Diagram shows addition to floor area and amenity provision by retaining and adding to the existing structure.

Grand Parc. Bordeaux, France. 2016. Lacaton & Vassal.

New buildings can employ recycled construction waste, such as the use of recycled aggregate in concrete, reducing material extraction by 35%.[15] Or, reuse existing building components – brick, stone, timber, steel – reducing carbon dioxide emissions by more than half.[16] A strategy employed by Rural Urban Framework at the Tongjiang Recycled Brick School, reusing the brick from a previously dilapidated school building in the new one. An environmentally sound tactic that also continues the memories and traditions of the local area in a resolutely modern way.

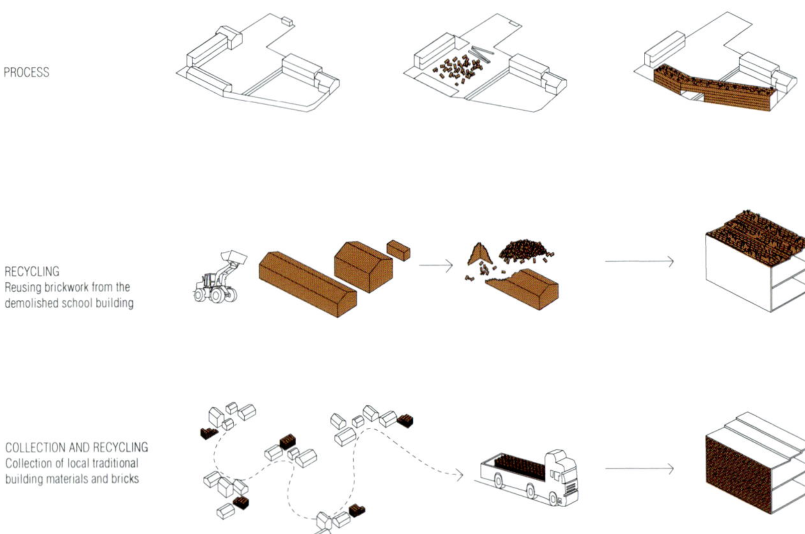

RECYCLE

Tongjiang Primary School. Jianxi Province, China. 2012. Rural Urban Framework.

When we do build anew, we must reappraise the tendencies that the practice of architecture relies upon. A desire to "conquer nature"[17] in the pursuit of profit and a supply chain dominated by global conglomerates. This begins with architects specifying local materials over those that require to be shipped.[18] This is challenging in practice, where the tendency is to risk-aversely specify materials and employ construction methods substantiated by comprehensive documentation, technical support, and legal warranties more commonly found with larger producers. However, using local materials not only makes environmental sense but helps strengthen local skills bases and economies, reducing the reliance on globalised labour and the siphoning of profit by multinational conglomerates.[19]

Challenge these hegemonies by finding local building materials and techniques, encouraging those who produce them to develop the same operational standards. Such as Herzog & de Meuron's Parrish Art Museum in New York State, a "direct expression of readily accessible building materials and local construction methods",[20] or their Ricola Kräuterzentrum in Switzerland, "built largely out of locally sourced earth".[21] Environmentally conscious design is embedded in both the concept and the reality.

LOCAL TECHNIQUE AND MATERIALS

Parrish Art Museum. New York, USA. 2012. Herzog & DeMeuron.

Ricola Kräuterzentrum. Laufen, Switzerland. 2014. Herzog & DeMeuron.

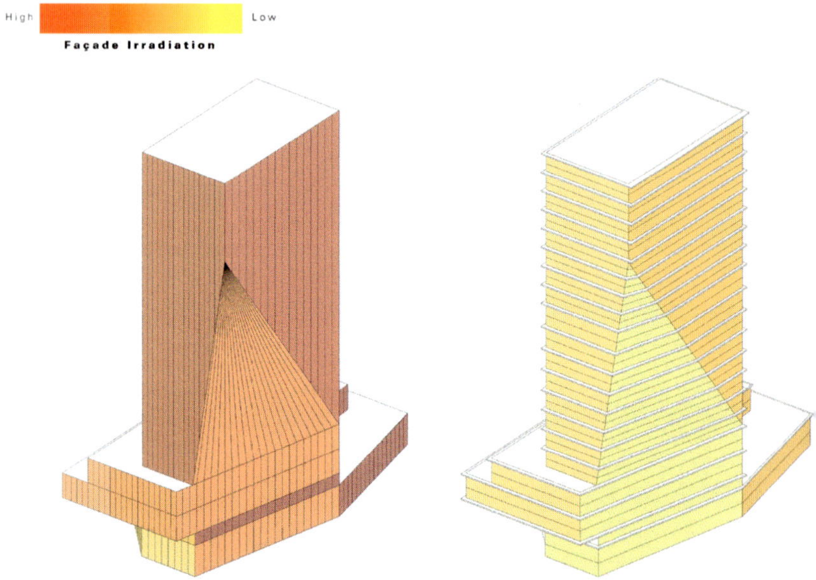

OPTIMISE

Diagram shows design options taken to extend floor slab to act as shading device significantly reducing façade irradiation as well as enhancing the form of the design architecturally.

Sustainable Bank HQ. Shanghai, China. 2018. Mecanoo & Buro Happold.

This approach must be fused with the latest advancements in technology to ensure it does not become retrograde. Not the solutionism that sees technology as a profitable panacea, but the considered employment of it throughout the design process. At an early design stage, use Integrated Building Performance Simulators which model the ventilation, thermal comfort, daylight, moisture flow, building controls, occupant behaviour, and renewable energy systems acting within a building design.[22] Thus allowing practitioners to identify which adjustments (in scale, form, orientation, fenestration, construction type, etc.) are required to optimise energy performance and assess future environmental impact during the design stage. An approach taken by Mecanoo in their competition proposal for the New Development Bank Headquarters in Shanghai, testing and discovering variations in the form and detail of the envelope for optimised energy performance.

In the developed design stages, embrace off-site digital fabrication tools which minimise material waste and achieve complex forms with little on-site construction. A technique applied by Pencil Office at their 'Simple Factory Building' in Singapore. An intricate façade of complex geometries and intersecting profiles was created by CNC (computer numerical control) routing and computer-controlled hot wire cutting.[23] A 1.2m deep veil reconciles the age-old demands of shading and views out, using contemporary technology.

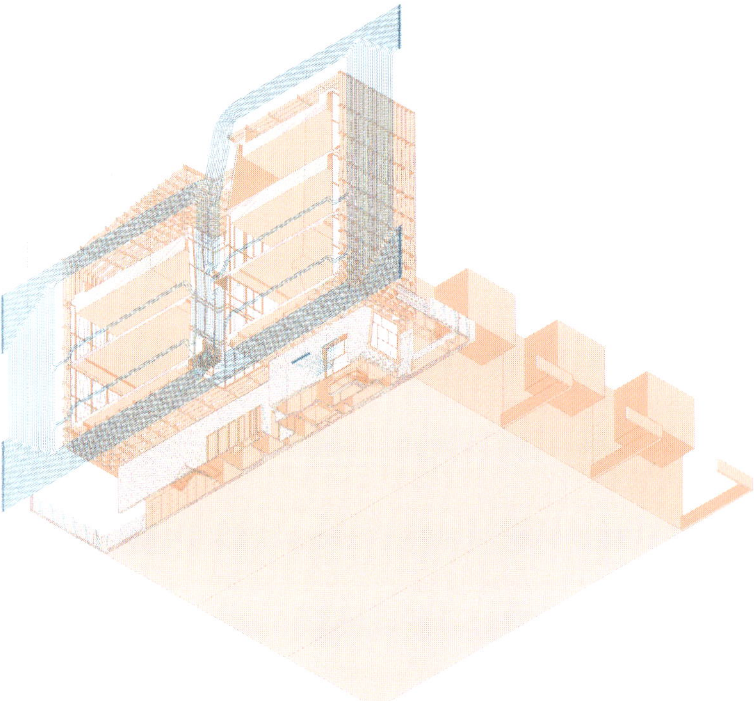

MINIMISE WASTE

A Simple Factory Building. Singapore. 2012. Pencil Office.

OKP HOLDINGS LIMITED

In the post-occupancy phase, where energy use is high, Baumschlager Eberle's 2226 office building eschews all heating, cooling, or mechanical ventilation. The simply constructed building employs only the use of vent shutters in the façade operated by the building users or software-controlled to ensure a sufficient supply of fresh air to prevent the building from cooling out in winter or overheating in summer.[24]

If these systems and approaches do not exist within your working environment, they should. The future environmental performance of what you will be involved in creating depends on it. This is now real. What you do in practice will affect the lives of others. Do you want to be complicit in the profligacy of one of the most wasteful and environmentally damaging industries on the planet, or proactively effect change? By responding to the need to wean ourselves from our dependency on growth,[25] and staying alert to those who see climate change as an economic opportunity, we can develop more engaging and enriching design responses. Design responses which are climatically appropriate, value reuse, employ local materials, embrace new technologies, and above all respect and improve the host environments within which they are situated.

facing page

MINIMISE ENERGY USE

2226. Lustenau, Austria. 2013. Baumschlager Eberle Architekten. Photographer: Eduard Hueber.

Notes

1 Kostof, S., 1977. The Architect in the Middle Ages, East and West. In: *The Architect: Chapters in the History of the Profession*. New York: Oxford University Press. p. 64.
2 Le Page, M., 2019. *Destruction of nature is as big a threat to humanity as climate change*. [Online] Available at: https://www.newscientist.com/article/2201697-destruction-of-nature-is-as-big-a-threat-to-humanity-as-climate-change/ [Accessed 18 May 2020].
3 Cornell, S. & Gupta, A., 2020. Is climate change the most important challenge of our times? In: M. Hulme, ed. *Contemporary Climate Change Debates: A Student Primer*. Abingdon: Routledge, p. 12.
4 Nolan, H., 2019. *New York's Hudson Yards is an ultra-capitalist Forbidden City*. [Online] Available at: https://www.theguardian.com/commentisfree/2019/mar/13/new-york-hudson-yards-ultra-capitalist [Accessed 18 May 2020].
5 Marx, K. & Engels, F., 1888. *The Communist Manifesto*. Penguin Classics ed. London: Penguin Random House. p. 10.
6 Atkin, E., 2019. *Climate change is the symptom. Consumer culture is the disease*. [Online] Available at: https://newrepublic.com/article/154147/climate-change-symptom-consumer-culture-disease [Accessed 18 May 2020].
7 Engels, F., 1876. *The Part Played by Labour in the Transition from Ape to Man*. Moscow: Progress Publishers.
8 Arendt, H., 1998. *The Human Condition* (2nd ed.). Chicago: University of Chicago Press. p. 126.
9 Tait, J., 2019. *Laurieston Lectures* [Interview] (30 November 2019).
10 Global Alliance for Buildings and Construction, 2017. *Global Status Report 2017: Towards a Zero-emission, Efficient, and Resilient Buildings and Construction Sector*. Nairobi: United Nations Environment Programme.
11 Ibid.
12 Arendt, *The Human Condition*, p. 152.
13 Slessor, C., 2019. *Grand Parc, Bordeaux review – a rush of light, air and views*. [Online] Available at: https://www.theguardian.com/artanddesign/2019/may/12/grand-parc-bordeaux-lacaton-vassal-mies-van-der-rohe-award [Accessed 18 May 2020].
14 Ibid.

15 Pavlu, T., Koci, V., & Hajek, P., 2019. Environmental Assessment of Two Use Cycles of Recycled Aggregate Concrete. *Sustainability*, November, p. 17.
16 Wainwright, O., 2020. *The case for ... never demolishing another building.* [Online] Available at: https://www.theguardian.com/cities/2020/jan/13/the-case-for-never-demolishing-another-building [Accessed 18 May 2020].
17 Rudofsky, B., 1964. *Architecture without Architects: A Short Introduction to Non-pedigreed Architecture.* New York: Doubleday. p. 4.
18 Awan, N., Schneider, T., & Till, J., 2012. *Spatial Agency: Other Ways of Doing Architecture.* Abingdon: Routledge. p. 60.
19 Ibid., p. 60.
20 Herzog & de Meuron, 2012. *Parrish Art Museum.* [Online] Available at: https://www.herzogdemeuron.com/index/projects/complete-works/326-350/349-parrish-art-museum.html [Accessed 18 May 2020].
21 Herzog & de Meuron, 2014. *Ricola Kräuterzentrum.* [Online] Available at: https://www.herzogdemeuron.com/index/projects/complete-works/351-375/369-ricola-kraeuterzentrum.html [Accessed 18 May 2020].
22 Clarke, J., 2019. Foreword to the second edition. In: J. Hensen & R. Lamberts, eds. *Building Performance Simulation for Design and Operation.* Abingdon: Routledge, p. i.
23 Pencil Office, 2012. *A simple factory building.* [Online] Available at: http://penciloffice.com/project/projecta-simple-factory-building/ [Accessed 18 May 2020].
24 Skoof, J., 2014. *House without heating: office building in Austria.* [Online] Available at: https://www.detail-online.com/article/house-without-heating-office-building-in-austria-16667/ [Accessed 18 May 2020].
25 Harper, P., 2019. *"Our dependency on growth, like on concrete, must be abolished"*. [Online] Available at: https://www.dezeen.com/2019/09/25/oslo-architecture-triennale-architecture-degrowth-phineas-harper/ [Accessed 18 May 2020].

TECHNICAL ADVICE NOTE

03

SURVEYING

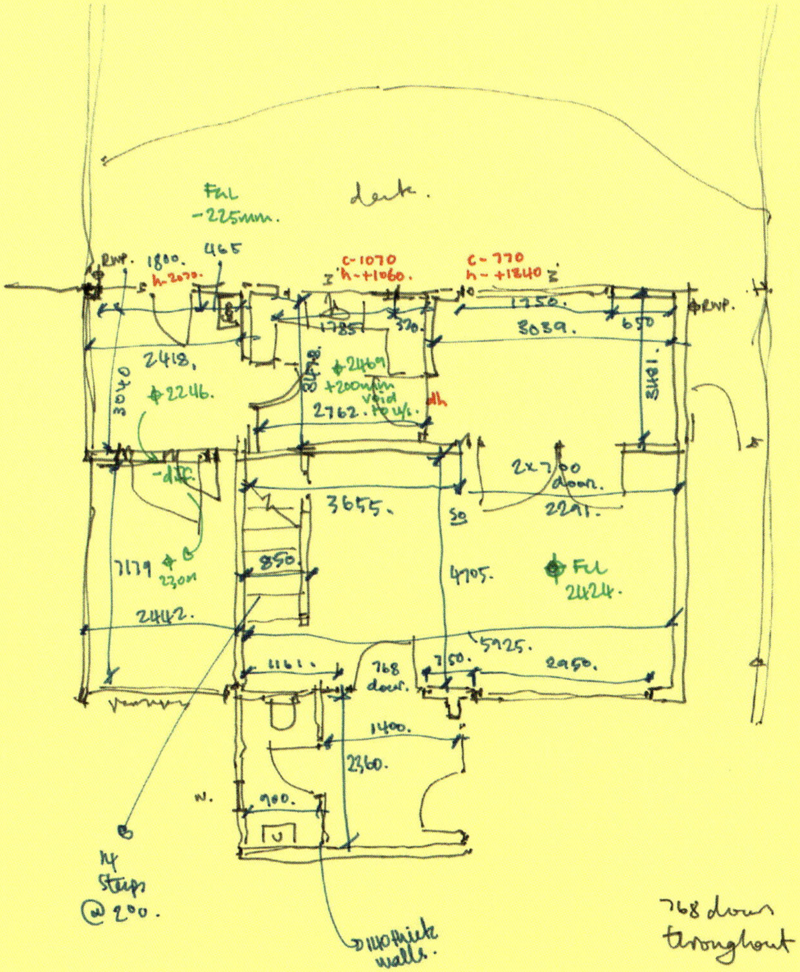

OPENING HEIGHTS

CEILING / FLOOR LEVELS

DIMENSIONS

INTERVIEW C

↘ Kengo Kuma

You spent eight years after graduation, before setting up an office of your own. What did you learn during this period?

When I graduated from architecture school, I felt I had no experience in society. I thought for architects – to know the reality of society is very important. Then I decided to work for a big firm. Before, when I was a student I worked as an intern for Fumihiko Maki and Hiroshi Hara's office. I already knew their working style and way of thinking. But I wanted to know society, the reality of the system so worked in a large office for some years. During this period, I also wanted to stay in a different country so I decided to go to New York to attend Columbia University. I stayed one year in New York – it was a very fruitful experience for me. In that year I wrote a book about architects (Jutaku-ron), where I interviewed 12 architects – Philip Johnson, Peter Eisenmann, Michael Graves, etc. I visited their offices, it was fun to see their working environments, it was a fun experience.

facing page

Nakagawa-machi Bato Hiroshige Museum of Art. Nakagawa, Japan. 2000. Kengo Kuma + Associates.

Photographer: Qingyue Li.

How has the practice of architecture changed in the last three decades since you founded Kengo Kuma & Associates?

It has changed a lot. When I started my practice in 1986 the economy was booming in Japan. We call that era 'The Bubble Era'. I started my office at the age of 32 and luckily many clients came to me for some big projects. But after four years, by 1991, the bubble economy burst. Suddenly every project in Tokyo was cancelled. I decided then to travel out to the countryside of Japan. In the 1990s I didn't do any projects in Tokyo. Instead I travelled a lot to small villages and towns where I created some very small but interesting projects. This experience of ten years was very important. After the year 2000 many of my countryside projects had been published and many clients came to me again to build in Tokyo. Then I began to get some work also outside of Japan. So, I experienced three unique periods – the bubble era, the burst of the bubble era and lost decade, then globalisation. From the countryside to the global.

Can you tell me about your design process? How does an idea develop into a built reality?

At the beginning of the design process, we try to find the material for the project. For example, we think – for this project we should use stone, or for this project we should use wood. That approach is very different from the common approach. Architects normally start the project from planning, the form and the programme, the last phase of the design is the specification of the material. My approach is to start from the material. If we can find a unique local material, then we are very happy.

China Academy of Arts' Folk-Art Museum. Hangzhou, China. 2015. Kengo Kuma + Associates.

Photographer: Eiichi Kano

You value collaboration and teamwork. What do you expect from those you collaborate with?

I believe architectural design is teamwork. How to communicate with team members is the most important thing. I used to play basketball. I always tell my team to 'pass' the ball not to 'dribble'. It is similar to soccer, or any team sport.

How can technology re-connect architecture with craft?

Craftsmanship is about materials. We try to find the essence of the material, the spirit of material. A good craftsperson can get to the heart of the material. To work with good craftspeople is very important to us. At the same time, with technology a new side of the material can be shown. For example, we have combined wood with carbon fibre. By using carbon fibre we can show a very different face of wood. Combining craftsmanship with new technology is very important for us. Sometimes when we work in certain countries, I take Japanese craftspeople with me. For example, I brought Japanese carpenters to France and I brought Japanese plasterers to Paris to make a unique façade in plasterwork. But this is not always the case. I like to work with local craftspeople because the 'Genius Loci' (spirit of a place) is embedded in both the local materials and the people who work with them.

China Academy of Arts' Folk-Art Museum. Hangzhou, China. 2015. Kengo Kuma + Associates.

Photographer: Eiichi Kano

Fond Regional D'art Contemporain. Marseille, France. 2013. Kengo Kuma + Associates.

Photographer: Fred Romero.

What interests outside of architecture do you have? Do they influence your work?

Music. I love music, I love Jazz very much. I used to play the piano, and my sister is a composer. Music is very familiar to me. In my design, rhythm is very important. The instrument is very important too. Material is a kind of instrument. I feel a connection with musicians – not sculptors or painters. Sculpture and painting are static. Music is movement, it is flowing.

Your projects span all four corners of the globe. How do you respond to each local context in a globalised world?

My best experience was a trip to the Sahara Desert as a student. At that time, I was very disappointed with Modern architecture and I didn't agree with recreating traditional Japanese design either. It was too nostalgic for me. So, I tried to find something at the edge of the world, not what I learned in architecture school or Japanese tradition. The Sahara Desert was my dream place. What I always do with every project is to try to learn many things from new experiences. You find new things in new places.

What future challenges do you think architecture faces? How should it respond to them?

Our lifestyles need to totally change after this Coronavirus pandemic. We should forget the idea of dense cities, we need to find another way of living and another way of working. Architecture has been supporting this system. Architects build big boxes and shut people up in them. This is a product of the Industrial era – but even after the Industrial era has passed, we still don't want to change our ways of living. Society needs to change its way of life, and architects should find a new way of creating for this new way of life. This new way of living is very much related with the environment. The importance of outdoor space, and semi-outdoor space is now much greater than before. The pandemic will attack us more than the climate crisis, every ten years we will have a pandemic. Our designs must change drastically, if not, we will not survive as a species.

What advice would you give students dealing with these issues then in the future?

To travel to the edge of the world. Only students have time to do that. The edge of the world is where you can find hints for a new lifestyle. Walk on foot and meet new people. It is more important than reading books, and more important than attending architecture school!

facing page

V&A. Dundee, United Kingdom. 2018. Kengo Kuma + Associates.

2.2 ETHICS

IN PRACTICE, ALMOST EVERY design decision has the capacity for dilemma. Architects have a dual responsibility to respond to the needs of society at large, and the needs of those who commission their designs.

↓

To negotiate "a balance between legitimate public concerns and private demands is at the heart of the architect's professional obligation".[1] Neither flexible spinelessness nor stubborn rigidness is tenable in the rush and reality of practice. Neither response engages with the nuanced complexities of the matters at hand – one blindly accepting and facilitating them; the other myopically neglecting them.

While working on a residential project in the Middle East, each apartment contained a maid's room, which we were ordered was to have no windows. Shocked and naïve I complained to my superior at having to facilitate this inequality – "just draw it". We arranged the maid's room on plan towards a narrow courtyard, which created a ten-storey high solid stone wall. Its aesthetic qualities were undeniable, providing a strong and bold counterpoint to the lighter glazed main façade. It looked good – but I couldn't get the image of the trapped maid out of my head. We presented the elevation to the design partner, who loved it – "whatever you do ... keep that", admiring its strength and boldness. No one told him the dark truth it was concealing. Aesthetics overruled ethics.

Most of the ethical dilemmas which architecture faces, besides cultural and political, concern money. Money

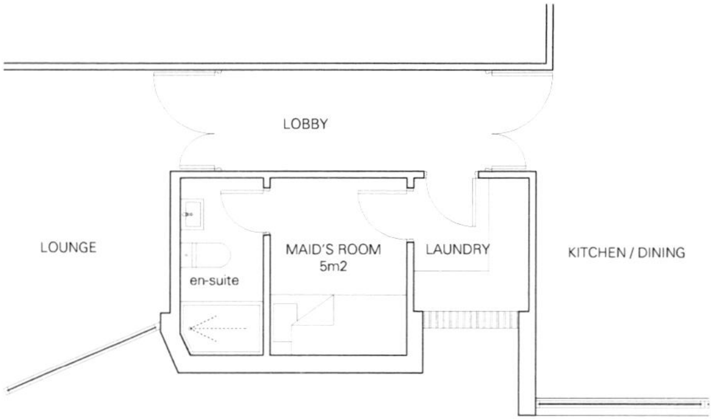

FLOOR PLAN

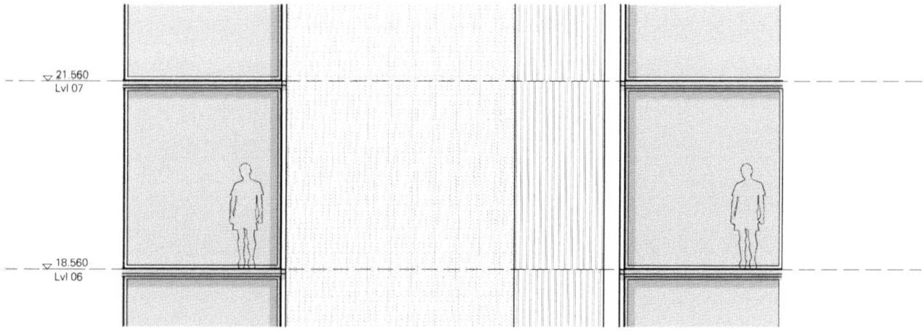

ELEVATION

"JUST DRAW IT"

5m² windowless maid's room. Middle East. 2012.

dominates the profession and its output. Since the early Modernists sought to align with the building industry by relying on standardised elements[2] – economy has become embedded as a necessity of the design process.[3] Something I encounter in housing design where the accepted standard ceiling height is a barely adequate 2.4 metres – the exact same vertical length as a sheet of the plasterboard material used to construct the walls. Any attempts to increase this height will mean another board has to be used and cut, usually vehemently resisted on grounds of economy. Standardisation and profit overrules quality of space.

The consequences of money become most apparent when design becomes participatory in the inequalities of the economic status quo. Whole sections of society are denied access to decent housing;[4] neighbourhoods become socially cleansed to make way for more profitable buildings for more affluent residents;[5] dwellings become smaller[6] and less durable; the public realm becomes privatised with increasingly sophisticated design strategies and technology in an effort to exclude an unwitting population;[7] while the contractor-led provision of public buildings[8] values efficiency and economy above quality or even safety concerns.[9] These inequalities and unethical practices are facilitated by architects, caused by the professions' uneasy pact with capital.

There are routes out of this pact. The first principle is that architecture should never compromise safety. To paraphrase Vitruvius, it is better to be at expense than to be in danger.[10] Any cost-related design decisions (use of the site, materials, construction methods, size, and plan arrangements among others) should never compromise the safety of its users or wider public. There are building regulations and codes which govern these issues, but they are not infallible. To which the recent school building collapses related to poor construction methods,[11] and the devastating fires related to the use of cheap and flammable architect-specified cladding in the UK attest.[12] It is essential that vigilance and diligence is exercised in assessing the claims of suppliers offering more economical materials or methods; or cost consultants and contractors offering project savings. The ethical and professional priority is safety.

AN ARCHITECTURAL MANIFESTATION OF SYSTEMIC INEQUALITY

Grenfell Tower. London, United Kingdom. 2017.

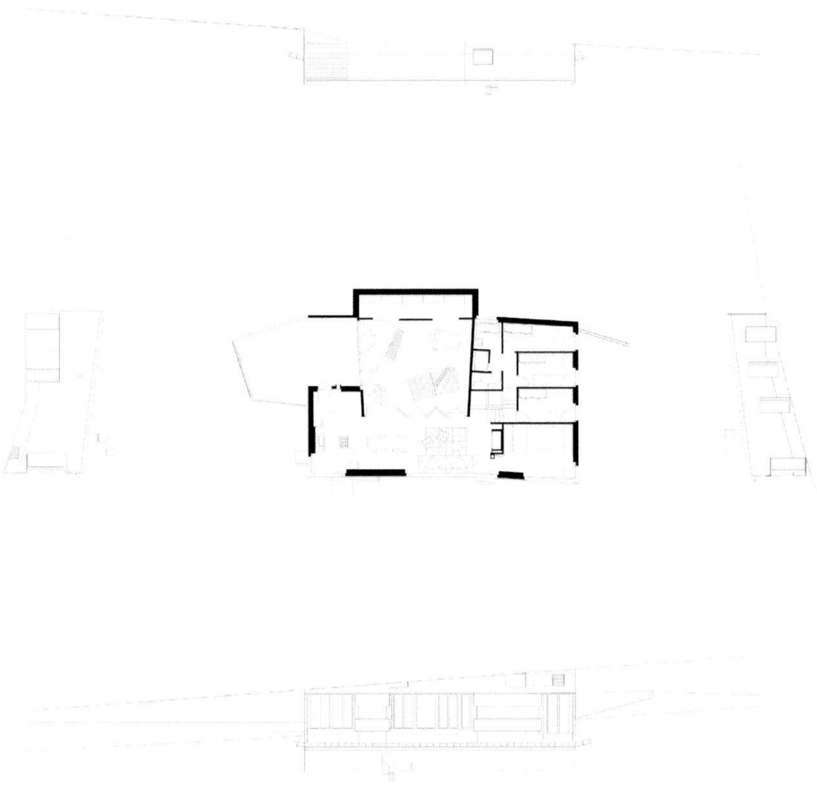

It is essential to know what is feasible within any given situation. Then to operate within the economy of means suitable to the financial parameters of each project. Further, to regularly assess how this economy of means interfaces within any latent or patent ethical issues; to pause and reflect, judging while doing, creating a more "ethically satisfying result".[13] Architect Peter Märkli has said that the "budget has nothing to do with the art of building. The question is whether the architect can handle the budget or not."[14] The more experience I have of designing in practice, the more I tend to agree. I have been involved

AN ECONOMY OF MEANS
Not one inch of space was surrendered in the face of budget cuts, instead focussing on simple strategies such as placing the basement to the front of the house to minimise the removal of land; using simple, exposed finishes throughout; and employing the use of exposed linear guttering instead of expensive concealed guttering. This ascetic approach is inherently ethical in that it promotes the appropriate use of materials and methods minimising resources used. More importantly, that the spatial and aesthetic qualities of the original house design are retained, if not amplified.
Atelierhaus Weissacher. Rumisberg, Switzerland. 2013. Studio Märkli

in many projects which proposed bloated schemes with value-adding and wilful forms, employing bespoke or inappropriately expensive materials. Often then forced to become leaner, more appropriate versions of themselves while still retaining their essential qualities of space, use, and form.

Beyond resourcefulness, the ethical challenge is to find ways for positive and responsive agency within the means of a project. Agency in architecture asks the question: "what can we hope for?"[15] within the financial limits and structures that each architectural project operates. What positive changes or differences can be achieved? An approach exemplified at the Quinta Monroy housing project at Iquique, Chile.

Low salaries, high land prices, and high construction costs hamper access to decent housing for the low-income families and workers of much of Latin America.[16] In this context, the client's limited budget could only stretch to

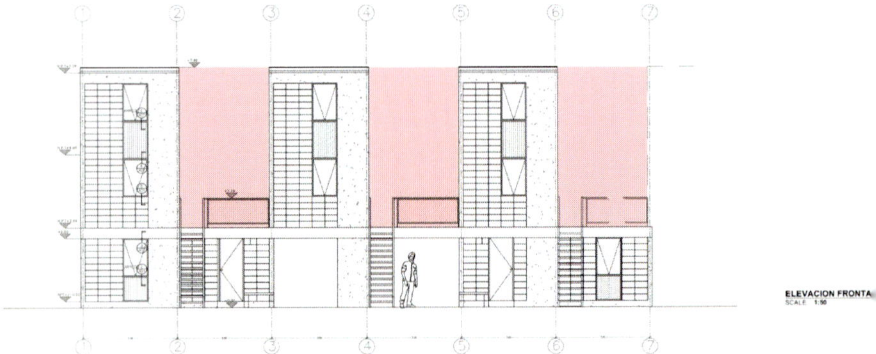

FUTURA AMPLICACIÓN

Areas in pink highlight zones for future additions / infill.

Quinta Monroy Housing. Iquique, Chile. 2005. Elemental.

half of the number of units required to deal with a local housing shortage. Rather than walk away, or propose a smaller number of homes, the architect proposed to build only the essentials: the structure, kitchen, and bathroom.[17] This approach allowed the families to inhabit a project that would otherwise not have been built, but also offered the ability to customise and add to it over time. The essential house was then augmented and personalised by its inhabitants. Here architect Elemental worked within their means, while still achieving their client's original intention and addressing the housing shortage. The unethical thing would have been to have walked away, or proposed fewer complete houses.

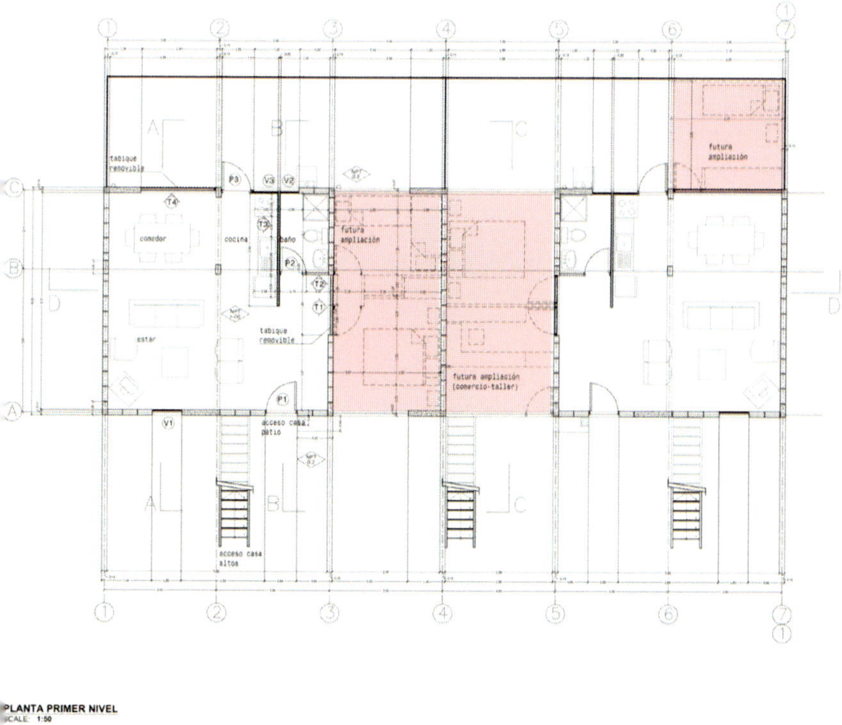

Another approach is that of Dutch architects MVRDV at the Silodam in Amsterdam. A fluctuating housing market led the client to pursue a development of different tenures and financing models,[18] to mitigate further fluctuations in different housing markets: 157 apartments and homes comprised of luxury penthouses and low-income dwellings; family dwellings and apartments for the elderly; artists' studios and office worker crash pads; office accommodation and communal facilities. Rather than create a homogeneous block of the same appearance comprising of simply bigger or smaller units,[19] or separating the different tenures into separate societal groups, MVRDV allowed the financial constraints

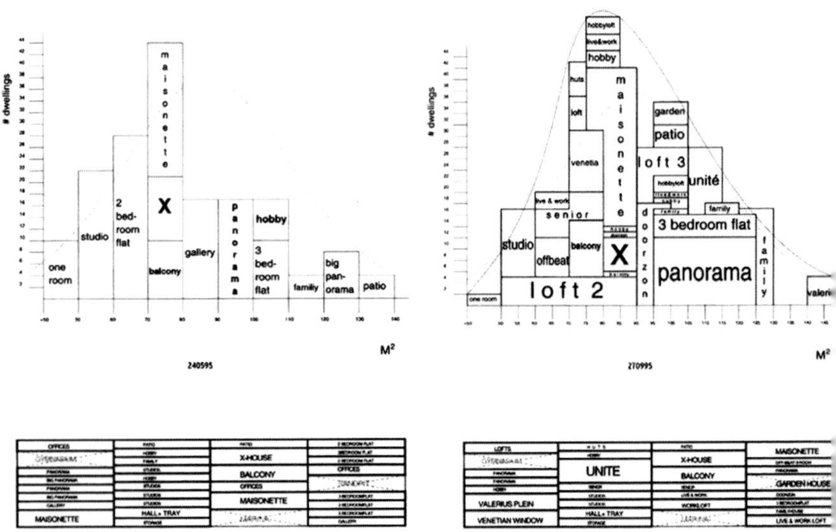

DWELLING TYPES

Early graphs indicating housing mix and how this informs the design strategy.

Silodam. Amsterdam, Netherlands. 2000. MVRDV.

to generate the architectural approach and form. Semi-public routes connect the different house types creating "a three-dimensional neighbourhood".[20] A variety of dwellings – some double aspect, some double height, some with a balcony, some with a patio, some with direct access to the street, others with access to a dock – create a tapestry of form and function. The client's financial risk was minimised, but more importantly the building became a physical manifestation of the social diversity of the city. A design approach which attempts to positively address the inequalities and social stratification often inherent in developer-led regeneration.

A FLOATING MICROCOSM

Silodam. Amsterdam, Netherlands. 2000. MVRDV

Both examples engage with the ethical dilemmas which finance had imposed. In Elemental's case, the easier option would have been to do nothing or not enough; in MVRDV's, to do simply what was expected. In both instances a different path was followed by applying creative and – crucially – realistic solutions. Both took a principled yet flexible approach which actively engages with the ethical dilemmas that inevitably arise when architects are required to respond to the needs of society at large, and the needs of those who commission their designs.

Notes

1 Spector, T., 2001. *The Ethical Architect: The Dilemma of Contemporary Practice.* New York : Princeton Architectural Press. p. 7.

2 Corbusier, L., 1925. *Almanach d'architecture moderne.* Paris: Editions G. Crès. pp. 114–115.

3 Benton, T., 2004. Pessac and Lège revisited: standards, dimensions and failures. *Massilia* , Issue 3, pp. 64–99.

4 D'Ottaviano, C., Pasternak, S., Bassani, J., & Amore, C., 2020. The institutionalisation of self-build governance: exemplifying governance relationships in São Paulo/Brazil/Latin America. In: W. Salet, C. D'Ottaviano, S. Majoor, & D. Bossuyt, eds. *The Self-Build Experience: Institutionalization, Place-Making and City Building.* Bristol: Policy Press. p. 38.

5 Lees, L. & White, H., 2019. The social cleansing of London council estates: everyday experiences of "accumulative dispossession". *Housing Studies.* p. 2.

6 The Royal Institute of British Architects, 2011. *The Case for Space: The Size of England's New Homes.* London: The Royal Institute of British Architects. p. 4.

7 Kimmelman, M., 2019. *Hudson Yards is Manhattan's biggest, newest, slickest gated community.* [Online] Available at: https://www.nytimes.com/interactive/2019/03/14/arts/design/hudson-yards-nyc.html [Accessed 24 May 2020].

8 Awan, N., Schneider, T., & Till, J., 2012. *Spatial Agency: Other Ways of Doing Architecture.* Abingdon: Routledge. p. 30.

9 Cole, J., 2018. *Report of the Review Panel on Building Standards Compliance and Enforcement.* Edinburgh: Scottish Government. p. 6.

10 Vitruvius, 1960. *The Ten Books on Architecture.* New York: Dover Publications. p. 57.

11 Cole, *Report of the Review Panel on Building Standards Compliance and Enforcement*, p. 6.

12 Booth, R., 2020. *Grenfell architect says cladding focus was on appearance and cost.* [Online] Available at: https://www.theguardian.com/uk-news/2020/mar/11/grenfell-architect-says-cladding-focus-was-on-appearance-and-cost [Accessed 06 April 2020].

13 Sennett, R., 2009. *The Craftsman.* London: Penguin Books. p. 296.

14 Markli, P., 2018. *My Profession, The Art of Building.* Cambridge, MA: Harvard Graduate Design School.

15 Doucet, I. & Cupers, K., 2009. Agency in Architecture: Rethinking Criticality in Theory and Practice. *Footprint,* Issue Spring, pp. 1–6.

16 D'Ottaviano et al., The institutionalisation of self-build governance, p. 38.

17 Schneider, T. & Till, J., 2012. *Elemental.* [Online] Available at: https://www.spatialagency.net/database/elemental [Accessed 21 May 2020].

18 Frearson, A., 2015. *MVRDV's Silodam block contains a cross-section of Amsterdam society says Nathalie de Vries.* [Online] Available at: https://www.dezeen.com/2015/07/28/silodam-mvrdv-housing-amsterdam-harbour-movie-nathalie-de-vries/6/ [Accessed 24 May 2020].

19 Ibid.

20 MVRDV, n.d. *Silodam.* [Online] Available at: https://www.mvrdv.nl/projects/163/silodam [Accessed 24 May 2020].

2.3 CONSTRAINTS

IN PRACTICE THE FORCES acting upon your design are often uncontrollable. A host of unexpected and active external constraints need to be addressed in every project.

↓

A considered response to these forces can enrich or even define a project. I have been involved in projects where an external courtyard was created due to a high voltage electrical cable running through the site which couldn't be built upon; where a leisure facility design was distilled due to a change in the client's financial circumstances; or where a bloated house design became more contextual and appropriate due to local authority intervention. Architects often have no option but to accept a loss of control as an inevitable condition to be dealt with in a positive light.[1] Each project has a unique set of conditions which can become opportunities if handled correctly:

- Financial (restricted budget or fluctuating economy affecting type, size, and quality of building)
- Legal (height restrictions, historic requirements, building code/regulations)
- Technical (limitations in software or materials or the ability of other project members to achieve the design concept)
- User (completion time frame, use of building and functions to be provided, relationship between needs of different groups)
- Environmental (climatic conditions, protection of nature, contextual relationships).

One architect who has built a career on accepting and often capitalising on the constraints acting on an architectural project is Rem Koolhaas, founder of the Office of Metropolitan Architecture. In his book, *Delirious New York*, Koolhaas detailed how the financial decision to carve the land into a cheap and convenient grid system created an "un-dreamt freedom of three-dimensional anarchy"[2]; how the parameters of its complex zoning laws meant the creation of familiar architectural forms was "impossible"[3]; how conflicting user needs and functions afforded architects' the freedom[4] to break from the idea that the relationship between the interior and exterior should be reflective of one another. What Koolhaas revealed was a city of architects not only wrestling and juggling with the constraints surrounding them but harnessing them to create a uniquely dynamic city. This revelation has been a consistent concern in his work since the late 1970s, since passed on to the cohorts of architects who have passed through his office. Architects such as Jeanne Gang, Bjarke Ingels, Zaha Hadid, Joshua Prince-Ramus, and Farshid Moussavi.

NEW YORK: A CITY GENERATED BY CONSTRAINTS

Study for Maximum Mass Permitted by the 1916 New York Zoning Law.

New York, USA. 1922. Artist: Hugh Ferriss.

FINANCIAL

LAVEZZORIO COMMUNITY CENTER

A limited budget on a central gathering and services hub for a residential village of foster families prompted the architect to solicit donations from various suppliers and manufacturers,[5] thereby obtaining internal floor finishes, wood panelling, external brick, and even concrete. A reversal of the typical approach where the architect

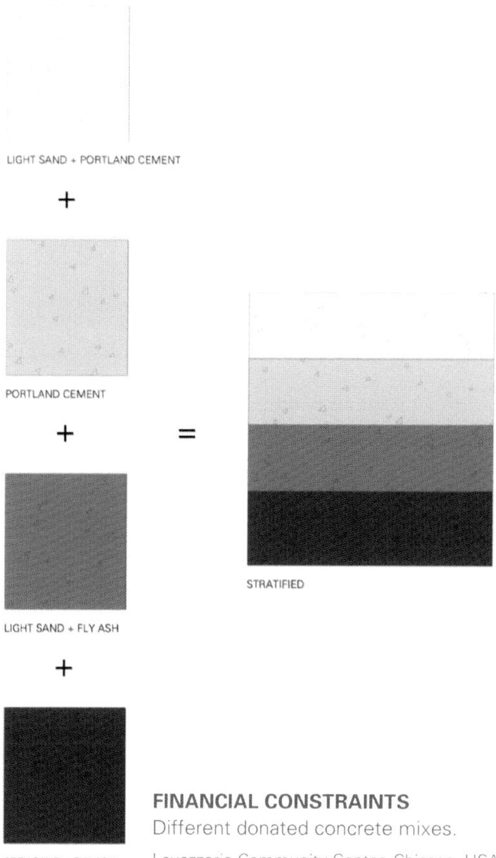

FINANCIAL CONSTRAINTS
Different donated concrete mixes.
Lavezzorio Community Center. Chicago, USA. 2008. Studio Gang.

specifies and is in control of the materials at their disposal. Instead of a limitation, it became a generator. The different mixes of donated concrete were exposed in the "geological stratification"[6] of its façade – which expressed a visual guide of donations, while providing a lively and solid counterpoint to the restrained curtain walling and brick comprising the remainder of the exterior. Such a resourceful approach to a limited budget allows the project to be successfully realised by actively seeking donations. Then, allows the nature of these donations to be expressed architecturally, defining the image of the building and the materials it is fabricated from.

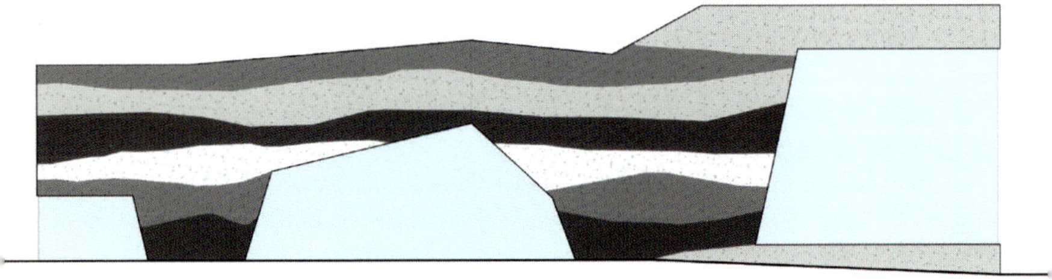

FINANCIAL CONSTRAINTS HARNESSED.
Elevation view of how these different donations were incorporated in the façade design.

Lavezzorio Community Center. Chicago, USA. 2008. Studio Gang.

LEGAL

MARITIME MUSEUM OF DENMARK

When approached to design a Maritime Museum, BIG found the site subject to a unique legal constraint owing to its proximity to Kronborg Castle, a UNESCO World Heritage site. The new 6000m^2 museum building would have to be hidden from view, the only possibility a disused underground dry dock. The new building was not permitted to rise an inch above ground level – meaning a

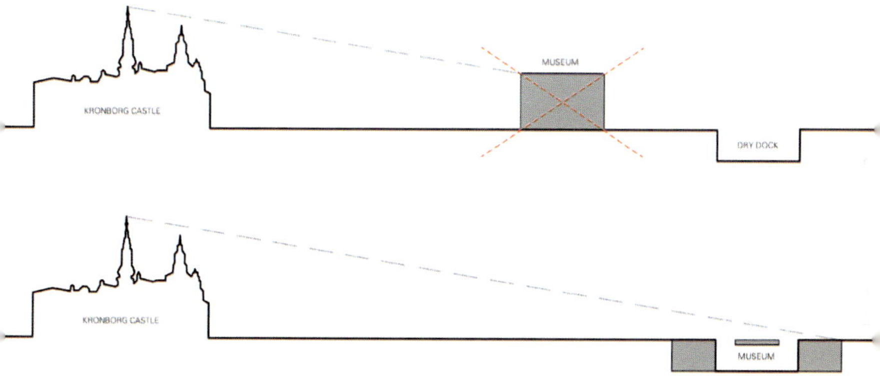

LEGAL CONSTRAINTS

Section showing design approach responding to proximity of Kronborg Castle.

Maritime Museum of Denmark. Copenhagen. 2013. Bjarke Ingels Group.

public building in a concealed basement with no views or direct access to sunlight.[7] Realising the dry dock would collapse if drained to make way for the new building, the architects effectively turned it into a courtyard, building new underground accommodation to either side. This would not only stabilise the existing dock but allow building users a unique perspective of this industrial, cathedral-like space. By creating the courtyard, workspaces and other functions would gain access to light and views despite being underground. The unique legal constraints acting on the project allowed the architect to create a unique building while connecting the museum with its maritime past.

LEGAL CONSTRAINTS HARNESSED

Maritime Museum of Denmark. Copenhagen. 2013. Bjarke Ingels Group. Photographer: Johan Wessman.

TECHNICAL

PHAENO SCIENCE CENTRE

Zaha Hadid conceived the project as an "artificial landscape",[8] a careful orchestration of space, movement, and form. The technical challenge, of supporting the 154 x 130m elevated structure without affecting the purity of space and form required at ground level, strengthened the original architectural concept. The structure became a technical solution which offered new opportunities in the organisation and form of the building. Ten structural 'cones' were developed, made large enough to become inhabitable for the various functions required at ground level. Their sculpted amorphous forms providing a sense of weight

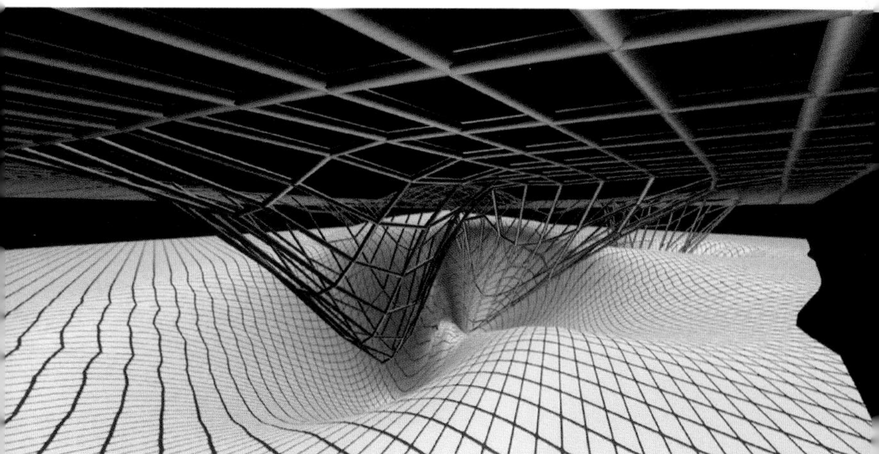

TECHNICAL CONSTRAINTS

Structural analysis diagram.

Phaeno Science Centre. Wolfsburg, Germany. 2005. Zaha Hadid Architects.

and solidity to the building and richness of space and light from underneath. These forms were not wilfully shaped; complex finite element analysis[9] software (which predicts how the structure reacts to forces imposed on it) was developed to create tailored forms. Through interrogation and analysis, the solution to the technical constraint valorised the architectural concept.

TECHNICAL CONSTRAINTS HARNESSED

Phaeno Science Centre. Wolfsburg, Germany. 2005. Zaha Hadid Architects. Photographer: Florian Schäffer.

USER

VAKKO FASHION CENTER

At the Vakko Headquarters in Istanbul, the client required the project to be completed within 11 months. Knowing that designing and constructing a new building from scratch within the given time frame was almost impossible, REX noticed that a previously unbuilt scheme offered potential as an approach to the Vakko Fashion Center in its scale, organisation, and form. They showed the new client the unbuilt science centre scheme and said that if they liked it, they could adapt the drawings for construction issue within one day. The client agreed and construction was started within three days of the client first approaching the architect. This allowed the adapted 'outer ring' to proceed. REX then designed a series of steel boxes, which could be configured on-site, to create the bespoke interior

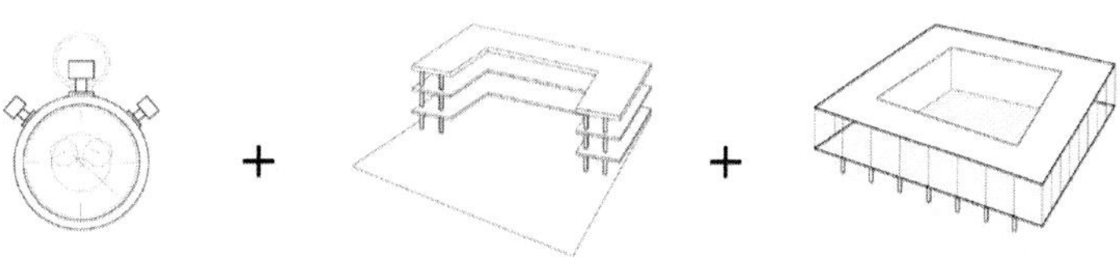

USER CONSTRAINTS

Time + existing structure + adapted historic design = a solution.

Vakko Fashion Center. Istanbul, Turkey. 2010. REX.

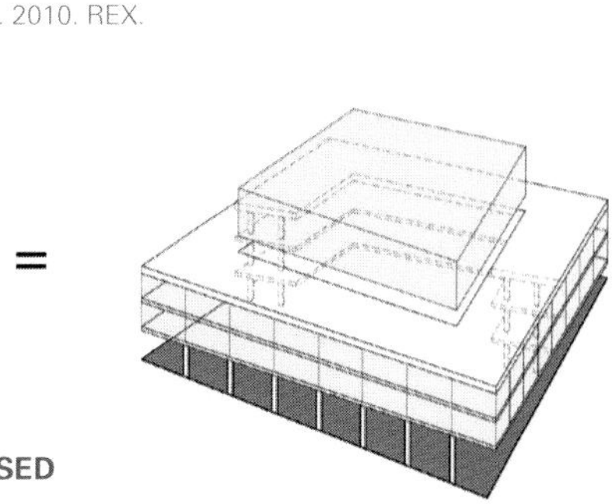

USER CONSTRAINTS HARNESSED

Vakko Fashion Center. Istanbul, Turkey. 2010. REX.

and circulation spaces – submitting them within 2 weeks of receiving the commission, to catch the steel mill order in time for completion.[10] Thus, the user constraints imposed create a design at once pragmatic and loose; prefabricated and bespoke.

ENVIRONMENTAL

LA FOLIE DIVINE

This residential development exploits both synthetic and natural environmental constraints surrounding the site to create an elegant tower form in stark contrast to its more traditional, prosaic neighbours. A masterplan for the site dictated that the maximum number of storeys any building could rise to would be nine. Despite being surrounded by low rise dwellings of one or two storeys, Moussavi decided

ENVIRONMENTAL CONSTRAINTS

Plan drawing (right) illustrating usage of site, a minimal footprint enhancing green space by 40% compared to a typical 4–5 storey block (left).

La Folie Divine. Montpellier, France. 2017. Farshid Moussavi Architects.

to build to the maximum height that the masterplan allowed. By pushing the limits of this constraint, the footprint is minimised allowing the majority of the site to become a garden space, while rising above its neighbours to provide coastal and city views.[11] Using this constraint 'loophole', a site which may have otherwise been occupied by a lower, longer and deeper volume becomes a stark,

ENVIRONMENTAL CONSTRAINTS HARNESSED

La Folie Divine. Montpellier, France. 2017. Farshid Moussavi Architects. Photographer: Jeff Nastorg.

elegant counterpoint. The small footprint allows for cross-ventilation of apartments – essential in a Mediterranean climate. The floor plate is then extended creating curvilinear balconies which provide 180-degree views while addressing the need for outdoor space. The design pushed to the limits of its constraints to reveal the full potential of the site and brief.

The parameters present within any architectural project do not limit opportunities or diminish agency – instead, they provide a framework for them. A crucial role of the architect is to read between the lines of any given set of instructions or limitations, to add social, spatial, functional, or aesthetic value to any given project. Students of architecture entering professional practice need not see this new professional realm as a landscape of unnavigable constraints stunting the purity and integrity of the design. If taken as they are[12] and handled correctly, constraints present opportunities. The practice of architecture is a balancing act of forming the core of your architectural response to a brief and site, and then allowing that core to be protected from or enriched by the forces acting upon it.

Notes

1 Awan, N., Schneider, T., & Till, J., 2012. *Spatial Agency: Other Ways of Doing Architecture.* Abingdon: Routledge. p. 39.

2 Koolhaas, R., 1994 . *Delirious New York.* New ed. New York: The Monacelli Press. p. 20.

3 Ibid., p. 114.

4 Ibid., p. 110.

5 Hall, S., 2009. *Lavezzorio Community Center by Studio Gang Architects, Chicago, USA.* [Online] Available at: https://www.architectural-review.com/today/lavezzorio-community-center-by-studio-gang-architects-chicago-usa/8601039.article [Accessed 25 May 2020].

6 Ibid.

7 Bjarke Ingels Group, 2010. *Yes is More: An Archicomic on Architectural Evolution.* Koln: Taschen. p. 227.

8 Zaha Hadid Architects, n.d. *Phaeno Science Centre.* [Online] Available at: https://www.zaha-hadid.com/architecture/phaeno-science-centre/ [Accessed 25 May 2020].

9 Anstey, T., 2008. Discourse networks and the digital: structural collaboration at the Phaeno Science Centre. In: H. Kara, ed. *Design Engineering: AKT.* Barcelona: Actar, p. 78.

10 Forbes, K., 2015. *Site Specific.* San Francisco: ORO Editions p. 87.

11 Farshid Moussavi Architecture, n.d. *La Folie Divine, Montpellier.* [Online] Available at: https://www.farshidmoussavi.com/node/29 [Accessed 26 May 2020].

12 Markli, P., 2018. *My Profession, The Art of Building.* Cambridge, MA: Harvard Graduate Design School.

TECHNICAL ADVICE NOTE

04

MATERIALS

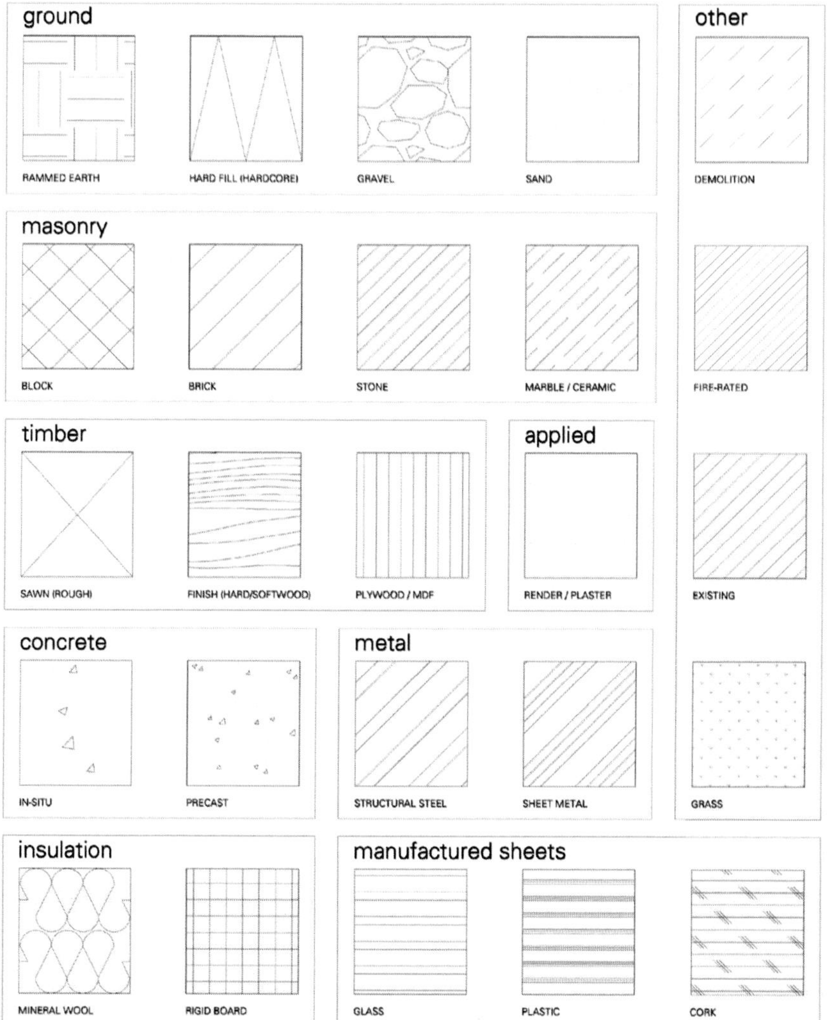
ground
RAMMED EARTH
HARD FILL (HARDCORE)
GRAVEL
SAND
other
DEMOLITION
masonry
BLOCK
BRICK
STONE
MARBLE / CERAMIC
FIRE-RATED
timber
SAWN (ROUGH)
FINISH (HARD/SOFTWOOD)
PLYWOOD / MDF
applied
RENDER / PLASTER
EXISTING
concrete
IN-SITU
PRECAST
metal
STRUCTURAL STEEL
SHEET METAL
GRASS
insulation
MINERAL WOOL
RIGID BOARD
manufactured sheets
GLASS
PLASTIC
CORK

INTERVIEW D

↘ Špela Videčnik (OFIS ARHITEKTI)

You started your own practice as soon as you left architecture school, what lessons did you learn at such a young age?

After Slovenia became independent in 1991, the economy grew quite rapidly. Under the previous system, all architects worked in big state offices which were then privatised. Everyone was new on the market, the old architects and the young ones were on the same playing field, and we won some competitions. The clients that we dealt with were tough – people who got a lot of money very quickly. Not easy to talk to, especially not for architects of the older generation used to the old ways of working. We learned that to be an architect you must do everything – design, manage, administer contracts, talk to clients … We had to be flexible.

What are the differences and similarities between academia and practice?

Through teaching you get deeper into the research – you don't have enough time in practice. I would not like to just be a teacher or just a practitioner. Academia is sometimes very disconnected from how you work in practice. However, I think there needs to be a distinction. Only in academia do you have the time to be aware of certain questions, to be critical about what is going on, to think deeper about

Alpine Shelters. Skuta, Slovenia. 2015. OFIS Arhitekti + Harvard GSD.

Photographer: Tomasz Gregoric.

Alpine Barn Apartment. Bohinjska Bistric, Slovenia. 2015. OFIS Arhitekti.

Photographer: Tomasz Gregoric.

what you want to contribute as an architect. On the other hand, students graduating from very academical schools are not in touch with the reality of practice. It is difficult – there are certain things you can learn at school and certain things you can learn in practice. I would advise students to take a break at some point in their studies, for at least a year, and go to a practice. Learn as much as they can then go back and study more. Learning from both sides.

You do combine both …

Yes, our way of teaching combines practice and academia. We try to ensure that the students develop a conceptual, research-based approach but also develop an understanding of how a project works. We also involve structural engineers and services engineers in the studio. There should be diversity in architecture school so that through the years a student can learn different things from different teachers. Some teachers are extremely theoretical, some teachers combine theory and practice like we do. We also encourage students to work in a team with other students who come from different environments and cultural backgrounds.

How do you deal with constraints and parameters in the design process?

Our education was very traditional modernist and we still follow that approach. We start each project with very pragmatic questions. What is the site like? Where are the nice views? What are the climatic conditions? Then of course you have all the restrictions – height, the width, and the programme. When we work in Alpine areas, we try to learn from local vernacular architecture, to keep Slovenia's identity alive through building. We want to do every project differently so that we are excited about it. We really try to explore different materials, different structures in steel, concrete, wood, cladding. In each project we try to explore something.

How do you achieve consistency in your work regardless of budget?

It's a very hard question – sometimes we think we don't! It needs a good client who is open-minded. From our side, we need to understand the pragmatic economic restrictions. In between this, we try to find creativity even if it is very restricted. Otherwise, it doesn't make sense. If the client isn't open-minded and there is no scope for creativity, we just don't take the project. Each project takes two years of your life ... you must ask yourself if it is really worth doing?

What technical design challenges have you faced in realising your architectural ambitions?

The 'Glass House' project in Spain was a small research project, our own contribution to understanding habitation in extreme environments. We asked, "Can you do a glass house in the middle of the desert where someone can live without air conditioning?" We pushed everything to the limit. Structurally the building is only glass, no columns or mullions. There are two wooden decks (above and below) and triple-glazed panels between them – no vertical supports other than glass, even though the winds in this area are very strong. The whole structure was prefabricated in Slovenia, so we could control how it was made. Then brought to Spain and assembled on the site which is very remote and inaccessible for construction machinery. Environmentally, even if the temperature is 50 degrees outside it remains a maximum of 28 degrees without air conditioning inside. They put a transparent coating on the three layers of glass to minimise glare and heat transmission. This building

Social Housing. Izola, Slovenia. 2006. OFIS Arhitekti.

Photographer: Tomasz Gregoric.

Farewell Chapel. Lukovica, Slovenia. 2009. OFIS Arhitekti.

Photographer: Tomasz Gregoric.

Glass House. Gorafe, Spain. 2018. OFIS Arhitekti.

was a combination of knowledge – structural, services and glazing knowledge to achieve a 360-degree glazed building in the desert from minimal prefabricated elements.

What future challenges do you think architecture faces? How are you dealing with them in teaching and practice?

There are so many! We have focused lately on small research projects looking at how to create buildings in harsh climates. This is research for the future, because of climate change. I would say in America, thinking green is not yet the main issue. Energy is still quite cheap, so they haven't yet learned. We are also concerned with inequality. At Harvard, the design studios were in Manila and Kuala Lumpur. Very big cities that are growing rapidly but have extreme economic inequalities in how people live. In Manila there is a minority who are very wealthy, then a majority who are homeless – surviving on a few dollars a day. This is one of the great challenges for cities. How to diversify in a way that the city can become more integrated – not divided. It's extremely important. People who are not aware of this are just bums! I think climate change and inequality are the central questions that are bothering us. We work at both the small scale and urban scale to try and address them.

2.4 TECHNICALS

"NICE DRAWING ... BUT HOW DO you expect me to build it?!"

↓

"What do you mean?" I asked the carpenter. "There's no way I'll be able to get my hand in there to fix that in place, how am I supposed to screw it in ... and what about future maintenance? If the sliding door gear needs to be replaced, you'll need to take down the whole wall and rebuild it!" I could tell by the decades of scrapes on his chisel he knew better than me. In obsessing over the aesthetics of the detail of a neatly recessed sliding door I had neglected its buildability and practicality. My lack of knowledge and experience was exposed.

This was my first experience of theory and practice colliding on-site. Architects cannot rely on the thought process itself to make tangible their conceptions.[1] Thought and production depend on each other for their respective realisation and value. This is true of all made things, including architecture.

The importance of this production phase is evident in its dominance in the design process and the allocation of resources. Architects in the United Kingdom structure their projects using the 'RIBA Plan of Work'. This "organises the process of briefing, designing, constructing and operating building projects into eight stages and explains the stage outcomes, core tasks and information exchanges required at each stage".[2] Of these eight stages, three relate to the early design stages that you will be used to from architecture school (see image on p. 240). Beyond

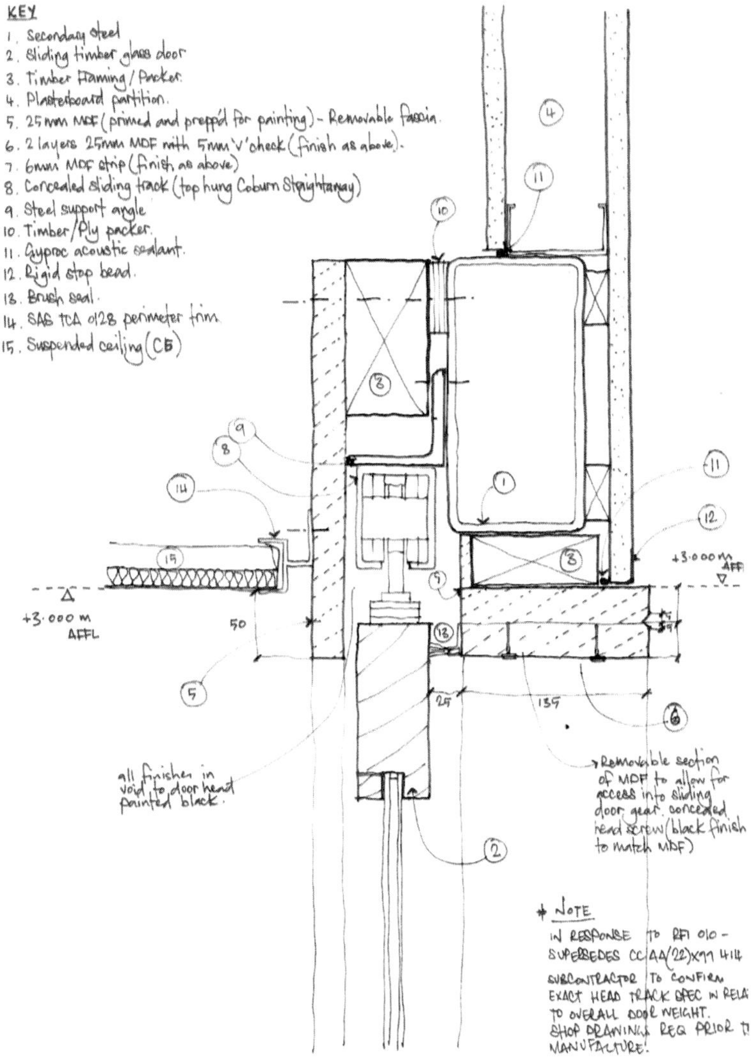

A SOLUTION DISCUSSED

The modified detail, developed through discussion, featuring a removable section to allow for access and maintenance to the door mechanics.

TASKS YOU WILL NOT BE ACQUAINTED WITH

Diagram illustrating proportion of time in practice on each design stage in relation to the RIBA Plan of Work and AIA Project Checklist.

these three initial stages, it is unlikely you will have had any experience in the requirements of the following five production stages. This is mirrored in the American Institute of Architects' equivalent 'Project Checklist'[3] (see facing page). Beyond Schematic Design, the student entering practice will have little to no experience of the five production phases from Design Development to Post-Construction Services.

The first three early stages of design comprise only 15% of an architects' fee resource and time.[4] So 85% of architectural time and resource are expended on the final five production phases and the tasks they entail. Coordinating, economising, complying, detailing, checking, scheduling. Not thinking, sketching, and creating like you are used to in architecture school. On entry to the profession, 85% of your time will be spent learning new skills, related to the production phase of architecture.

The predominance of this long, complex phase in architecture reinforces its importance to the original idea. Here, a project can soar or sink. The technical strategies adopted either crystallising or sullying the original intention. 'Great' architecture has always relied on a foundation of technical knowledge which affords a platform for "advanced building modes"[5] which realise the architectural intention. Not relying on local precedent or traditional technique, instead harnessing them to introduce experimentation and innovation. Like the pioneering use of limestone[6] piled up in six levels which created the first stepped pyramid at Saqqara.[7] Or the revival of Ancient Roman concrete construction which allowed Donato Bramante to create vast new conceptions of spatial

ADVANCED BUILDING MODES

The earliest use of large-scale ashlar construction. A proto-pyramid.

Step Pyramid and Chapels. Saqqara, Egypt. c.2610 BC. Imhotep.
Artist: William Henry Goodyear.

organisation.[8] Or in Ludwig Mies van der Rohe's pursuit of a new monumentality, achieved through the precise proportioning and arrangement of glass and steel.[9] Dreams validated by means.

Few architects since the modern era have defined questions of the importance of the architectural detail more than Ludwig Mies van der Rohe. His control of the production phase, the 85%, elevated his architecture. Through command of proportion and sensitivity to both craftmanship and industrial technique, he ensured that the grand vision of any project was represented in the smallest of details: "nothing should be built that is not clearly

ADVANCED BUILDING MODES

Column/Beam junction. The valorisation of technique: of screws, joints, gaps, and junctions.

Neue Nationalgalerie. Berlin, Germany. 1968. Ludwig Mies van der Rohe.

constructed ... to elevate it to structure ... By structure we have a philosophical idea. The structure is the whole from top to bottom, to the last detail – with the same ideas."[10]

This philosophical approach was founded on the building site. Aged 14, he followed his father into stonemasonry,[11] working as an apprentice. Later attending technical college, by age 19 Mies could not only draw but knew how to lay brick and carve stone.[12] Unlike many of his contemporaries trained in architectural offices and technical schools in the 'Jugendstil' arts and crafts tradition,[13] the act of designing and construction were combined in his architectural education.

There is a deep current in architectural thought that design and construction should be separated – evident in Leon Battista Alberti's statement that the "manual Operator" is no more than "an Instrument to the Architect".[14] A viewpoint embedded in intellectual and class distinctions. Head and hand separated, such that the architect knows the theory behind what is done, the operator unthinkingly does it.[15] This current still courses through practice today, in my experience, with many architects disregarding the innate practical experience that 'operators' have.

The gap between architect and builder is created during our education. A student can progress through three to seven years of education without having any dialogue with a builder. It may then take the graduate a further few years until afforded the opportunity to emerge from the drawing office onto a building site. Architects can spend from seven to ten years of training without interfacing with the people who make their ideas, drawings, and visions. Unsurprisingly the young architect gets a rude awakening when first faced with technical problems on-site.

If the majority of tasks you will be involved in concern the coordination, resolution, and verification of technical concerns, surely bridging this gap should be of concern to architectural education and practice. As the late modernist architect Andy MacMillan has noted: "contact with the building profession at an early age is the best way to learn about architecture, a builder can make your job. Building is after all a team effort."[16]

This requires a fundamental shift in how architecture is taught, but there are immediate things you can do. When at architecture school, forget the bar job or shifts in the local café out of term. Get a job on a building site. Pick up a dust-covered, coffee-stained drawing with tiny 6pt text on it and try to build from it; lift up and lay down the 20kg concrete blocks the architect has specified for four straight hours; try and usher a 10m high piece of glazing into place on a crowded construction site.

Absorbing the tacit knowledge of suppliers, consultants, and contractors will allow you a sound platform to consolidate your dreams with the reality, then introduce experimentation and innovation. This is not about subservience to the building industry, but engaging with it to produce better results.

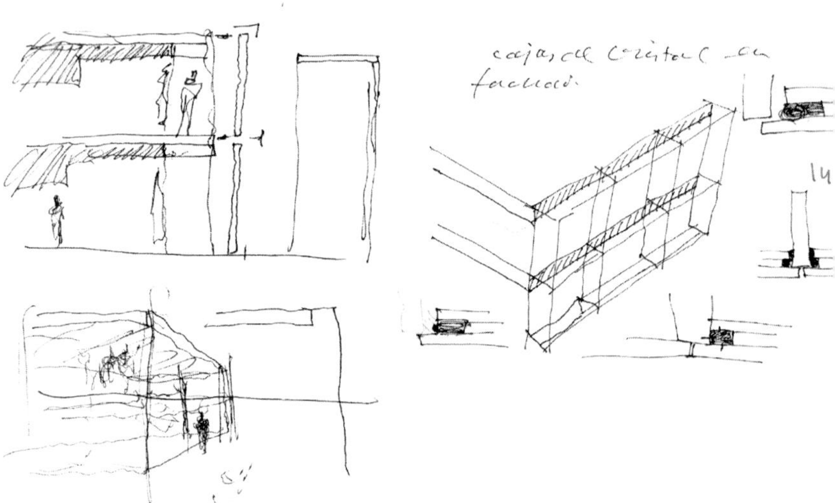

DEVELOPMENT OF AN IDEA

Sketching: from concept to detailed solutions.

Office building. Zamora, Spain. 2012. Alberto Campo Baeza.

Such an approach is evident in the office building at Zamora, designed by Alberto Campo Baeza, who had the lofty ambition to "build with air".[17] As Campo Baeza describes, the key to resolving the technical challenges was collaboration:

> *We tried to create a contemporary dialogue with the medieval cathedral. We inserted a box of glass. Very simply, we separated two glass walls to create a corridor. Then, because we designed the building to have only two levels, it was possible to use only one sheet of glass vertically without any joints or divisions. My first question, before I started designing, was to an old friend working for a glazing company. He said it would be very easy if we did these two things. We followed his advice and the results are astonishing. One day in New York, the architect James Polshek (who spent his career designing glass boxes) said to me 'Alberto, how did you make that glass box without metallic pieces?'. It's simple – I consulted the engineer and he told me how to do it. Collaboration, it's simple. To be sharp you must have good people, more knowledgeable, around you – this is the secret.*[18]

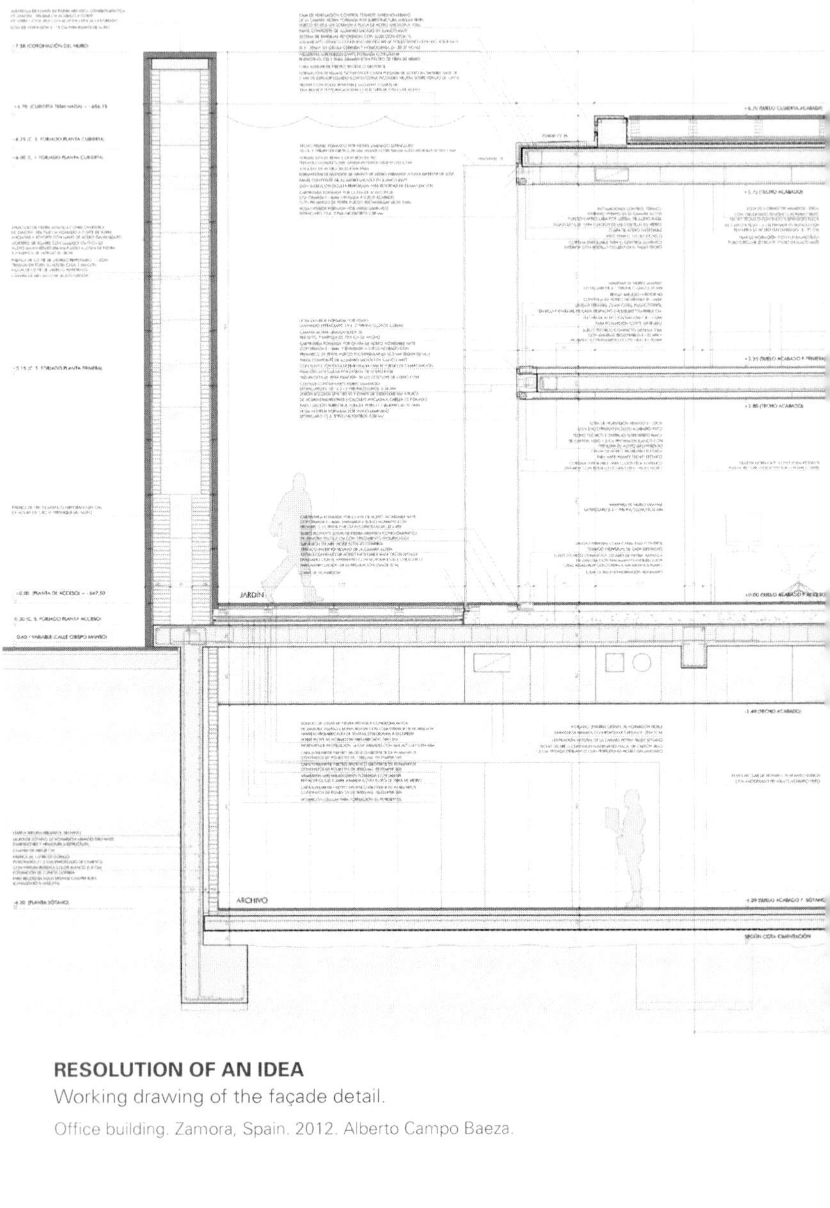

RESOLUTION OF AN IDEA

Working drawing of the façade detail.

Office building. Zamora, Spain. 2012. Alberto Campo Baeza.

BUILDING WITH AIR

The idea and resolution of it in built form.

Office building. Zamora, Spain. 2012. Alberto Campo Baeza. Photographer: Javier Callejas.

Armed with this collaborative attitude, architects can engage with technology in the production phase. At the Cattedrale di Santa Maria del Fiore in Florence, architect Filippo Brunelleschi led an army of craftsmen[19] in the pursuit of achieving this architectural wonder. Brunelleschi often spontaneously carved turnips to illustrate his intentions for each complex detail.[20] The margin for error and misinterpretation between the two-dimensional representation of the drawing and three-dimensional reality were eliminated. A small piece of carved turnip or moulded wax bridged the gap.

Technology has developed such that we no longer need turnips to explain our designs. Building Information Modelling, Virtual Reality, and Digital Fabrication all allow architects to quickly represent their designs in three dimensions. These tools are largely used only at design stage, shared between other designers and consultants. Not to create physical manifestations of exactly what is intended to be built to be issued to the people building it. Instead these three-dimensional models are flattened and facsimiled as a series of simplified two-dimensional line drawings. Architecture is not reaping the full benefits of co-creation that many other industries do.[21]

Imagine a future world where Brunelleschi's approach is updated for the twenty-first century. The architect is posed with a problem on-site, architect and builder discuss solutions to the problem, the architect then quickly models (perhaps on a hand-held device) the agreed solution, tweaking what has already been modelled previously. The architect then sends the model to an on-site 3D printer creating an instant physical representation, any doubt dismantled.

There is of course a danger with an over-reliance on technology. If introduced too early in the design process expression and thought can be limited.[22] Architecture becomes detached from its humanist ideals, its creation dependent on the capabilities of the machine.[23] Introducing technology during the 85% production phase as a means to test, experiment with, and successfully realise the established concept becomes all the more critical.

Technology can help realise our dreams if the dreams are there. Like at Groupwork + Amin Taha's oneiric 168 Upper Street where the "choice of construction and fabrication processes was key"[24] to ensure the realisation of a concept to erect a monument to the building which previously completed the urban block but had been destroyed during World War II. The architect uses a double skin in-situ terracotta/cement mix structural shell. Every single component of the building was modelled in three dimensions, then robotically routed into expanded polystyrene formwork before the mix was poured in. Inherent imperfections in the digital fabrication process were embraced, to crystallise their original concept to "misremember" the original building. Neither a facsimile of history nor an erasure of it, a playful bricolage using the tools of our time.

The appropriate and timely use of technology could help bridge the gap between two-dimensional representation and three-dimensional built reality, and the gap between the intentions of our designs and their physical reality. In the production phase, the architect must have an approach to every detail. What am I trying to express here? How do I want these materials to meet? How is the detail contributing to the overall experience of the building? How is the philosophical idea materially expressed? Through our approach to collaboration, using technology as a vital tool, we can elevate our work in practice through the development of advanced building modes. Like great architecture always has.

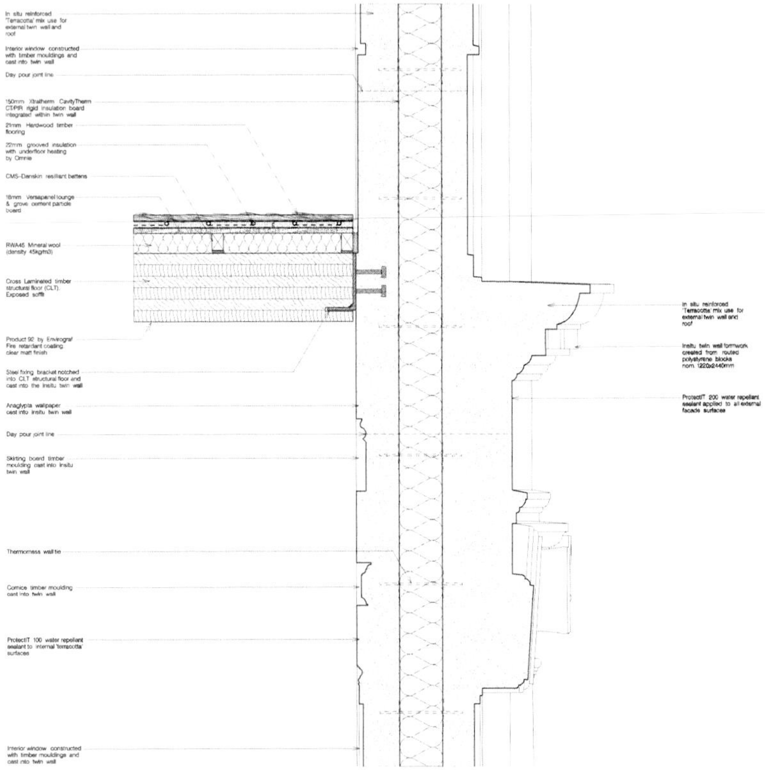

RESOLUTION OF AN IDEA

Technical detail.

168 Upper Street. London, United Kingdom. 2017. Groupwork + Amin Taha.

facing page – bottom

SKEUOMORPHIC MEMORY

The idea and resolution of it in built form.

168 Upper Street. London, United Kingdom. 2017. Groupwork + Amin Taha.

PROCESS

The architects' CAD information is robotically routed into expanded polystyrene formwork before the concrete and terracotta mix is poured in.

168 Upper Street. London, United Kingdom. 2017. Groupwork + Amin Taha.

Notes

1 Arendt, H., 1998. *The Human Condition* (2nd ed.). Chicago: University of Chicago Press. p. 169.
2 Royal Institute of British Architects, 2020. *RIBA Plan of Work 2020*, London: RIBA.
3 American Institute of Architects, 1995. *AIA Document D200™ – 1995*, Washington: AIA.
4 Beale, M., 2018. *Architects' Fees*. Cambridge, University of Cambridge.
5 Kostof, S., 1977. The Practice of Architecture in the Ancient World: Egypt and Greece. In: S. Kostof, ed. *The Architect: Chapters in the History of the Profession*. New York: Oxford University Press. p. 4.
6 Verner, M., 2002. *The Pyramids: The Mystery, Culture, and Science of Egypt's Great Monuments*. New York: Grove Press. pp. 108–109.
7 Van De Mieroop, M., 2010. *A History of Ancient Egypt*. Hoboken, NJ: Wiley-Blackwell. p. 56.
8 Wilkinson, C., 1977. The New Professionalism in the Renaissance. In: S. Kostof, ed. *The Architect: Chapters in the History of the Profession*. New York: Oxford University Press. p. 136.
9 Frampton, K., 1992. *Modern Architecture: A Critical History* (3rd ed.). London: Thames and Hudson. p. 237.
10 Ibid., p. 161.
11 Ibid., p. 161.
12 Zimmerman, C., 2016. *Mies van der Rohe: 1886–1969*. Koln: Taschen. p. 7.
13 Frampton, *Modern Architecture*, p. 161.
14 Alberti, L., 1726. *The Architecture of Leon Battista Alberti in Ten Books. Of Painting in Three Books and of Statuary in One Book*. London: Thomas Edlin. Preface.
15 Sennett, R., 2009. *The Craftsman*. London: Penguin Books. p. 45.
16 MacMillan, A., 2008. Gillespie, Kidd & Coia: 1956–1987 Learning, Building, Teaching. *Paperspace*, pp. 74–87.
17 Estudio Campo Baeza, n.d. *2012 Offices in Zamora*. [Online] Available at: https://www.campobaeza.com/offices-zamora/ [Accessed 28 May 2020].
18 Campo Baeza, A., 2020. *Interview with J. Tait* [Interview] (26 May 2020).

19 Mueller, T., 2014. *Brunelleschi's Dome.* [Online] Available at: https://www.nationalgeographic.com/magazine/2014/02/Il-Duomo/ [Accessed 28 May 2020].

20 Ibid.

21 Moser, C., 2014. *Architecture 3.0: The Disruptive Design Practice Handbook*. Abingdon: Routledge. p. 222.

22 Pressman, A., 2019. *Design Thinking: A Guide to Creative Problem Solving for Everyone*. New York: Routledge. p. 55.

23 Arendt, *The Human Condition,* p. 169.

24 Groupwork + Amin Taha, 2017. *168 Upper Street: Project Information,* London: Groupwork + Amin Taha.

TECHNICAL ADVICE NOTE

05

SCALE

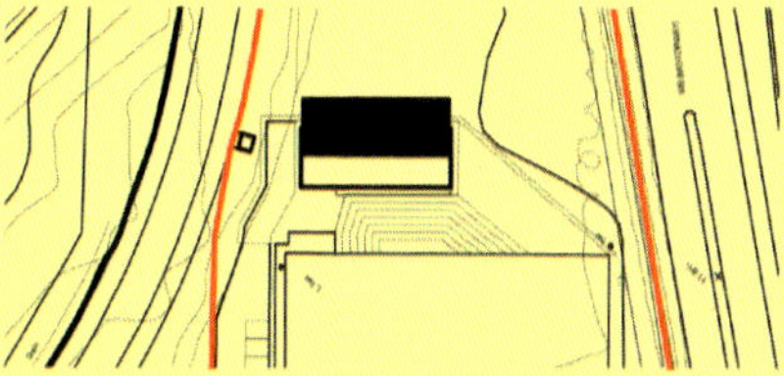

0
25
50
75
100
125(m)

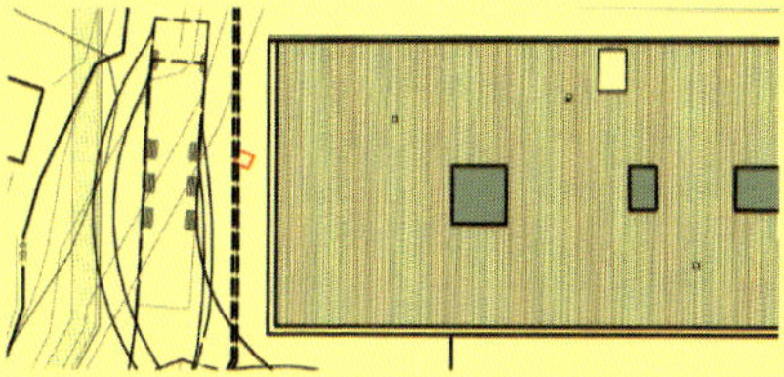

0
5
10
15
20
25(m)

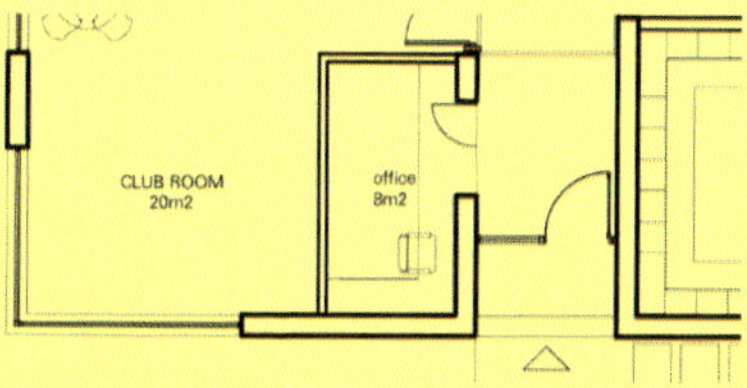
CLUB ROOM
20m2
office
8m2

0
2
4
6
8
10(m)

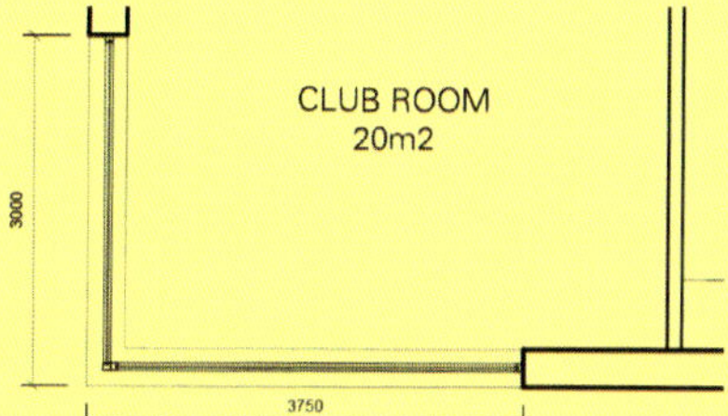
CLUB ROOM
20m2
3000
3750

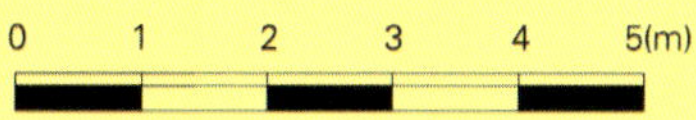
0
1
2
3
4
5(m)

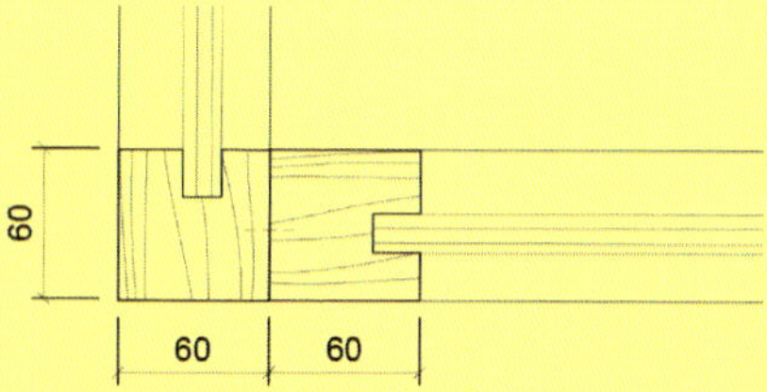
60
60
60

0
50
100
150
200
250(mm)

2.5 TIME

I REMEMBER MY FIRST TASK in practice. "Is it ready yet?", "Yep, 5 minutes" eyes fixed on the cursor chasing itself across my screen.

↓

"You said that ten minutes ago", "What are you mucking about with that for?!" gesturing towards the stylised outline of a building I have taken it upon myself to Photoshop a new graphic identity for. Do I tell him the original presentation adversely affected my aesthetic sensibilities? "Just put together the drawings like I asked and give it a title page. No bells, no whistles, no fancy fucking outlines. Just plain text ..." He scribbles, pen squeaking across the page, what he wants. I stay silent hoping he will go away ..."Let me see it again ... that outline highlights we are above the existing roofscape, exactly what we are trying to convince the planning department we are not doing. This needs to go now, it was supposed to be gone by three o'clock ... the planning consultant needs to comment on it before it is submitted." My mind says: "you didn't tell me any of that ...". My

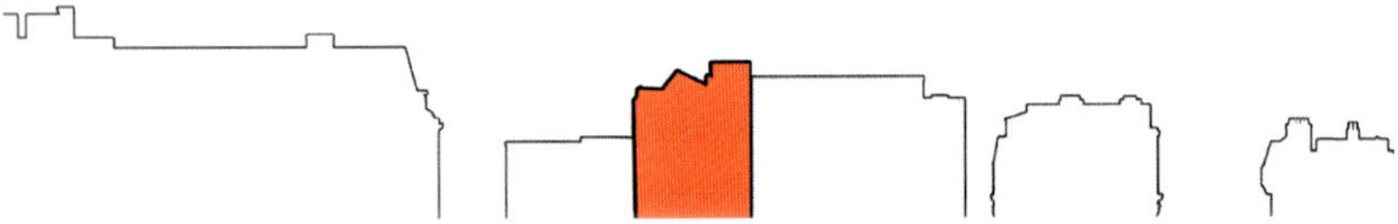

"STOP FUCKING ABOUT"
Irrelevant tasks waste time.

mouth says: "OK." I take another ten minutes and get the task done. I am not asked again. I hadn't appreciated the importance of meeting the deadline or the core tasks required. Distracted and diverted by something I thought was important, but was inconsequential, if not detrimental. Sometimes you need to focus purely on the task at hand.

I remember my first presentation in practice. A community group are looking to acquire a site. If they acquire it, we will design the building. I am meeting my boss there at 4pm, the pressure building each time the small hand reaches the next digit. I have been obsessing over various options for the site expressed in diagrammatic form. It is 2.30pm and nothing is done yet. I have been refusing help in a vainglorious attempt to do it myself, concealed by a feigned concern 'not to bother' anyone. I finally finish these four pristine, paltry diagrams and realise I have four slides for an hour-long presentation. Nothing on the context, history, or capacity of the site; the programme, schedule, or permissions required; no tangible vision the client can invest their hopes in before they invest their money. My colleague makes an intervention. We try to salvage the unsalvageable, adding slides from previous jobs. "What

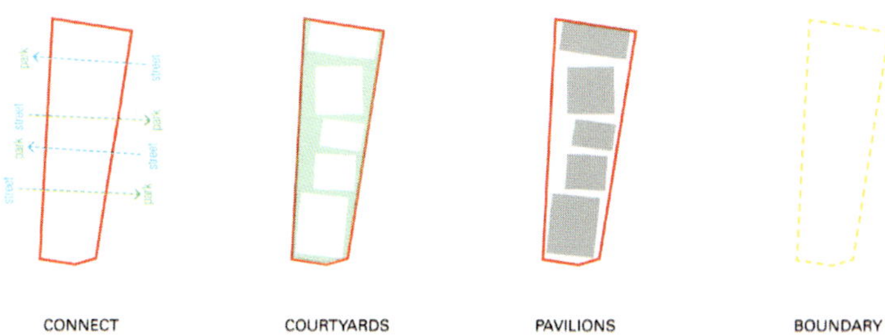

FOUR DIAGRAMS FOR AN HOUR-LONG PRESENTATION

The unblinkered pursuit of perfection limits production.

time do you need to be there?" she asks ... I get to the meeting a half-hour late. "This had better be good", the collective thought bubble above their heads tells me. It wasn't. The pristine diagrams were masking a lack of preparedness and depth. In the pursuit of perfection, I had nothing. Sometimes an unblinkered pursuit of perfection limits production.

Time is one of architecture's inconvenient demands[1] dictating when and how it is produced. "Architects must co-ordinate things in time as well as in space",[2] perpetually reconciling the demands of the design process with the design itself. The pressures of time elicit different responses. Either to remain outside of it; or to allow it to shape what you do. The second, more pragmatic approach being the most common.

The development of ideas takes time, requiring immersion in the issues creating it and periods of gestation allowing responses to emerge and develop over time. This immersive gestation approach is inseparable from the idea that "architecture is an art";[3] a creative endeavour whose deeper meaning and purpose lie outside of time. Representative of Portuguese architect Álvaro Siza's projects, which are "never finished ... because we never have enough time."[4] Evident too in the works of Swiss architect Peter Märkli, "slowly built, considerate pieces of architecture"[5] exemplified by the exquisitely crafted La Congiunta, house for sculptures. Märkli defies 'fast architecture' dictated and impacted by the inconvenient demands of time and money. He would be happy to work in the two places where these demands are most keenly felt – Dubai and China – "as long as they gave him enough time".[6]

ARCHITECTURE IS AN ART

Nadir Afonso Museum. Chaves, Portugal. 2015. Álvaro Siza.

THE ART OF BUILDING

La Congiunta House for Sculptures. Giornico, Switzerland. 1992. Studio Märkli.

DUBAI: ARCHITECTURE AS A SERVICE

"Yesterday I went to the site, it's a massive project – 120,000m2. We need to do a full design for some dude in America – in 5 weeks! All the design needs to be done in about two and a half weeks at the most ... then it's modelling and rendering. Maybe we can get another week's extension ..."[7]

Various presentation models. Killa Design.

The demands of time and money can diminish periods of immersion and gestation created by architecture's primary role in these contexts as "vehicles for investment".[8] Time is money – the shorter the design and construction phase, the longer the renting or selling phase. This forces another design approach of forced clarity. Time becomes an agent of change,[9] a constant stream of deadlines forcing decisions amid the multiplicity of options and iterations any architectural project generates.

The embracement of this approach is typified by Reiser + Umemoto who see architecture as the management of material processes, working like chefs at incomprehensible speed, with quantity and precision.[10] Reiser + Umemoto build in Dubai. Also, with typical laissez-faire acceptance, the OMA's CCTV building, whose accelerated design programme was necessitated by the need to appear finished in time for the 2008 Beijing Olympics.[11] This meant a chaotic stream of frozen design moments, forced by endless deadlines.[12] A six-year-period of design and construction, matching Märkli's La Congiunta project, despite being around 2000 times larger.[13]

CHINA: ARCHITECTURE AS A SERVICE

CCTV building development models. OMA.

CHINA: ARCHITECTURE AS A SERVICE

CCTV under construction. Beijing, China. 2008. OMA.

Design takes time regardless of approach, requiring "hours of mental and manual effort",[14] further complicated by the abortive efforts and endless refinement which characterise every architectural project. Time influences output too. How time management and design information are reconciled at each stage can impact quality. At the early design stage, time pressures may mean a vital technical restriction is not picked up, later affecting the design as it develops. Or, at a later stage, a constricted design programme may mean a crucial aspect of a design is not described or drawn and therefore included within the building contract, invariably becoming an 'extra' to be paid for by the client during the construction phase with limited funds. Time management has an accumulative effect on the built outcome.

Lack of time can be one of the main sources of error in architecture. Busy senior members are often unable to review or check everything that 'goes out the door' within the required time frames. Time pressures exert an overriding fear of making mistakes when they can't be caught in time – limiting experimentation and the ability for less experienced members of staff to learn from them.

Time is also a catalyst for change. A set of promotional plans and images can garner support from political or community groups, validating proceeding to the next stage. A successful planning application can release the funding required to build a project before tax deadlines or other regulatory cut-off dates. A timeous detailed design package allows works to commence well in advance of the promised completion date, as much as the prompt response to construction phase queries does too. The output of architects and the time frames within which they are completed are critical to the success and delivery of a project.

The dual impact of time on quality and delivery mean it is perhaps the greatest source of pressure in practice. Time is a source of personal stress too, staff becoming dominated by the feeling of too many things to do in not enough time.[15] Deadlines can force panicked production as you attempt to square the oft-competing demands of time and quality. Deadlines can be self-administered to get through a body of work efficiently or, more commonly, imposed by others – your superiors passing on external project demands from clients and project managers. In either situation you must give realistic assessments of how long a task, or accumulation of tasks, will take.

This requires prioritisation. Ascertain what the core output is of the task you are involved in. If it is not made clear to you, ask. This will allow you not to be diverted or distracted by extraneous tasks. Secondly, be realistic about the time available and what can be achieved within it. Don't abandon perfectionism – never abandon that – but pursue it selectively. There are certain tasks where perfectionism is not essential like ancillary tasks or some more conceptual ones like sketching. This allows more time for when perfectionism is required such as in the technical detailing of a façade or the creation of complex three-dimensional models shared amongst other designers for coordination. This will give you a realistic chance of meeting the unrealistic deadlines set, without compromise.

There is also the aspect of managing change. One of the largest sources of last-minute time pressure is change. One change means multiple revisions to multiple drawings. That entrance sequence to the building isn't quite right on the ground floor plan? Bear in mind if it is changed, then two maybe three elevations, two building sections, the first-floor plan, the technical façade section, as well as the three-dimensional computer model, perspective views, and physical models will need to be changed also for consistency of information. Not to mention the changes other consultants may be required to make to their structural or services designs. Changes which they will justifiably seek further remuneration from the client for. Changes and revisions should never be made in a knee-jerk manner. Their value needs to be harmonised with their implications.

This again involves time. As Sir John Soane implored: "lay the entirety aside, until it ceases to be familiar to the mind ... If on re-examination, the whole still appears clear and satisfactory",[16] only then should one proceed. Unlike architecture school these pause periods are less available, if tolerated at all. Carve out time for reflection in any situation, before getting sucked into the next phase of a project, or a different one entirely. Review a design collectively with colleagues of different viewpoints to discover latent opportunities or problems, prior to pressing ahead to the more detailed stages. Or carry out post-project evaluation of successes and failures to ensure any mistakes are not repeated in the next project. I have been encouraged and discouraged in practice when seeking these moments of reflection. A good practice will always allow them, provided they can be executed within the wider constraints of time on any project. Only by pausing the constant flow of time can our understanding, of what we are doing and why, be deepened.

ARCHITECTURE AND TIME
J.M. Gandy's aerial view of Sir John Soane's Bank of England in ruins. 1830.

Notes

1 Koolhaas, R., 2004. Universal HQ: Babylon falling. In: R. Koolhaas, ed. *Content*. Koln: Taschen, p. 118.
2 Yarrow, T., 2019. *Architects: Portrait of a Practice*. Ithaca, NY: Cornell University Press. p. 216.
3 Jodidio, P., 1999. *Álvaro Siza*. Koln: Taschen. p. 48.
4 Siza, A., 2014. *Álvaro Siza: "Emotion is very important" in architecture* [Interview] (1 June 2014).
5 Galilee, B., 2008. Peter Märkli: An interview with the Zurich-based architect. *Icon*, 59 (May) [Online].
6 Ibid.
7 Killa, S., 2020. Interview with J. Tait [Interview] (9 June 2020).
8 de Graaf, R., 2017. *Four Walls and a Roof: The Complex Nature of a Simple Profession*. Cambridge, MA: Harvard University Press. p. 5.
9 Yarrow, *Architects*, p. 145.
10 Reiser, J., 2006. *Atlas of Novel Tectonics / Reiser + Umemoto*. New York: Princeton Architectural Press. p. 168.
11 Etherington, R., 2008. *China Central Television Headquarters by OMA*. [Online] Available at: https://www.dezeen.com/2008/08/06/china-central-television-headquarters-by-oma/ [Accessed 31 May 2020].
12 Yaneva, A., 2016. Diamonds and sponge. In: R. Dalton & C. Hölscher, eds. *Take One Building : Interdisciplinary Research Perspectives of the Seattle Central Library* . Abingdon: Routledge, p. 17.
13 Koolhaas, R., 2004. CCTV. In: *Content*. Koln: Taschen. p. 496.
14 Lewis, R., 2013. *Architect? A Candid Guide to the Profession* (3rd ed.). Cambridge, MA: MIT. p. 36.
15 Yarrow, *Architects*, p. 223.
16 Soane, J., 1787. *Plans, Elevations, and Sections of Buildings*. London: The Architectural Library. p. 7.

communicating

3.0 COMMUNICATION

WE HAVE ALL DONE IT.

↓

The stock phrase in your resumé about how you "embrace teamwork", "thrive in a collaborative environment", or are an "integral team member" usually followed by a proclamation of your "excellent communication skills". What do these glib phrases mean in practice?

Most students of architecture are not used to working in a team.[1] The focus in architecture school is on your own approach to design, skill set, and ethos. This period of development is critical to "liberate the pupil's individuality from the dead weight of conventions",[2] allowing the acquisition of "personal experience and self-taught knowledge".[3] To realise the potential and limitations of our own individual creative powers before they are applied in a group setting. The reliance on this process of 'individual liberation' in education doesn't prepare the student for the "social construction of architecture".[4] For the negotiations, debates, judgements, coordinations, and compromises.

The habits we learn in education die hard. Students, unchecked by tutors, describe their collection of drawings and models representative of a design, as 'my building'. It is the host city or landscape's building, the users' building, the client's building – not your building. A hubristic and myopic view that continues in practice. As architect W.W. Caudill asked: "I read a newspaper account of the opening of a public building ... the architect said 'I did this', or 'I did that' six times, and 'my building' twice. Yet did he really do the building? Didn't he just a little help? Did he program the needs of the client himself? Did he draw every line? Make every engineering calculation? Specify the cement,

LIBERATED FROM THE DEAD WEIGHT OF CONVENTION
Life at Bauhaus Dessau: Students in the Department of Architecture. Lotte Beese and Helmut Schulze at the Tracing Table. c.1928.

IT'S NOT "YOUR" BUILDING

Casa Ensamble chacarrá, Pereira, Colombia. 2015. Ruta 4 Arquitectura.

aggregate, and texture of concrete? Estimate the cost? Nurse the building through construction?"[5]

These habits are at odds with both architecture itself, and the role of the architect in practice. Architecture is a collective body of knowledge. A language of concomitant experiences and responses to the question of being human. Adding to or adapting this body of knowledge is, itself, a diachronic collaboration[6] with the past and the future. What has architecture been? What will it be? In the daily practice of it, too, architecture is an "embroiled world",[7] where the "question of creative ownership is moot".[8] Architecture is not possible in isolation, needing others to bring it into being and validate its worth in society.

Any architectural project depends on how effectively aims and intentions are communicated then implemented in concert. Architects' designs are executed by a multitude of others,[9] needing hundreds of diagrams, working drawings, models, specification clauses for it to be explained to the hundreds of other hands and minds that will execute it. Not to mention the influence of other design and construction professionals during the pre-construction phase. Questions of design ownership become murky if not futile. Architecture is only achieved through collaborative effort.[10]

This need not breed communal sameness and sterility, but instead increase the capacity for analysis and invention in any given situation at an increased rate.[11] Nor need it extinguish the flame of individual agency and creativity. As Hannes Meyer affirms, "The more contrasted the abilities of the designing brigade, the greater its abilities and creative power."[12]

A DIACHRONIC COLLABORATION

Pilgrim's Route. Jalisco, Mexico. 2010. Tatiana Bilbao ESTUDIO.

Collaboration needs to be tempered with a need to remain critical, objective, and inquisitive. Not to simply convert competing demands of others into a design, but to find ways in which they can be unified in a coherent whole. This raises the question of compromise. Architects who say they never compromise are self-deluded liars. Architecture is a process of resistance and compromise. The skill of knowing what to compromise and when to compromise it, as much as what and when to resist. As Paul Shepheard observes: "compromise sounds weak, but it means bind – as in promise – together ... the fitting together of the parts."[13] A successful project relies on the complex coordination of competing demands or parts into a coherent whole.

This requires communication. Of universal principles and individual desires through thought; thought into tangible representations by drawing, modelling, and writing; and the translation of these representations into instructions. If good architecture can be defined as "a human need clearly understood and imaginatively served",[14] and not a thundering statement of individual personality,[15] then it is best achieved through collaborative communication. The fluency of our communication and the ideas it represents sharpens our capacity and our instruments of judgement and innovation. This is the basis of the practice of architecture.[16]

HUMAN NEEDS CLEARLY UNDERSTOOD AND IMAGINATIVELY SERVED

Angdong Hospital Project. Hunan Province, China. 2011. Rural Urban Framework.

Notes

1 Yarrow, T., 2019. *Architects: Portrait of a Practice.* Ithaca, NY: Cornell University Press. p. 33.
2 Gropius, W., 1965. *The New Architecture and the Bauhaus.* Paperback ed. Cambridge: Massachusetts Institute of Technology. p. 71.
3 Ibid., p. 71.
4 Cuff, D., 1991. *Architecture: The Story of Practice.* Cambridge, MA: The MIT Press. p. 44.
5 Caudill, W.W., 1971. *Architecture by Team: A New Concept for the Practice of Architecture.* New York: Van Nostrand Reinhold. pp. 31–33.
6 Ghidoni, M., 2013. Editorial. *San Rocco,* 6(Spring), pp. 3–5.
7 de Graaf, R., 2017. *Four Walls and a Roof: The Complex Nature of a Simple Profession.* Cambridge, MA: Harvard University Press. p. xii.
8 Yarrow, *Architects,* p. 154.
9 Jenkins, F., 1961. *Architect and Patron.* Oxford: Oxford University Press. p. xv.
10 Frearson, A., 2019. *"We banned renders" from the design process says Tatiana Bilbao.* [Online] Available at: https://www.dezeen.com/2019/12/04/tatiana-bilbao-banned-renderings-architecture-interview/ [Accessed 1 April 2020].
11 Angelillo, A., 1997. *Álvaro Siza: Writings on Architecture.* Milan: Skira. p. 27.
12 Hays, M. K., 1990. *MODERNISM AND THE POSTHUMANIST SUBJECT: The Architecture of Hannes Meyer and Ludwig Hilberseimer'.* PhD Thesis. Cambridge, MA: MIT.
13 Shepheard, P., 1994. *What is Architecture?.* Cambridge: MIT Press. p. 86.
14 Banham, R., 1975. *Age of the Masters: A Personal View of Modern Architecture.* New York : Harper & Row. p. 154.
15 Ibid., p. 154.
16 Angelillo, *Álvaro Siza,* p. 27.

TECHNICAL ADVICE NOTE

06

LINEWEIGHTS

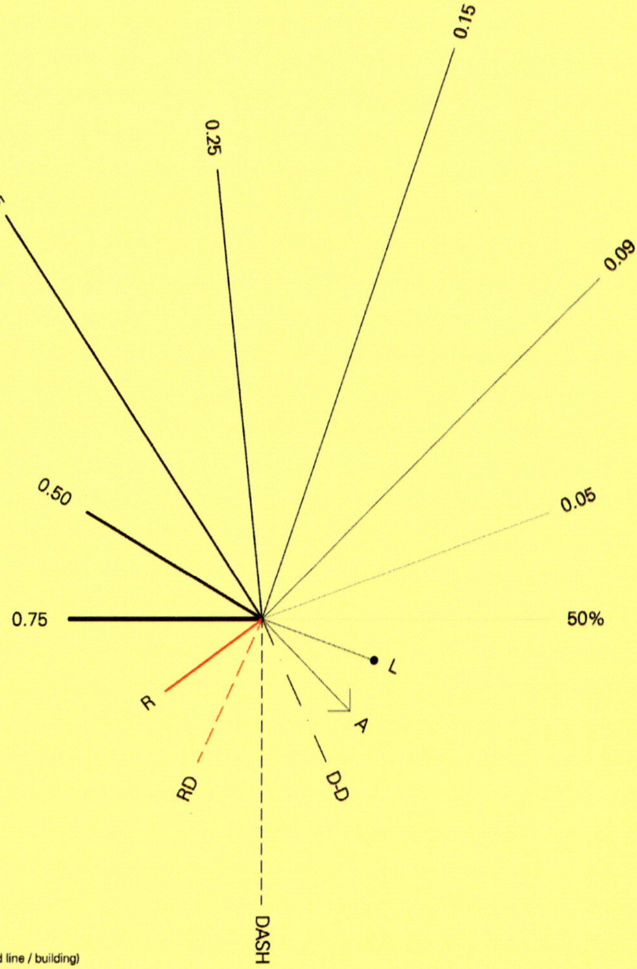

0.75 - section cut (ground line / building)
0.50 - primary external elements (loadbearing walls / structure)
0.35 - secondary external elements (non-loadbearing walls / roofs/ existing buildings)
0.25 - primary internal elements (partitions / timber / windows)
0.15 - secondary internal elements (doors / wall finishes / floor finishes/ ceilings)
0.09 - tertiary elements (services / landscaping / roads)
0.05 - detailed elements (notes / furniture / hatching)
50% - background elements (people / vegetation / vehicles)
L - leader call-out for notes/annotation
A - arrow indicating slope or level change
D-D - dash-dot line indicating: drainage / grid-line
D - dashed line indicating something above the plan cut
RD - downtakings / demolition
R - site / plot boundary

3.1 TOOLS

AT MY FIRST ARCHITECTURAL office we occupied a shopfront where two clients had acquired a unit next door and planned to convert it into a music studio.

↓

Something of which they had no prior experience. Upon finalising the design, we issued a full set of plans, details, furniture layouts, and lighting diagrams. We asked if they wanted us to assist in getting costs from local contractors. They were "going to do the work themselves". Sensing our scepticism, they replied with the optimism of someone who has never built anything before, "how hard can it be?!". Each week they would 'pop in', regaling us with their successes and failures. The sixth week, they almost bust the door off its hinges. "We've finished!", breathlessly explaining that "we even did that detail for the lights you wanted ... it looks brilliant ... we weren't sure about the curves, but they look great – you've got to trust the designers, eh?!", with a knowing wink. Curves?! "What curves?", "The curved shelf for the wall mounted lights ... took us all night". He's starting to panic, fatigue setting in, and the effects of the 'special' cigarettes he was accustomed to now wearing off. I suddenly realise what has happened. He has literally built the lighting connection diagram (a dashed annotation line showing how the wiring of the lights should be connected) as a curved shelf. Not the sleek rectilinear pelmet which concealed the cheap lighting fittings. Instead, this poor guy has spent all night using a borrowed jigsaw to celebrate them by putting them on a thin, curved wall-mounted plywood plinth. "Come round and see it". I couldn't say no, it was ten steps away. He's staring at me intently now ... "what do you think, good eh?". I can't lie, nor can I tell him how awful it

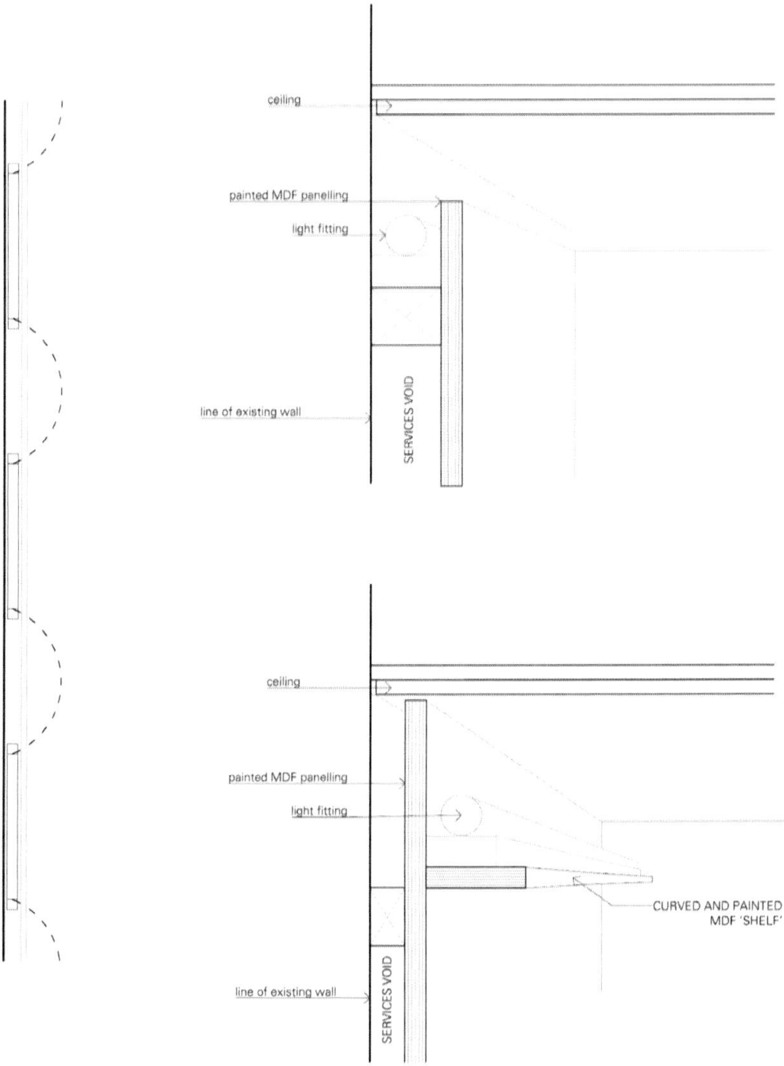

"OH, FOR FU..."

Plan detail (left) showing lighting connections in a dashed line. Miscommunicated intention (top right). Built reality (bottom right).

looks now knowing that this situation is largely our fault. How could we have expected someone with no technical knowledge or experience of reading architectural drawings to know that the curves were only for annotation? I carry out a quick post-mortem back at the office. The lighting drawing has no notes to say what the dashed 'curves' indicate, the dashes tighter than they should have been – to the untrained eye it could easily be a solid line. Further, they had never understood the intended detail anyway, a more appropriate medium – a three-dimensional diagram or image – would have been more effective in communicating the idea.

This painful experience taught me two things about communication in practice – Clarity and Selectiveness. Reliability of information is paramount, as is selecting the appropriate means of communication relative to the fluency and capabilities of the intended audience. An architect or contractor may instantly understand the intricacies of standard technical annotation, but a client may not. Each person has a different capacity to understand different forms of communication.[1] Architects must communicate in the most clear and selective way possible using the most appropriate medium.

Our methods of representing and instructing are also our working tools. Our tools of communication allow us to experiment with, test, and learn about what we are creating. In this capacity, versatility is more important than mastery. A rough concept model can give a fresh perspective on the totality of a design that a beautifully drawn elevation may not.

DRAWING

Our primary medium of communication is drawing. Whether generated from a three-dimensional model, precisely drafted in two dimensions, or loosely sketched by hand, a drawing is the most ubiquitous method for an architect to express the physical features, spatial relations, and material nature of any imagined reality. Beyond the role of representing what something will be, drawings in practice are also a set of instructions for those tasked with bringing them into material existence. A set of drawings for any project slowly develops from purely representational to largely instructional. The outline of a building filled in gradually with expanded detail on construction methods, materials employed, the incorporation of others' designs, manipulated too for the various forces acting on a design through time. Through this process, the drawing package expands, providing more instructive detail at smaller and smaller scales. Some drawings get populated with more detailed information – levels, detail references, exact representation of componentry. New ones are created to provide separate instructions for each condition.

The shift from 'what' to 'how' will dominate your time in practice. One of the first things you will notice in practice is how skeletal most drawings appear. A collection of black and white lines often devoid of any of the materiality, atmosphere, or human scale that drawing in architecture school had. Most drawings in practice are instructive – produced as a means rather than an end. If a drawing in architecture school is a fleshy life drawing, in practice they are diagrammatic X-rays.

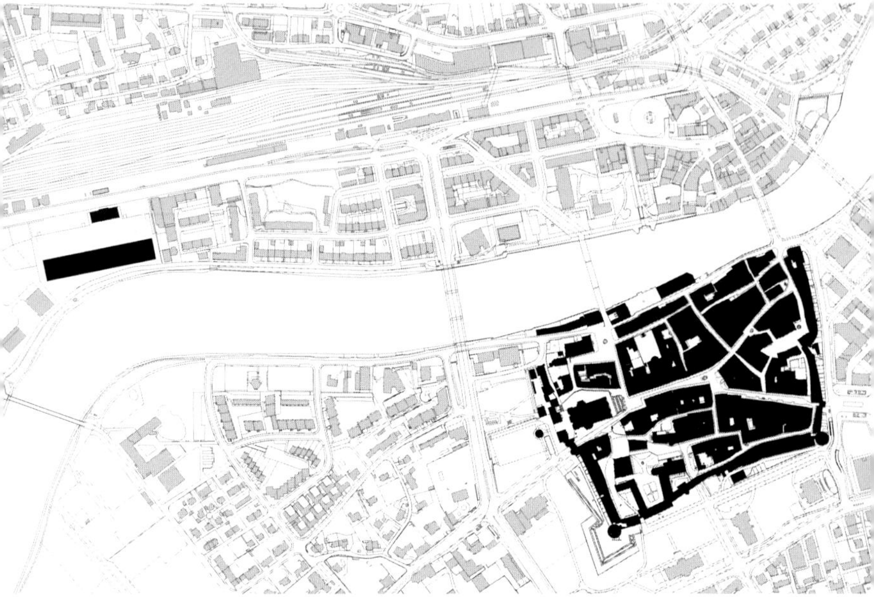

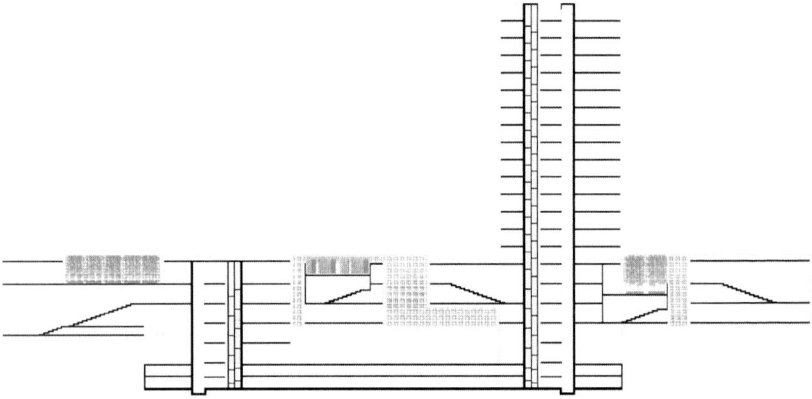

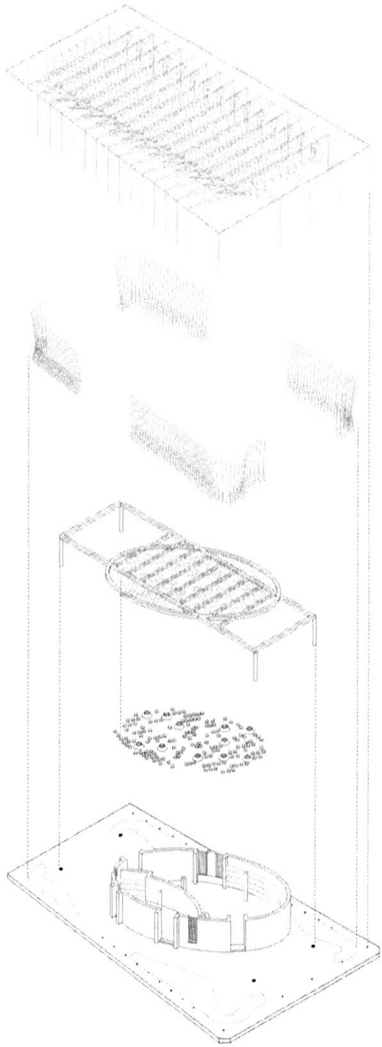

FROM "WHAT" TO "HOW"

Site Plan. Solothurn Synthes. Basel, Switzerland. 2012. Studio Märkli (facing page, top).
Section. La Maison du Savoir. Esch-sur-Alzette, Luxembourg. 2015. Baumschlager Eberle Architekten + Christian Bauer & Associés (facing page, bottom).
Axonometric. Bibliothèque scolaire Gando. Gando, Burkina Faso. 2010. Kéré Architecture (this page).

What elevates many designers is their ability to represent and instruct simultaneously. Like the details of John Ruskin or sectional perspectives of Paul Rudolph. The instructive drawing in their hands retains the capacity for poetry and evocation. Exploration, representation, and instruction intertwined.

POETIC INSTRUCTION

Construction view. Lambie Beach development (Lamolithic houses). Florida, USA. c.1950. Paul Rudolph.

IMAGE

If the drawing moves towards instruction over time, the image rests in representation. Images are imperfect imitations of objects,[2] idealised views of what a building should be. The use of the image in communicating a physical reality began in Renaissance Italy with the perspective, and proliferated during the Industrial Revolution where the architect was increasingly required to produce realistic images for 'lay-clients' who could not read architectural drawings without the aid of "naturalistic perspectives".[3]

THE BIRTH OF THE REALISTIC PERSPECTIVE

Architectural Veduta. c.1495. Francesco di Giorgio Martini.

This continues to be the communicative power of the image today. The architectural visualiser translates raw architectural data (CAD drawings, digital models, sketches), sculpting a snapshot of the imagined building to be easily digested and understood by the multitude of people that any one building project affects or interests.[4] The image becomes the 'real' in an otherwise abstract story. You will encounter many situations where clients will not 'get' the drawings but 'get' the image.

The idealised image can bring dangers. The author can represent the building how they would *like* it to appear. Tricks are played with scale and texture; lighting and cloud effects animate the building more intensely than it would be; shadows create false depth and mass; nature softens, occludes, and obscures; birds, vehicles, mist animate the foreground to distract. Concerns raised in the Victorian era[5] and echoed again now.[6] The degree of artistic license can lead to disappointment, the delusion only detected until it is too late.[7] The final product always judged by earlier communications of it. With so much at stake for so many people, it is important to communicate images honestly and accurately.

Honesty and accuracy are difficult to provide in an ever-shifting design process. While still in flux, the exploration of options throughout a design process would be better represented through the looseness and freedom of collage, its ambiguity leaving open possibilities rather than shutting them down.[8]

AERIAL VIEW

Powerhouse Parramatta. Sydney, Australia. 2019. Moreau Kusunoki.

COLLAGE

Mexican architect Tatiana Bilbao bans renders in the office until the design process has reached a certain point and the client and designer can be sure of the final outcome.

(Not) Another Tower. Chicago, USA. 2018. Tatiana Bilbao ESTUDIO.

MODEL

The historical role of the model has been representation, regarded as "the most satisfactory medium for showing an architects' proposals".[9] Models give the most faithful impression of how a design will look. Not only to clients and others, but to the architect themselves, ensuring that no aspect of the three-dimensional totality of a design is overlooked. The architect can stand over, or zoom and pan around, all aspects of a design to understand its full implications and potential.

Whether digitally generated or physically produced, architects may continually test and detect the consequences of a model's actions.[10] Either countering or confirming the intention – or offering new ones. This aspect of modelling, as an exploratory tool, is afforded the least amount of time in practice in my experience. Often there is deemed not enough time in the design process, much to the frustration of students previously encouraged to communicate and explore in this medium. How can we communicate the full implications of what we design, if we can't fully communicate it to ourselves?

MODELS IN PRACTICE: CONTEXT, TESTING, PRESENTING

6a Architects, London

EXPERIMENTAL MODEL

How to Carve a Giant. Helsinki, Finland. 2018. Sonia Magdziarz.

SPECIFICATION

Pre-Renaissance, the communication of architecture required no visual aids.[11] Owing to the architects' historic role as a 'master builder' the main method of communication was the written specification. This would typically state the size, format, provenance, properties, method of procurement and installation, as well as the finish of all elements of a building. Different parts of the document would be consulted by different trades.[12] This remains the fundamental role of the written specification in practice today. Further evolving to become the foundation of pricing documents and supplementary to working drawings to expand on the information contained in them.

This supplemental role is the root cause of the misuse of specifications in practice with over half of architects admitting to copying and pasting specifications from previous projects.[13] This is malpractice. Each project has a unique set of conditions, and standards and regulations evolve constantly. Can you really trust the information contained in a project elsewhere from five years ago? I have found this problem in most of the offices in which I have been employed. A specification should be developed in tandem with the drawings, not only to ensure consistency of information but to ensure that all material and technical possibilities have been explored then embedded in the visual information once settled on.

In Building Information Modelling (BIM), there is a drive to bring these four, principal means of architectural communication together. Ideas are sketched, then modelled digitally, from which two-dimensional hard-line drawings are produced, each modelled building component

FOR CONSTRUCTION

Architectural Specification_Rev03

12 December 2011

This document includes:

Code	Section	Revision	Dated
C20	Demolition	A	7 Jan 2011
C40	Cleaning masonry/ concrete	A	7 Jan 2011
C41	Repairing/ Renovating/ Conserving masonry	A	7 Jan 2011
C51	Repairing/ Renovating/ Conserving timber	A	7 Jan 2011
C90	Alterations - spot items	A	7 Jan 2011
F10	Brick/ block walling	B	1 Aug 2011
F30	Accessories/ sundry items for brick/ block/ stone walling	A	7 Jan 2011
G10	Structural steel framing	A	7 Jan 2011
H11	Curtain walling	B	18 Apr 2011
H14	Precast concrete and glass lens/ paver rooflights/ floor lights/ pavement lights/ security panels	B	5 Jul 2011
H51	Natural stone slab cladding/ lining/ features	A	7 Jan 2011
H62	Natural slating	A	7 Jan 2011
H71	Lead sheet coverings/ flashings	A	7 Jan 2011
H75	Stainless steel strip/ sheet coverings/ flashings	A	7 Jan 2011
J10	Cementitious mortar tanking/ damp proofing	B	15 Sep 2011
J21	Mastic asphalt roofing/ insulation/ finishes	B	12 Aug 2011
J40	Flexible sheet tanking/ damp proofing	A	7 Jan 2011
J42	Single layer polymeric sheet roof coverings	A	7 Jan 2011
K10	Plasterboard dry linings/ partitions/ ceilings	D	22 Nov 2011
K11	Rigid sheet flooring/ sheathing/ decking/ sarking/ linings/ casings	B	15 Sep 2011
K13	Rigid sheet fine linings and panelling	A	7 Jan 2011
K40	Demountable suspended ceilings	A	7 Jan 2011
K41	Raised access floors	B	22 Nov 2011
L10	Windows/ Rooflights/ Screens/ Louvres	C	27 May 2011
L20	Doors/ shutters/ hatches	B	1 Aug 2011
L30	Stairs/ ladders/ walkways/ handrails/ balustrades	B	18 Apr 2011
L35	Fixed utilitarian access systems	A	7 Jan 2011
L40	General glazing	A	7 Jan 2011
M10	Cement based levelling/ wearing screeds	B	15 Sep 2011
M20	Plastered/ Rendered/ Roughcast coatings	A	7 Jan 2011

FOR CONSTRUCTION 1

CLAUSES UPON CLAUSES

Typical architectural specification.

then containing detailed written specifications. The fundamental tools of communication remain the same, just organised and produced in a different way.

Around 70% of practices currently use BIM.[14] This figure will only increase as more project teams demand its coordinative capacity. Just as hand draughting (not sketching, it will never die) died a slow death in the 1980s, 2D CAD draughting is today. Most practices can ill afford to wait until you become accustomed to the software they use. Some may not even look at your portfolio.[15] Learning the current tools of the trade is critical to your employability, but also to improve the efficiency of how architecture in practice is created. Having experienced both, I can only say I managed more of my daily list when using BIM than traditional CAD. Software is never a guarantee of quality, but its increasing complexity and algorithmic potential means visualising multiple design options as well as testing the performance of a design can be carried out in real time. This can only be of benefit to what we create, if used correctly.

The role of the architect is to communicate future conditions. "Architects work in the present towards an imagined future";[16] through their unique tools of communication – drawings, images, models, specifications – architects communicate imagined realities at different scales and stages of development. Whether a massing model of a potential site, a circulation diagram predicting use, or the detailed design of a soon-to-be fabricated door, these multiple imagined realities need to be communicated to the multiple actors and agents involved in the creation of a building. As representations of what it will be, or instructions of how it will be made. The clarity and reliability of this communication is central to the success of a project, forming informal and formal bonds between designer, client, and maker.

Notes

1 Yarrow, T., 2019. *Architects: Portrait of a Practice*. Ithaca, NY: Cornell University Press. p. 115.

2 Eco, U., 2017. *Chronicles of a Liquid Society*. London: Penguin Random House. p. 191.

3 Jenkins, F., 1961. *Architect and Patron*. Oxford: Oxford University Press. p. 210.

4 Hodgson, T., 2018. *"The role of the contemporary visualiser is deeply misunderstood"*. [Online] Available at: https://www.dezeen.com/2018/10/25/architectural-renderings-defending-visualisers-troy-hodgson-darcstudio-opinion/ [Accessed 6 June 2020].

5 Jenkins, *Architect and Patron*, p. 207.

6 Betsky, A., 2018. *"It makes no difference whether you draw with Rhino or a Pelikan"*. [Online] Available at: https://www.dezeen.com/2018/10/15/opinion-aaron-betsky-architecture-renderings-versus-real-buildings/ [Accessed 6 June 2020].

7 Jenkins, *Architect and Patron*, p. 210.

8 Frearson, A., 2019. *"We banned renders" from the design process says Tatiana Bilbao*. [Online] Available at: https://www.dezeen.com/2019/12/04/tatiana-bilbao-banned-renderings-architecture-interview/ [Accessed 1 April 2020].

9 Jenkins, *Architect and Patron*, p. 124.

10 Yaneva, A., 2009. *The Making of a Building: A Pragmatist Approach to Architecture*. Bern: Peter Lang. p. 188.

11 Kostof, S. 1977. The Practice of Architecture in the Ancient World: Egypt and Greece. *The Architect: Chapters in the History of the Profession*. New York: Oxford University Press. p. 12.

12 Ibid., p. 12.

13 Murray, C., 2019. *"It's time for architects to choose ethics over aesthetics"*. [Online] Available at: https://www.dezeen.com/2019/03/28/opinion-christine-murray-climate-change/ [Accessed 7 June 2020].

14 NBS, 2019. *National BIM Report 2019: The definitive industry update*. RIBA Enterprises.

15 Killa, S., 2020. *Interview with J. Tait* [Interview] (9 June 2020).

16 Murphy, K., 2011. Building Stories: The Embodied Narration of What May Come to Pass. In: J. Streeck, C. Goodwin, & C. LeBaron, eds. *Embodied Interaction: Language and Body in the Material World*. Cambridge: Cambridge University Press, p. 246.

INTERVIEW E

↘ Jane Hall (ASSEMBLE)

What did you do when you left architecture school? What was your first experience of architecture in practice?

We (Assemble) graduated in the recession, 2009, and managed to get jobs straight away. We were cheap labour as more qualified (and expensive) architects were being fired. I had a good time at my first job, working on a huge £80m office building, just me and a project architect. It was very different though – suddenly you are working 9 to 6 and doing what you're told. There's creativity, but you're not valued for your individual input and no one cares if you are learning anything really. We graduated from Tom Emerson's unit (of 6a Architects) at Cambridge where we really got into the craft and detail of making things ... suddenly that all stopped in practice. Assemble came from a desire to have a more hands-on architecture experience that augmented the one we were having in the workplace. We weren't trying to do something alternative, because we didn't even know what the normal traditions were. A big part of it was just to have fun with your friends. Architecture is a group activity.

Can you describe your design process at Assemble? How does an idea develop into a reality?

It depends. We have about 15 members, and we allocate two to each project. People are allocated completely based on interest – each of us only work on things we have an interest in. The design process begins with those two people and their intuitive response to a brief. Every Tuesday morning, the whole studio participates in design-oriented workshops on two or three projects. We'll usually be modelmaking or drawing. We don't have one standard way of approaching a project. Different individuals have different ways of working and often we will shape our process to suit each project.

Collaboration is at the core of what you do, either amongst yourselves or with others ...

Collaboration is mainly about having good conversations with people, and maybe not even about projects. It's best when your collaboration is a hybridity of two people's practices – like our collaboration with ceramicist Matthew Raw – we value skill a lot. In each collaboration we ask "how can we learn something from somebody or see something in a different way?". Even if a project comes to us in which we have no background – we will learn and find the right people to work with. Every project is an opportunity to learn something new and work with new people.

facing page

Granby Four Streets. Liverpool, United Kingdom. 2013. Assemble.

Granby Four Streets. Liverpool, United Kingdom. 2013. Assemble.

facing page

Granby Winter Garden. Liverpool, United Kingdom. 2019. Assemble.

Can you describe how you dealt with the jump in scale at the Goldsmiths CCA? Did your approach change accordingly?

When you jump a scale, it still feels like you are involved but that it is realised by someone else. We try to look for opportunities to do things that are more crafted. Like at the Goldsmiths façade – we could only afford a cheap material. We were never going to get the quality we were looking for, so that's where the idea for the green-stained cement board came from. We worked hard to convince the client we could do the façade package ourselves. That was quite a risk – I'm surprised we did that now! We developed details with the manufacturer and made 1:1 mock-ups – there was a lot of development. It's weathered very well. That led to doing the reception desk, a chair, tables, a lamp. Being able to introduce these more crafted elements rests on two things. Our collective ability as Assemble and our studio environment. We are in a big workspace – with carpenters, ceramicists, metalworkers – where we can have an idea, do a drawing then show it to someone. They have more ideas and then fabricate it for us. We can quite quickly design with the person who is going to make it. This allows us to do these things expediently. It gives an extra layer of human touch and care, rather than just using ready-made products.

How can the architectural profession address its many diversity issues?

Education is a huge barrier, the cost of it and the diversity of teaching staff. It's important students are taught by those representative of them. To provide a future model. Fundamentally, practice is structured against minorities too. You may become a licensed architect in your early thirties, with a whole load of debt, by which time you are thinking about having children. Most women then don't build in their

Goldsmiths CCA, exterior view. London, United Kingdom. 2018. Assemble.

Goldsmiths CCA, interior view. London, United Kingdom. 2018. Assemble.

thirties, when men get experience and progress to higher positions. You have so many barriers. The way to address that is moving away from the outdated idea of a meritocracy and taking more interest in training and educating staff. To use the potential of the person you have hired. Creating environments where people want to stay and learn is also good for diversity. It's the responsibility of practice, but it's so cut-throat they rarely have time. I'm in support of unionisation – architecture requires new institutions. I used to be an advocate for reform, now I think let's get rid of the RIBA. Start from scratch.

What advice would you give graduating students about to enter professional practice?

I would encourage students to think of that moment when they leave university as the start of their education. Go out and look for work and jobs that you want. Not simply think, "oh I've been given a job isn't that great" then adapt themselves to that environment. No, the industry is there for you to learn and you can find people you want to work with and who will support you. Don't just passively treat it as your job. Meritocracies don't exist – networking is a great skill, it's about getting to know people. Working and talking with people that you like. I wish they'd taught us at university to be more entrepreneurial. If you like a practice, try and talk to somebody from the practice. Students could build up confidence a lot quicker if they could talk to and learn from those in practice before entering it.

3.2 SPEECH

SPEECH REMAINS PERHAPS the most unique aspect of being human.[1]

↓

Speech has the capacity for poetry, instruction, clarity, and candidness; as much as it has the capacity for prose, delusion, obfuscation, and insincerity. It is those first four capacities of speech that architects must harness in practice. Poetry to convince and inspire; instruction to lead and guide; clarity to ensure complex ideas are communicated effectively; candidness to ensure trust and respect is earned. "Design emerges through interaction."[2] If these interactions are not underpinned by those four principles the aims and intentions of a design will become neutered, muddled, obscured, and falsified. Words and how they are used form the basis of how shared or divergent understandings will be negotiated or coalesced. Certain words open up possibilities, while others shut them down.[3]

The forum for this development of understandings is the meeting. Either internally – ad hoc meetings, weekly progress meetings, or design reviews. Or externally – client meetings, design team meetings, or site progress meetings. Meetings clarify design intentions, becoming clearer and more solidified. This solidification is often manifest by the architect agreeing to certain premises or solutions, then later confirming them with updated drawings, images, models, or specifications. Discussions reveal intentions to then be confirmed by further communicative action. Each issue raised in a meeting engenders multiple design implications. Implications that need to be assessed and tested prior to confirmation. Decisions are rarely made there and then; architects often say: "We'll check that and confirm back to you." Meetings

COMMUNICATING POSSIBILITIES

"... my job is to communicate many possibilities."

David Adjaye at Columbia University Graduate School of Architecture, Planning and Preservation, New York.

THE MEETING
Benedictine Sisters of Mary College meeting with Marcel Breuer (with the black glasses) in the early design process of their campus and monastery. c.1960.

are typically an information-gathering session, as one former boss used to say – "Don't agree to anything."

I remember my first meeting. I felt underprepared and overdressed. Say too much and risk creating a first impression of an ill-informed loose cannon. Say nothing and risk being dismissed as a mute bit part. I was also struck by how character, not just content, played a pivotal role in the discussions. Some loud and dominant, others humorous and deflective, some patient and insightful. The tempo and direction of the meeting dictated by the interplay between each character. I had conversed with each of these people by email but had not yet formed the bonds that collaboration in practice requires, by witnessing at first hand the content of their character. The multitude of issues raised and alien terms flying across the table, bamboozled me – until an outbreak of consensus emerged, and I had to take notes again. Almost every issue raised seemed to involve us to some degree.

The structural or services engineer may leave a meeting early after their input has been given – but the architect along with the project manager is usually there for the duration. That is not to say that the architect is more important; instead it is reflective of the more coordinating and holistic view of a project that they have. Taking detailed and comprehensive records of any meeting is then crucial. Not only as a means of capturing the full range of matters raised and the implications they have, but as a form of protection should divergences or agreements be disputed, or required as evidence, in the future.

DESIGN TEAM M

04.01.2012

5.0 CONTRA

5.1 Received

5.8 Received January. issued in

8.0 MISC.

8.4 wi

DESIGN TEAM MEETING

04.01.2012

1.0 STRUCTURAL/ARCHITECTURAL DISCOVERIES

1.5.6 provided setting out information on 20.12.2011. See attached SK.024. subsequently issued SI to .

1.5.7 Detail 1 opening to be filled with concrete pending confirmation from that this aligns with venting requirements. Colt confirmation on louvre depth and appearance through louvres.
Detail 2 opening to be investigated by to allow design team to ascertain exact solution.
Detail 3 as detail 2. to also ascertain whether door opening can shift to the right to allow commencement of concrete pier solution.

1.9.3 Will raise amended change notice for this based on 07.11.11 site visit agreements.

1.9.5 Have chased at by phone and email today and will alert team as to any indication of feedback ASAP.

1.14.1 **For cleaning methods** - report issued under CN0075 - awaiting instruction.
Balustrade Relocation - please see attached SK.025 for discussion purposes. This present an option of retaining and relocating the existing balustrade which we see as preferable to introducing any new elements.

2.0 INFORMATION REQUIRED SCHEDULE

2.1	5.12	CLOSED.	INSTRUCTED UNDER CAI122.
	7.01	CLOSED.	PREVIOUSLY ADVISED THAT POSITIONS GENERALLY AS INDICATED ON DRAWINGS. FINAL SET OUT BY TENANT.
	7.06	CLOSED.	CONFIRMED NO EXISTING MOVEMENT JOINTS.
	7.20	OPEN.	GROUT AND TILE SAMPLES ORDERED AND RECEIVED TO ENSURE MATCH PRIOR TO COLOUR SELECTION - WE SHOULD REVIEW WITH IN THE EARLY PART OF NEXT WEEK.
	7.23	CLOSED.	ISSUED UNDER CN0069.
	7.33	CLOSED.	HAVE PROVIDED POSITIONS ON DRAWINGS. SECTION N25/220A CLEAR THAT *'INSTALLER TO MAKE DETAILED PROPOSALS FOR SETTING OUT OF SOCKET POINTS FOR CA APPROVAL'*
	7.38	OPEN.	SENT PROPOSALS FOR EMERGENCY EXIT LIGHTING (24.11.11). HAVE RECEIVED NO INDICATION YET AS WHETHER TO PROCEED. NOTE WE ARE PROPOSING COMSIGN II.
	7.39	OPEN.	SENT PROPOSALS FOR EMERGENCY EXIT LIGHTING (24.11.11). HAVE RECEIVED NO INDICATION YET AS WHETHER TO PROCEED. NOTE WE ARE PROPOSING COMSIGN II.
	7.41	CLOSED.	ISSUED UNDER CN0069.
	7.42	CLOSED.	ORIGINALLY ISSUED UNDER CN0053, EHICH WAS SUPERSEDED BY CN0069. INFORMATION CONTAINED ON CN0069.
	7.44	CLOSED.	ISSUED UNDER CN0069.
	7.45	OPEN.	TO REVISE WHB'S SETTING OUT - BY 06.01.12.

4.0 REQUESTS FOR INFORMATION

4.3	133	OPEN.	TO REVISE INFORMATION FOLLOWING RECEIPT OF MARK UP - BY 06.01.12. FURTHER MEETING ARRANGED FOR W/C 9th JANUARY.
	157	CLOSED.	SETTING OUT PROVIDED BY + .
	158	ANSWERED	REMAINS OPEN DUE DEBATE ON RESPONSIBILITY FOR FINAL SETTING OUT OF M+E WORKS. NEED A MEETING WITH ON THIS ASAP.
	159	ANSWERED	NEEDS INSTRUCTED BY .
	160	ANSWERED	
	161	ANSWERED	NEED A MEETING WITH + ON THIS ASAP.
	170	ANSWERED.	
	176	OPEN.	ANSWERED - FURTHER QUERY, WILL RESPOND BY 05.01.12.
	178	ANSWERED	

MEETING NOTES

Even if you are not the designated minute taker – ALWAYS TAKE DETAILED NOTES!

Communication is required to be considered and thoughtful in practice. Architecture is a legally risky business. Every spoken word or written communication could be used as evidence for or against you in a legal dispute. It may never come to that, but it could. Careless communication can also harm the quality of a design. The use of prosaic language failing to capture the potential of a design, clients subsequently reverting to a safer option; muddled instructions opening up the possibility for confusion on-site; or deceitful or abrasive communication causing detachment between the architect and the rest of a design team no longer willing to go the extra mile to coordinate their designs with yours.

Further, loose talk harms the progress of projects. This applies as much outside of the meeting room as it does inside it. I have found this out to my cost on two early occasions. Once, when helping convert a residential property into a drug rehabilitation centre, a fact which I naively told an old family friend who lived on the same street. He subsequently mobilised a community campaign to halt the project. Another, where I stupidly participated in an impromptu meeting with other consultants prior to our client meeting, in a café in the very building we were planning to demolish – the owner suspiciously glancing over at the very familiar model of the existing building displayed on the table. His lawyers became involved and the design process stalled.

There is the wider question of how we communicate, too. Architects are notoriously bad at communicating their ideas to others. Too obtuse or obscurant for some;[4] not captivating or expansive enough for others.[5] Many assign this problem to the proliferation of jargon – the problem occurring when it is inadequately translated in public.

"...**charismatic** collection of cantilevers and **iconography**..."

"the poetic possibilities of their **architectonic** and **symbolic** composition..."

"Horizontal **"plates"** bring to mind the **tectonics** of the surrounding mountains."

"...the centre forms an **iconic marker** of global influence."

"...the **dynamic** becoming of its curves implies change"

"To **materialize** this elevated horizontal **plane**..."

"... with multiple ground **planes** and **sectional interconnectivity**"

"a synoptic **symbol**"

"the center goes beyond **program** to play an **iconic** role..."

"The **dynamic** structure is constructed animation, curiosity made concrete."

"Its form is **programmatic**..."

"...its **dynamic** landscape awakens the sense of wonder and kindles the zest for discovery."

GARBLED, OBSCURANTIST, HUBRISTIC. BULLSH...

It's only a building, mate. Not a "symbolically charismatic marker, dynamically materialised by sustainable innovation ..."

"...socially **sustainable**..."

"The main factor in the **innovation** and design quality"

"...**urban fabric**..."

"... an energy field pushes and pulls the building **dynamically** into a reiterative play of form, space, and function."

"tactics of **programmatic** organisation..."

"... offers maximum flexibility and a **sustainable** development capacity."

"...pushing them along in a **dynamic** flow of converging and diverging walls and ceilings that transmit the **dynamism** of the shell to the interior."

"...high **occupational density** and good **permeability**."

"...ten-story-high **urban envelope.**"

"...the complex geometries and program **architecturalize** the park."

"...challenges the generic architecture of the institution through **programmatic** and material **innovation.**"

"...unfolding the **formal composition** to reveal its content and maintaining the **fluidity** between interior and exterior..."

Jargon develops to communicate internal values and practices in a particular field. On one hand: "Architecture is a specialist subject with deep culture, long history, involved technologies and complex politics ... it needs specific types of language to talk about it!"[6] On the other: jargon is de-centrifugal and clumsy.[7] With the sole intention of occluding and excluding the uninitiated,[8] only serving to inflate the architects' pomposity while deflating their relevance.

The critical role of speech in architectural practice is one of translation. You are no longer communicating only to other architects or architecture students, but to a multitude of others unaccustomed to our often-arcane jargon. A building is no longer "an exploration of epistemological function"[9] nor is the creation of it a set of "formal relationships, organizational relationships, scalar relationships which articulate the oscillating space between the rigid tool and plastic matter".[10] These academic terms need to be translated in real terms, in practice.

This also comes down to the appropriate use of words. Architects often misuse them either to inflate the importance of something or distract from its real value. One of the most overused words in practice is 'innovative'. Used to describe anything from the mechanism on a door hinge, the detail of a façade, or whole building forms, this confuses its real meaning, the use of revolutionary ideas or methods, with novelty – the quality of something which is new and unusual. Has what you're doing never been done before? Is it a new and better way of solving a problem? Does it have the potential to shift future practices and attitudes? Or does it just look or act slightly differently to what has gone before? 'Innovative' is an example of a whole host of misused words in architectural practice

ARCHITECT AS TRANSLATOR

Cassia Co-op Training facility. Kerinchi, Indonesia. 2011. TYIN tegnestue Architects.

designed to oversell yet serving to undervalue the history and complexity of what we do.

Simple ideas need not be communicated in hyped, complex, or arcane language. Architects have a duty to explain complex ideas with clarity, conciseness, and candidness. Recognise that you have moved into a new realm, a more public one, where the translation of architectural intentions is key to their success. If design in practice emerges through interactions with others, the quality of these interactions is vitally important.

Notes

1 Arendt, H., 1998. *The Human Condition* (2nd ed.). Chicago: University of Chicago Press. p. 27.
2 Yarrow, T., 2019. *Architects: Portrait of a Practice*. Ithaca, NY: Cornell University Press. p. 135.
3 Murphy, K., 2015. *Swedish Design*. Ithaca, NY: Cornell University Press. p. 147.
4 Fairs, M., 2018. *"Poor communication skills" to blame for architecture's problems, says Tom Dyckhoff*. [Online] Available at: https://www.dezeen.com/2018/06/04/tom-dyckhoff-sam-jacob-twitter-row-architecture/ [Accessed 8 June 2020].
5 Winston, A., 2016. *Architecture has a serious problem with communication says Rem Koolhaas*. [Online] Available at: https://www.dezeen.com/2016/05/24/rem-koolhaas-architecture-serious-problem-communication-oma-american-institute-architects-aia-convention/ [Accessed 8 June 2020].
6 Jacob, S., 2018. [Online] Available at: https://twitter.com/_SamJacob/status/1002548075687239680 [Accessed 8 June 2020].
7 *Jonathan Meades on Jargon*. 2018. [Film] Directed by F. Hanly. United Kingdom: BBC Four Television.
8 Ibid.

9 Westcott, S., 2007. *Greenwich Perceptual Observatory*. [Online] Available at: http://www.presidentsmedals.com/Entry-20901 [Accessed 8 June 2020].

10 Hall, D., 2017. *Cycles of Toolmaking: An Optic, Tactile, Haptic, Material, Scalar and Pedagogic Study*. [Online] Available at: http://www.presidentsmedals.com/Entry-43391 [Accessed 8 June 2020].

TECHNICAL ADVICE NOTE

07

EMAILS

1 DON'T USE 'WEASEL WORDS'

~~'to the best of our knowledge'; 'it is our understanding'; 'perhaps'; 'maybe'....~~ Be clear and confident, not evasive and weak.

2 USE BULLET-POINTS

simplify your key points into:

- clear
- concise
- summaries

3 IT'S BETTER TO BE FORMAL THAN INFORMAL

Hi, Hiya, Alright, Yo, are not acceptable in the workplace. 'Dear John'; Hello Jane; or just the name will suffice. UNDER NO CIRCUMSTANCES SHOULD THERE BE ANY EMOJIS!

4 DETACH THE EMOTION

Never write an email in anger. These are considered, and traceable communications. Step away from your desk, go grab a coffee and take a deep breath... then write in a considered and factual manner. And no exclamation marks please!

5 DON'T SAY SORRY

Firstly never make the same mistake twice. This will limit the need to say sorry in the first place. If you do need to apologise, do so by phone call or in person. It will not only be more genuine, but also less likely to get you in trouble at a later date.

6 BE CAREFUL WHO YOU ARE CC'ING

Don't encourage private conversations within a project team, no-one likes a clique. Always check you are sending an email to the correct recipient too. Don't use the BCC function - it's sneaky.

3.3 OTHERS

IN ARCHITECTURE SCHOOL everyone cares in some capacity about design. In practice, this is not the case.

↓

This is a difficult concept for the architectural student entering practice to fathom let alone negotiate. You have spent five years or so collaborating, discussing, learning from, and engaging with people who value the creation of space, how it interacts with light, how these spaces are used, what qualities they possess and what functions they engender; how these functions are defined by form, how these forms interact with their context, the experiential or material effects of a building, or how the cityscape or landscape are enhanced by your proposals, and so on. In practice, architects can find themselves acting often as a sole defender of these principles, rather than dealing with them as absolutes.

EVERYONE CARES ABOUT DESIGN

Studio discussions. Avery Hall. Columbia University Graduate School of Architecture, Planning and Preservation. New York. New York City.

The others you collaborate with daily in the design and creation of any building will not have the quality of the architectural design as their primary priority. Why should they? That is your job. The client will often favour novelty and economy[1] over longevity and value; the project manager wants to achieve the project on time, on budget, and as agreed; the cost consultant suggests how to reduce expenditure or meet the budget; the structural engineer is busy making the building stand up[2] in the most efficient and risk-averse way; the services engineer needs space to locate and operate his/her ventilation, drainage, and heating equipment; and the contractor is motivated largely by the need to make a profit.[3] These are generalisations – many consultants, clients, and contractors pride themselves in their design intelligence and ability to appreciate and promote the functional, spatial, and aesthetic qualities of good design. However, in my experience these people are often thin on the ground. Each agent brings their own set of agendas, aims, and belief systems. In practice, "design hangs in the balance",[4] and at times comes under sustained attack. You are its primary defender.

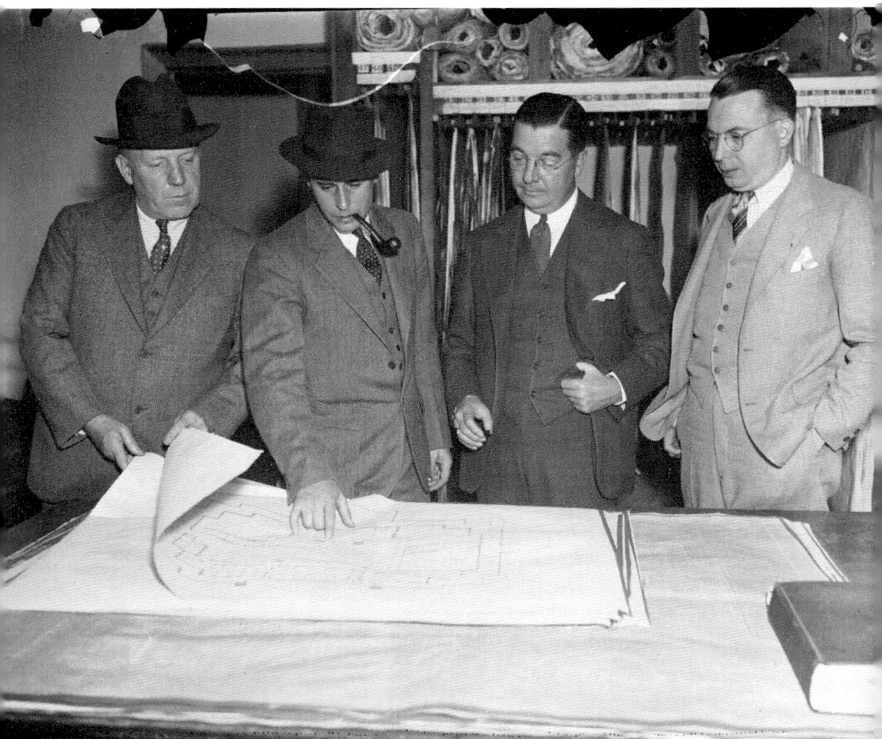

NOT EVERYONE CARES ABOUT DESIGN

From left: Contractor; Architect; Client; Engineer. c.1935.

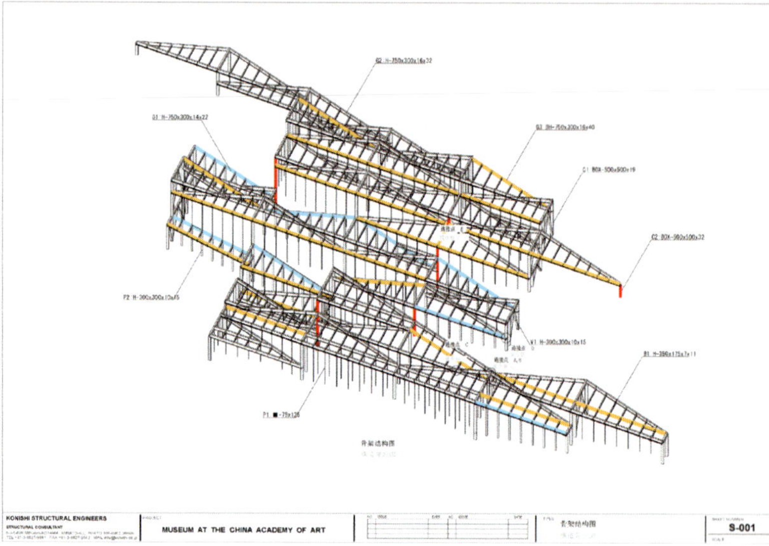

MAKING THE BUILDING STAND UP

Structural diagram. Museum at the China Academy of Art.
Hangzhou, China. 2009. Kengo Kuma + Associates / Konishi Structural Engineers.

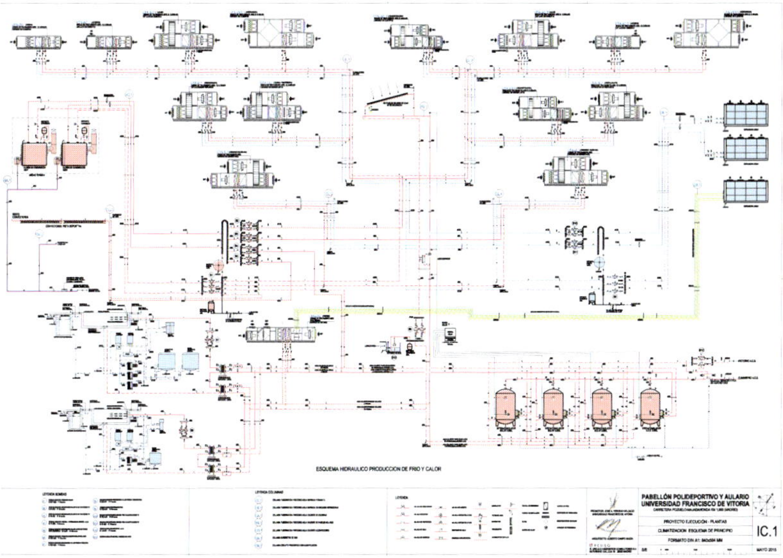

FINDING SPACE FOR THE EQUIPMENT

Services schematic. Francisco de Vitoria University Sports Pavilion. Madrid, Spain. 2016. Alberto Campo Baeza / R. Urculo Ingenieros.

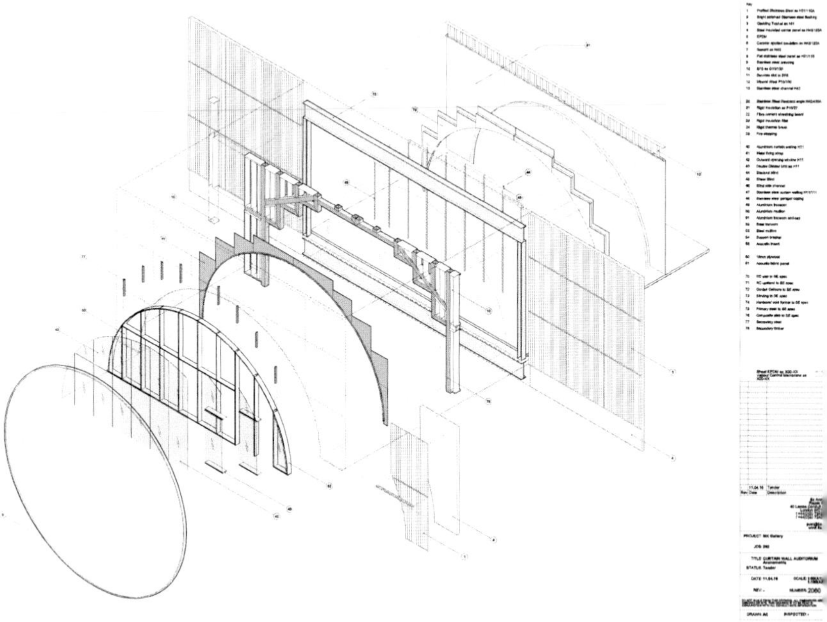

PROVIDING INSTRUCTIONS

Curtain wall axonometric. MK Gallery. Milton Keynes, United Kingdom. 2019. 6a Architects.

This situation inevitably leads to confrontation. There is an attitude in practice that conflict should be avoided wherever possible.[5] I don't agree with this pacifist approach. Avoiding confrontation can be counterproductive, forcing the architect to accept situations which injure the social, spatial, functional, or aesthetic integrity of a design. If the architect doesn't fight for these things – who will? Further, avoidance of confrontation can be viewed as weakness, the architect pliant to whatever other concerns in the design process begin to dominate solely to avoid conflict. It is more important in practice to be respected than liked. How can anyone respect you if you don't fight your corner in the melee that often ensues in the complex and stressful process of realising a building? Too much flexibility breeds spinelessness.

The apparent isolation in the fight for design and its qualities can be a positive. Allow this role as design defender to intensify and distil your love of architecture, not wear it down. Be clear what the driving principles are of the design, explain them clearly, and fight for them at every stage of the design process. Ensure that, despite the concerns and agendas of everyone else, you are involved in creating architecture of value and worth. That presumably is why you wanted to be an architect in the first place.

It would be false to say that this non-pacifist approach does not bring with it risks. My two most memorable experiences of conflict between others involve teacups (how British!). One teacup being launched at me across a meeting room by a contractor who took exception to my questioning his ability to build the project to the quality required. Another teacup being hastily filled with whisky by a colleague during the recess of a particularly rough meeting with a disgruntled client. Through these instances and countless others, as well as observing the actions of those around me, I realised a tempestuous disposition does not get you very far in the collaborative environment of practice. Promote and defend what you believe in and the architectural quality of what you are producing as a team – but do so with caution and care.

Timing is critical. Conflict at an early stage in the design process can cast a long shadow over the rest of the project, just as the wrong word at the wrong time can cause irretrievable damage to project relations too. Set off every project on an amiable and cooperative foot; and take time out to think when conflicts do arise before contributing to them.

Evidence is critical, too, never cast unfounded aspersions on the abilities of others – as I learned to my cost. You should only be concerned with their concomitant actions in relation to the project in which you are all involved. Not your opinions on their general capacity. When you are questioning those concomitant actions, make sure you have the facts and evidence to back up your claims. If not, leave it. More importantly you must know your own information intimately – its content, detail, and value. This will provide a solid foundation against any future attack, but also project an image that you and the practice you are employed by are confident in and fluent in their own work and in the production of architecture.

Thirdly, detach the emotion. Unlike my colleague who reached for the bottle, don't take professional criticisms as personal attacks. This can be difficult for someone who has been inculcated in the belief that their work and life are inseparable,[6] but it is essential. Professionalism involves a certain detachment from your individual self; be precise and measured. To disconnect, to some extent, who you are from what you know.[7] If conflict is not approached with timing, thoroughness, and restraint, it will be your individual reputation and that of the practice you represent that will suffer. Gaining a reputation as 'difficult to work with', or 'more trouble than they are worth'.

The best approach to dealing with conflict is prevention. The divergent interests of others can often enhance the architectural proposals, developing latent design possibilities that the architect's scope of knowledge could never have predicted. An enlightened and engaged client can set the standards for quality across a project, becoming a key ally and collaborator in the process. Fostering direct relationships with user clients is crucial, as modernist architect Kate Macintosh describes: "That's the way you get the most satisfactory product and the greatest level of client satisfaction."[8]

USER ENGAGEMENT

Weaving class. A House For All Seasons. Shijia, China. 2012. Rural Urban Framework.

A good engineer (structural or services) will operate somewhere between creativity and technical ingenuity,[9] contributing to the overall design integrity rather than simply solving problems within it. Such an approach was adopted by AKT II engineers in their structural design for the Heydar Aliyev Centre in Baku. They proposed an eight-storey concrete structure which eliminated the use of columns, allowing the original concept of a fluid interior space to be realised.

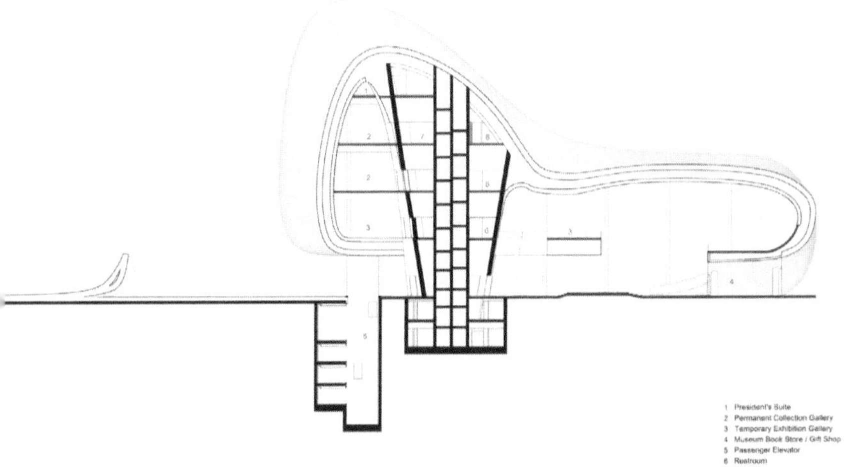

CREATIVE COLLABORATION

Heydar Aliyev Centre. Baku, Azerbaijan. 2012. Zaha Hadid Architects / AKT II.

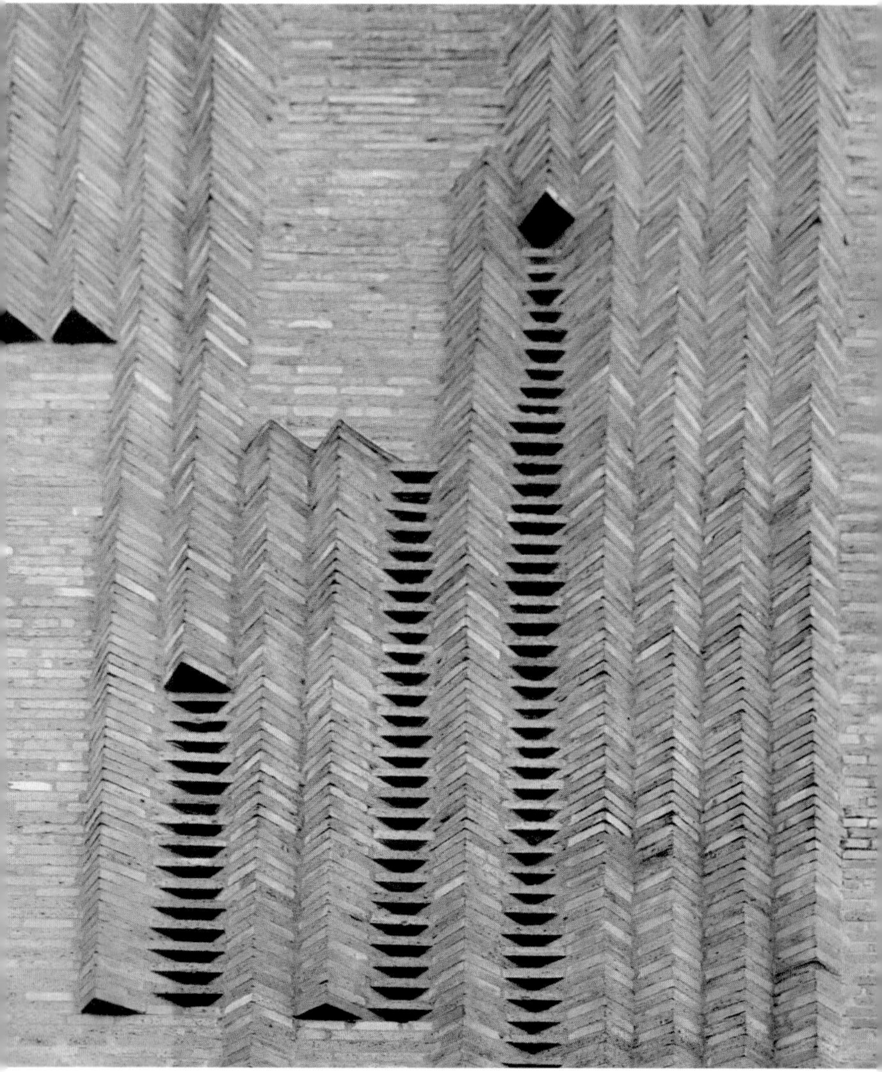

QUALITY THROUGH COLLABORATION

St Bride's Roman Catholic Church. East Kilbride, United Kingdom. 1964. Gillespie, Kidd & Coia.

An engaged and invested contractor will "often do things they wouldn't normally do"[10] if a collaborative, not dictatorial, approach is adopted and a shared vision forged. This is evident in the highly crafted details of Gillespie, Kidd & Coia, who used to work on-site with the bricklayers, surrounded by stacks of un-mortared bricks, in an open and physical dialogue of how to achieve their complex details.[11]

Others involved in the design and build process harbour as many generalisations about architects as architects themselves do about them. Successful collaboration, resting in the ability to resolve competing aims, is the only way to surmount these preconceptions. If divergences arise within this collaborative process they should be addressed, not avoided, with consideration and restraint. The success of what you design now, and in the future, depends on it.

Notes

1 Draper, J., 1977. The Ecole des Beaux-Arts and the Architectural Profession in the United States: The Case of John Galen Howard. In: S. Kostof, ed. *The Architect: Chapters in the History of the Profession*. New York: Oxford University Press, p. 214.

2 Mostafavi, M., 2008. Between engineering and architecture. In: H. Kara, ed. *Design Engineering: AKT*. Barcelona: Actar, p. 264.

3 Lewis, R., 2013. *Architect? A Candid Guide to the Profession* (3rd ed.). Cambridge, MA: MIT. p. 218.

4 Cuff, D., 1991. *Architecture: The Story of Practice*. Cambridge, MA: The MIT Press. p. 69.

5 Ibid., p. 183.

6 Judkins, R., 2015. *The Art of Creative Thinking*. London: Sceptre. p. 208.

7 Yarrow, T., 2019. *Architects: Portrait of a Practice*. Ithaca, NY: Cornell University Press. p. 213.

8 Macintosh, K., 2020. *Interview with J. Tait* [Interview] (3 June 2020).

9 Mostafavi, Between engineering and architecture, p. 264.

10 Metzstein, I. & MacMillan, A., 2008. Gillespie, Kidd & Coia: 1956–1987 Learning, Building, Teaching. *Paperspace*, pp. 74–87.

11 Ibid.

INTERVIEW F

↘ Alberto Campo Baeza

How important is teaching to your practice of architecture?

The ideal situation is to teach and to practice. My father was a surgeon, as a surgeon it is necessary to have a sharp scalpel for every operation. Teaching sharpens the scalpel, it allows you to criticise and refine. When they say "Mr Campo Baeza your buildings are very sharp, your buildings are very precise", it is because I am teaching. To teach is a gift.

You often cite poetry as a key inspiration in your work ...

It can be summarised in this – "omit needless words". In poetry every word has its place. I am composing not only a beautiful piece but solving the problems that Vitruvius set – Utilitas, Firmitas, Venustas. We must find the beauty. Beauty is truth. At the start of a project, the client is not asking for beauty – "Give me a house, three bedrooms and a nice kitchen ...". You must take these requirements, like words in a poem, and find the beauty. To not use more words than is necessary. Economy is important. In my latest project, a house, the original design was around 150m^2. The client couldn't afford it, so we reduced it to 90m^2 but it is still very well composed. It still resolves the function, is well constructed, and finds beauty.

Francisco de Vitoria University Sports Pavilion. Madrid, Spain. 2016. Alberto Campo Baeza.

Photographer: Javier Callejas.

**Museo de la Memoria de Andalucía. Granada, Spain. 2010.
Alberto Campo Baeza.**

Photographer: Javier Callejas.

The pursuit of beauty and truth is a common theme in your work regardless of location, typology, or budget …

Every project is an opportunity, an opportunity to create a masterpiece. Like when Michelangelo designed the Piazza del Campidoglio in Rome. It's only a square, but he created the centre of the world. As a designer you can profit in every occasion. Size doesn't matter. What is important is your intentions and your capacity to resolve the problem. The capacity to create emotion. We must try with every project to get this type of feeling and at the same time resolve the site, economy, the construction. It's about finding something more.

Is that your key role as an architect?

An architect whose work is worthwhile, will never become rich. A good architect never gets their satisfaction from money. Or fame. To try to become a 'star-architect' is dangerous – it's a guarantee to forget the history of our profession. Be more silent, more peaceful. Then maybe your work will remain through time. Don't try and do everything with your architecture. Be calm. Respect the rhythm of history.

Tell me about your design process. How do your projects develop from idea to reality?

There is not a list. It is like a doctor – you listen. You listen to the client, the place, its history, the budget, and many other things. Then you make a diagnostic. A diagnostic must be very precise to get the best result. Two days ago, I was in front of four renders with four different solutions trying to get the most appropriate, the sharpest result. You are investigating. It's not a question of fashion. An idea must mature. An idea is not something that appears from the sky. It

Casa del Infinito. Cadiz, Spain. 2014. Alberto Campo Baeza.

Photographer: Javier Callejas.

needs to distillate like my favourite liquor, Patxaran, grandmothers like it. When I need inspiration, I have a little glass of Patxaran and the ideas come immediately!

Do clients give you time for this distillation and maturation?

Clients, clients, clients! Sometimes, clients are very good. For example, my best clients are an American couple. I built a house for them in New York (Casa Olnick Spanu) and we are also making a museum of contemporary art for them. But it is always a battle. You must try not to say yes, yes, yes, or no, no, no. You must convince. At the Casa del Infinito, the client was an architect. She was trying to convince me to make the house in a green stone from Italy. It was beautiful, but my idea was to build with a stone made from the sand that surrounded the site. I won in the end. She now says, "you were right, Alberto". It is necessary sometimes to convince clients.

What is your main motivation as an architect?

There are a million motivations. I am 73 years old now but every day I am more and more happy to be an architect. I think being an architect is the most beautiful job in the world. You are dreaming and your dreams can be materialised. You are building dreams. In architecture, you are trying to make people living in these dreams happy. It's so beautiful! There is no comparison.

Entre Catedrale. Cadiz, Spain. 2009. Alberto Campo Baeza.

Photographer: Javier Callejas.

3.4 INTERNAL

AS MUCH AS DESIGN EMERGES from interactions with those outside the profession, it does too from within it.[1]

↓

Your working environment, and the people that you work with, will have a greater bearing on your concepts of professionalism and your design ethos than abstract professional codes – "it is infinitely preferable that these standards be embodied in a human being than a lifeless, static code of practice".[2] Through observation and participation, you will be able to make judgements on how to practise integrity and competence, and create meaningful relationships with others.

As a student I was fascinated by the work of Oscar Niemeyer, Marcel Breuer, and Rem Koolhaas. This led me to find out more about how they created it. Niemeyer depicted a working environment I recognised from architecture school, where they worked hard but always "found time for fun".[3] Robert F. Gatje's elegant account of his relationship with Marcel Breuer expressed a "family"[4] environment underpinned by a deep professional and personal respect for their humble leader, something which I saw in my best studio tutors. Koolhaas fostered a high-octane environment of chaos and unpredictability[5] – the two things I enjoyed most about the design process at architecture school. The distinct cultures which each architect cultivated, their internalised ethos, and modes of internal communication, became as interesting to me as their works. Hard work, fun, respect, exploration, and unpredictability. Did I find these aspects in practice? Sometimes, but not often.

THE MET

Whitney Museum of American Art (now Met Breuer). New York, USA. 1966. Marcel Breuer.

SCULPTURAL MODERNISM

Mondadori Headquarters. Milan, Italy. 1975. Oscar Niemeyer.
Photographer: Carlo Dell'Orto.

AFTER THE "CRIT"

Students at the National University of Singapore. 2006.
Photographer: Jonathan Lin.

Interaction in practice is formal and informal; work-oriented and social. A continual oscillation between the tasks you are involved in, and how you represent them and yourself. Formal interactions in practice centre around two different types of forums: the project review and the design review. The design review loosely follows your experiences of studio tutorials and 'crits' at architecture school. Either as an entire office or in smaller project-specific groups, the design review is a forum for ideas to be presented, debated, agreed, and refined in a collective and discursive environment. Design input will be welcomed from any direction but is generally led by those in more senior positions.[6] These forums are vital for the development of a design, highlighting opportunities and pitfalls while helping explore and refine a design at any stage of its conception, development, or realisation. Design reviews also allow participants the opportunity to establish themselves within the working environment. A careful yet bold intervention or statement alerting those in more senior positions to your potential for thought and action. As architect Shaun Killa recalls of a recent graduate employed on a temporary contract: "We have all of these options pinned up ... It gets to my option (and I'm the boss!), and she says 'I totally disagree, that doesn't work at all, if this is done or that is done, we can do it in a better way' everyone was shocked. I looked at her and said 'go straight to HR and ask for a new contract – you are now a permanent employee'. She's still here today and she's amazing."[7] The ability to freely speak your mind may not be afforded in every practice, but a good working environment will allow this – fostering rather than cowing talent.

A DESIGN REVIEW IN PRACTICE

Killa Design, Dubai.

The second formal internal forum, commonly known as the project review, is more focused on the operation and organisation of a project. Project reviews typically involve the entire office, the parallel worlds of different teams on different projects temporarily inhabiting the same room.[8] Usually organised weekly, they allow for those involved in each project to explain tasks completed, progress made, and future tasks pending, giving an assessment on its health and progress. Marked by brevity and conciseness, project reviews allow those in charge to quickly coordinate and allocate work. They are not opportunities to display your design nous or strength of character, but instead to display the other skills valued in architects – organisation and clarity. Honesty is vital in these forums, any attempt to occlude or circumvent will be discovered sooner or later.

There are also the informal interactions occurring on a continual and ad-hoc basis. A more senior member leaning over your shoulder to review a drawing or model (tweak this, shift that), a colleague asking you for a 'quick word' in another room or at their desk, or participating in general knowledge-sharing discussions – eyes still fixed on screens. These are equally as important as the more formal interactions owing to their frequency. A constant dialogue of assessment, opinion, and thought which translates into the design process. Design emerges in practice by informal and formal interaction.

INFORMAL INTERACTIONS

Killa Design, Dubai.

Interaction allows meaningful and close working relationships to form in practice. This requires you to absorb the environment, learning its methods, approaches, and language through the observation of the words and deeds of those around you who have internalised them. First, listen. Limit the use of headphones, ask to be involved in meetings, try to position yourself physically within the office near those you feel you can learn from. An educational eavesdropping. The interactions around you are invaluable to your development as a professional, even if they don't directly concern you. I once sat opposite a particularly cantankerous architect always taking phone calls from contractors on-site, exposing me to terms and phrases I had never come across and to the scepticism and caution required during the later stages of a project when so many things can go wrong. I once sat next to a poorly sound-proofed meeting room discerning the shift in tone and register required by my superiors when they were engaging with clients. Learning the need to charm, as well as inspire confidence in, those who pay for your services. After absorption and observation, you can then use the intelligence gained towards participation.

facing page

INDIVIDUALS WORKING TOGETHER TOWARDS A COMMON GOAL

Moreau Kusunoki, Paris.
Photographer: Moreau Kusunoki.

Participation requires collegiality. Close working relations are integral to the cultivation and dissemination of tacit knowledge and experience of any collection of people working towards a common goal. If you dislike someone you are less willing to share knowledge with, or seek knowledge from, them. A lack of collegiality can harm the ability to respond to the complex challenges faced daily, with the full capacity of the people involved. Over time, a carefully cultivated working relationship can develop into friendship. At the creation of the then new capital city of Brasilia, Oscar Niemeyer was given the ability to choose who he wished to work on the project; he hired "various friends from various professions".[9] This collection of architects, doctors, journalists, lawyers, footballers, and others allowed the team to become more versatile, the work more complete, with each member contributing their own speciality.[10]

Friendships in practice are formed first from respect. Respect for another's ability to deliver in a team environment, getting the right information at the right time, and to the expected standard. Respect for how they conduct themselves in certain situations – will they blame others for their own shortcomings or shoulder collective responsibility? Respect for how they communicate with others. Humility and reason have much more capacity to earn respect than arrogance and abrasiveness. One example is described by Gatje of Marcel Breuer: embarrassed by his poor draughtsmanship, he quipped, "I would never get a job in this office ...".[11]

Once a foundation of mutual respect is laid, familiarity and camaraderie can be formed. At Marcel Breuer's office, moments of "raucous informality"[12] were encouraged to punctuate the serious and efficient design work.[13] Architecture offices can often be serious and restrained

INFORMALITY

Party at Otti Bergers'. Bauhaus Students. 1930.

Photographer: Otti Berger.

environments reflecting the level of concentration required to carry out the complex and detailed work. However, my best experiences of practice have been ones where the seriousness has been punctuated with moments of informality and fun. A daily dialogue that breeds the informal and formal; personal and professional bonds that designing as a team requires. Evidenced in the emphasis placed on regular and inventive parties at the Bauhaus under Hannes Meyer, who saw them as a cornerstone of the institution.[14] My own career has been peppered with daily instances of pranks (where's my lunch?!), good-natured ribbing, and cynical banter. This combination of respect and camaraderie; seriousness and fun is encapsulated by Gatje: "We never joked about architecture, but we joked about everything else."[15]

In certain situations, a 'bunker mentality' can also develop as it did when I worked in a small architectural satellite office on a construction site. Surrounded by others with different agendas, our bond strengthened, collectivising under the strain of the almost hourly disputes we had with contractors, engineers, and quantity surveyors. Beware not to lose the support of your colleagues, you will need it. What underpins all internal communication – friendly or formal; informal or heated; between superiors or equals – is the ability to ask questions. A well-run practice should "balance tacit and explicit knowledge",[16] its leaders implored to "explain themselves ... if only they could and only they would".[17]

In architecture school you are taught to question everything, often told 'there are no right answers'. This is not the case in practice. Often there are right answers. There are clear-cut building regulations or laws that cannot be misinterpreted or construed in another way; there are manufacturers' guidelines which need to be followed to maintain guarantees; there are certain standardised ways of organising office documentation; or through years of practice an experienced practitioner can instinctively know the right answer to a particular issue or problem that he or she has encountered previously.

Outwith these absolutes, you will also encounter those in practice who see a question as a threat, especially from younger members of staff, moments where gaps in their knowledge could be exposed. Architecture is a continual dialogue. Fresh perspectives occur through rigorous questioning.[18] In my experience, some architectural practices regurgitate the same designs or details from previous similar projects that they have carried out, rolling out a set of 'standard details' each time. This is to limit risk – if a roof has been designed in a certain way before, and never leaked, then let's do it again. Or to increase office efficiency – the less time spent poring over the intricacies of a detail the quicker you can get onto the next project. However, it can also create staleness in an office – only by the injection of new inquisitive faces asking 'why?' or 'how?', will the office stay fresh.

ASKING QUESTIONS

A good working environment encourages discussion.

Moreau Kusunoki, Paris.
Photographer: Moreau Kusunoki.

The practices where I have worked which have not valued regular and rigorous questioning are the ones where the impulse was repetition, leading to sterility. A handful of self-appointed arbiters of design preventing the trickling down of knowledge and experience as well as the upward flow of curiosity and passion. Design idiosyncrasies and prejudices become the default rather than perpetual discovery and engagement. Keep asking questions, it is the only way you will learn why you are doing something, but more importantly it may make others in the office re-evaluate why or how they are doing something – only serving to improve the quality of what we produce.

Notes

1 Yarrow, T., 2019. *Architects: Portrait of a Practice*. Ithaca, NY: Cornell University Press. p. 135.
2 Sennett, R., 2009. *The Craftsman*. London: Penguin Books. p. 80.
3 Niemeyer, O., 2000. *The Curves of Time: The Memoirs of Oscar Niemeyer*. London: Phaidon. p. 28.
4 Gatje, R., 2003. Working with Marcel Breuer. In: A. von Vegesack & M. Remmele, eds. *Marcel Breuer: Design and Architecture*. Weil am Rhein: Vitra Design Museum, p. 313.
5 Wagenaar, F.H., 2004. Astrology: Protect us from what we want. In: R. Koolhaas, ed. *Content*. Koln: Taschen. p. 204.
6 Yarrow, *Architects*, p. 28.
7 Killa, S., 2020. *Interview with J. Tait* [Interview] (9 June 2020).
8 Yarrow, *Architects*, p. 222.
9 Niemeyer, *The Curves of Time*, p. 71.
10 Ibid., p. 71.
11 Gatje, Working with Marcel Breuer, p. 316.
12 Ibid., p. 318.
13 Ibid., p. 315.
14 Bergdoll, B. & Dickerman, L., 2009. *Bauhaus 1919–1933: Workshops for Modernity*. New York: The Museum of Modern Art, p. 333.
15 Gatje, Working with Marcel Breuer, p. 315.
16 Sennett, *The Craftsman*, p. 78.
17 Ibid., p. 78.
18 Townley, B. & Beech, N., 2010. *Managing Creativity: Exploring the Paradox*. Cambridge: Cambridge University Press. p. 31.

3.5 PUBLIC

ARCHITECTURE IS A REFLECTION of what society wants it to be. So too the role of the architect.

↓

The public image, cultivated by home improvement shows, of a gifted individual who can furnish them with a bespoke dream as an expression of private wealth, reflects an increasingly materialistic society eager to display its wealth.[1] This cliché of the architect is at odds with reality. Only a fraction of architects conform to this TV dinner of a stereotype,[2] most are busy creating the buildings that really matter to our collective public lives – mass housing, schools, colleges, transport infrastructure – as well as the privately owned hotel, residential, and office complexes that dominate our skylines.

Another assumption is that the architect is wealthy. I have lost count of the friends and family discreetly shocked at the fact that they earn more than I do. Architecture almost always has been a profession that only the socially elite and wealthy could afford to embark on,[3] leading to an ingrained assumption by those outwith the profession that it must therefore be well remunerated. A small, elite band of architects are, but the majority are not. Instead architects earn average salaries,[4] and much less than other professionals who undertake similar lengths of study and hurdle over similar barriers of entry.

ARCHITECT AS HOME RENOVATOR

"Justin and Charlotte are converting this dilapidated Second World War air control tower into a stunning tranquil hideaway … Are they? Very good …"

Former control tower at RAF Fearn, Scottish Highlands, United Kingdom. Photographer: Peter Moore.

The most pointless stereotype is 'all architect's wear black'. There is enough pseudo-intellectual waffle on this subject – some suggesting that we wear black because we are in mourning for the life we once had,[5] too busy making decisions all day to decide what colour to wear, because we lack imagination, or even because we have something priestly about us.[6] Architects wear black as much as anyone else – who cares anyway?!

Another is the architect as misunderstood artist. This view is embedded in historical reality. Like Le Corbusier's design struggles at the Carpenter Center for the Visual Arts at Harvard University, prompting collaborator Josep Lluís Sert to note "he is an unusual man ... but so was Michelangelo".[7] This view of the architect is as outdated as it is unattainable for most architects subsumed in the collaborative team environment that architecture demands. Most architects cannot afford to be misinterpreted; finding nimbler, more pliant means to be understood.

Closely related to this outdated cliché is that architects are out of touch with popular aesthetic tastes. Since at least Vitruvius,[8] architects have railed against popular taste but if we only mirrored them, would anything of real ambition ever be built? Sir Christopher Wren's now much-loved St Paul's Cathedral was denigrated in its day by the general public.[9] Much of what endures beyond any moment in time in any creative endeavour – art, music, literature – once shocked and appalled contemporary public taste. The stereotype is neither unique to architects nor helpful to the evolution of creative thought.

ARCHITECTS DON'T ALL WEAR BLACK

The Architect Hans Heinz Luttgen and his Wife Dora. 1926.

Photographer: August Sander.

"AN UNUSUAL MAN"

Le Corbusier at Chandigarh, India. 1955.

Photographer: Lucien Hervé.

ONCE DESPISED BY "UNBELIEVERS"

St Paul's Cathedral. London, United Kingdom. 1715. Sir Christopher Wren.

From The New York Public Library.

Finally, there is our perceived arrogance. Architects are characterised as egotistical, only concerned with pushing their own principles on an unwitting and unwilling client or public. This cliché is not helped by architect Louis Sullivan who, when asked by a client to design a colonial house, replied "Madam, you will take what we give you".[10] Nor is it helped by claims that architecture is about the "ordering of social processes"[11] and that one particular architect's adopted style is the only relevant way to achieve it. This is not representative of the profession as a totality. There are as many egoists in architecture as there are pragmatists, romanticists, and humanitarians. And as many egoists in other professions where a degree of power and influence can be gained – Politics, Law, and Finance to name a few. Many more architects listen to the needs of others, engaging in collaborative dialogue with humility and objectivity.

Not all stereotypes of our profession rest on shaky ground. Some are true.

Owing to our long working hours[12] and the belief that our life and work are inseparable,[13] we tend to mix largely with other architects. This creates the impression of an insular, protective profession. There is truth in this impression. Architects at present are in danger of communicating only commensally. Often, we remain ambivalent to and un-sustained by outside influences, only giving time to architecture, trading in empty learned rhetoric passed down by other architects in a closed and self-serving manner. Yet to engage with the communities within which we are involved and improve the value of what we create, a more symbiotic relationship with the rest of society is vital.

FOR AESTHETICS AND EXPERIENCE. NOT PRACTICALITY.

Exposed lifts. The Lloyd's building. London, United Kingdom. 1986.
Rogers Stirk Harbour + Partners.
Photographer: It's No Game.

Another view is of impractical dreamers, happy to waste clients' money on folly and experimentation. The world needs dreamers. Maybe now more than ever. However, many of the issues that arise in the post-occupancy phase of a building come from a failure to communicate the true meaning and value of these dreams, or to understand their practical implications. Many architects create convenient constructs to justify purely aesthetic or experiential goals in falsely practical terms. Like Richard Rogers' Lloyds building whose lifts were apparently located on the outside of the building to make them easy to replace.[14] Yet, the building has a maintenance bill double that of neighbouring properties largely because the "lift cradles carrying the cleaners, bang against the cladding, leaving dents".[15] The placement of the lifts was always an aesthetic and experiential move, its perceived practicality used as a convenient construct not discovered until too late.

Most importantly, is the professions' racial and social uniformity and inherent gender imbalances. Architecture is a "professional microcosm"[16] where professional socialisation irons out many of the idiosyncrasies that embody the diversity of the human condition. This begins and ends with barriers of entry. From increasing tuition fees and course expenses,[17] to post-study exams and interviews to gain professional registration or licensure. My own experience of this interview was surreal and humiliating, three ageing men in suits silently assessing whether my character was worthy of entry. In an empty hotel room – a neatly folded bed occupying the background.

The act of "getting in and getting on"[18] in the profession is made more difficult for those already marginalised by society as a whole: women, those of black and ethnic minorities, and the working class. The stereotype of architecture as a predominately male, white, and privileged profession, is backed up by the figures.[19] Being the first two, I will not begin to postulate on the experiences of the people who remain marginalised in the profession. All I can relate is my observations of this issue in practice.

Only four of my fellow students in the first year of architecture school were of black and ethnic minority origin, a 4% representation in a city with an overall proportion of 12%.[20] Worse, I can count on one hand the number of black and ethnic minority architectural colleagues, out of a total of around two hundred, I have worked with in the past 15 years in practice. That both the RIBA and AIA have mobilised specific task forces to address these systemic issues is encouraging but will not be enough unless fundamental societal change occurs simultaneously.

I have overheard my superiors ruefully discuss a female colleague who "could have been a director ... if she hadn't decided to go and have babies". I corrected a contractor who mistakenly assumed I was the qualified architect and the brilliant project architect whom I was shadowing, and ten years my senior, was an assistant. Work–life balance and lack of recognition are the primary reasons women architects in the US become disillusioned with the profession.[21]

Less than half of the eight architectural practices where I have worked were fully accessible to those with impairments to their physical mobility – a historically under-represented group in architecture.[22] In a profession which caters for this issue every day through its work, this seems like hypocrisy.

I have often had to alter my regional, working class accent to be heard, or not dismissed, in a profession dominated by those of higher social standing. Only 10% of architects in the UK come from working class backgrounds.[23]

Addressing these anecdotal imbalances, backed up by figures, begins with addressing the primary barrier to entry – tuition fees. With their continual rise (doubling in the UK since 1999, and at $30,000 a year in the US) the architectural profession could well become even less represented by marginalised communities unable to afford the exorbitant admission fees.

Secondly with education. We were only taught a Western, male, and privileged version of architectural history. Learning nothing of the rich architectural heritage of west and east Africa or of the incredible stone and earth dwellings of the Ancestral Puebloans established long before the European invasion of North America. We remained oblivious to the immeasurable influence that women had in the development of Modern Architecture – from the private houses of Eileen Grey to the poetic functionalism of Lina Bo Bardi. We focused only on grand architectural expressions of power and wealth – temples, churches, opera houses – and never on the majority, everyday architecture inhabited by most of the population. I only learned about these aspects of our diverse and rich collective architectural history outwith formal education. This selective history is corroborated widely. That many involved in academia for decades are only recognising this issue now[24] is not good enough. Bernard Rudofsky[25] and Joseph Esherick[26] warned the profession over half a century ago. To paraphrase author and activist Akala, architectural education should not be a place which reproduces social, societal norms but instead a place to

IT BEGAN IN AFRICA

The Great Mosque of Djenné. Djenné, Mali. c.1200–1907. Photographer: Jurgen.

POETIC FUNCTIONALISM

SESC Pompéia. São Paulo, Brazil. 1982. Lina Bo Bardi.
Photographer: Paulisson Miura.

AN ASSET FOR ALL

Parc National du Mali. Bamako, Mali. 2010. Kéré Architecture.
Photographer: Francis Kéré.

encourage those previously marginalised in its stories to become active participants in its future.[27]

The architectural profession does not currently reflect society in its diverse totality. Nor do we all fully engage outwith our professional domain, to help enrich it. Nor do we all have the capacity to translate our dreams into believable, supportable aims. Architecture gains its ultimate value from its use in public. How can architecture hope to reflect and communicate the needs and desires of society when it is a domain only occupied by a privileged section of it? If the realm of the architect is as expansive as that of human life itself, we must too have the diversity and ability to communicate with all sections of it.

Notes

1 Monbiot, G., 2013. *Materialism: a system that eats us from the inside out.* [Online] Available at: https://www.theguardian.com/commentisfree/2013/dec/09/materialism-system-eats-us-from-inside-out [Accessed 11 June 2020].

2 Architects' Council of Europe, 2018. *The Architectural Profession in Europe 2018,* Brussels: Architects' Council of Europe.

3 Kostof, S., 1977. The Practice of Architecture in the Ancient World: Egypt and Greece. *The Architect: Chapters in the History of the Profession.* New York: Oxford University Press. p. 21.

4 Office for National Statistics, 2019. *Employee earnings in the UK: 2019.* [Online] Available at: https://www.ons.gov.uk/employmentandlabourmarket/peopleinwork/earningsandworkinghours/bulletins/annualsurveyofhoursandearnings/2019 [Accessed 4 May 2020].

5 Wainwright, O., 2019. *"It's in complete crisis" – architects form trade union amid fury and despair over exploitation.* [Online] Available at: https://www.theguardian.com/artanddesign/2019/oct/30/architects-form-trade-union-uvw-saw [Accessed 3 May 2020].

6 Rau, C., 2017. *Why Do Architects Wear Black?.* 2nd ed. Basel: Birkhauser. [Online]

7 Corbusier, L., Zaknic, I., & Staff, L.C., 1997. *Mise Au Point*. New Haven, CT: Yale University Press. p. 31.
8 Vitruvius, 1960. *The Ten Books on Architecture*. New York: Dover Publications. p. 211.
9 Campbell, J., 2007. *Building St. Paul's*. London: Thames and Hudson. p. 21.
10 Lloyd Wright, F., 1931. *Two Lectures on Architecture*. Chicago: The Art Institute of Chicago. pp. 40–41.
11 Schumacher, P., 2012. *Parametric Order—21st Century Architectural Order*. Cambridge, MA: Harvard Graduate School of Design.
12 Wainwright, *"It's in complete crisis"* [Online]
13 Judkins, R., 2015. *The Art of Creative Thinking*. London: Sceptre. p. 208.
14 Shepheard, P., 1994. *What Is Architecture?*. Cambridge, MA: MIT Press. p. 3.
15 Thompson, J., 1993. *Lloyd's counts cost of keeping "The Espresso Machine" sweet: Jay Thompson on more dents in a battered institution*. [Online] Available at: https://www.independent.co.uk/news/uk/lloyds-counts-cost-of-keeping-the-espresso-machine-sweet-jay-thompson-on-more-dents-in-a-battered-1489999.html [Accessed 12 June 2020].
16 Cuff, D., 1991. *Architecture: The Story of Practice*. Cambridge, MA: The MIT Press. p. 157.
17 Jolliffe, E., 2018. *The hidden costs of studying architecture are causing profound suffering*. [Online] Available at: https://www.bdonline.co.uk/opinion/the-hidden-costs-of-studying-architecture-are-causing-profound-suffering/5094592.article [Accessed 11 June 2020].
18 Brook, O., O'Brien, D., & Taylor, M., 2018. *Panic! Social Class, Taste and Inequalities in the Creative Industries*. London: Arts and Humanities Research Council. p. 7.
19 The Royal Institute of British Architects, 2019. *Equality, Diversity and Inclusion (EDI) Strategy: Creating Opportunity and Enabling Success*. London: RIBA.
20 Office for National Statistics, 2011. *2011 Census: Ethnic group, local authorities in the United Kingdom*, London: UK Government.
21 American Institute of Architects, 2015. *Diversity in the Profession of Architecture: Key Findings*, Washington, DC: AIA. p. 10.

22 Williamson, B., 2019. "It's time to take off the blindfold". *Icon Magazine*. June #192, pp. 26–36.

23 Brook et al., *Panic!*, p. 11.

24 Betsky, A., 2020. *The opening of our architectural history.* [Online] Available at: https://www.architectmagazine.com/practice/the-opening-of-our-architectural-history_o [Accessed 12 April 2020].

25 Rudofsky, B., 1964. *Architecture without Architects: A Short Introduction to Non-pedigreed Architecture.* New York: Doubleday. p. 1.

26 Esherick, J., 1977. Architectural Education in the Thirties and Seventies: A Personal View. In: S. Kostof, ed. *The Architect: Chapters in the History of the Profession.* New York: Oxford University Press, p. 257.

27 Akala, 2018. *Natives: Race and Class in the Ruins of Empire.* London: Two Roads. p. 74.

4.0 ANTICIPATING THE REALITY

I see, Prometheus, and I wish to give thee
My best advice, all subtle though thou be.
Know thou thyself …
(Aeschylus, *Prometheus Bound*)[1]

WE HAVE EXPLORED THE question of what it means to be an architect in practice.

↓

Grappled with the shock of the transition from architecture school to practice. Addressed the multiple factors that impact the purity and integrity of design. Discussed how best to communicate the opportunities and possibilities of architectural thought into architectural action. We heard too from across the profession. From solo practitioners to multinational offices; from Mexico City to Tokyo. Each interviewee portraying a unique approach to the practice of architecture – their priorities, methods, and strategies. Portrayed too, was a clear echo of my own frustrations between the anticipation of the profession and the reality of it.

It is clear a more synergetic relationship must be found between practice and theory if the profession is to realise its full potential. Architecture schools need to equip students for the challenges design faces in practice; just as practice needs to defend the universal principles and Humanist values inculcated in architecture school.

If good architecture is a projection of life itself,[2] architecture schools could bring more of 'life itself' into the design studio. Engage more with the societal, circumstantial, and technical issues architects face in practice to limit the disconnection identified by Fernanda Canales between architecture school and "the actual needs of cities and citizens". Incremental introduction of these issues (site constraints, budgets, time pressures) would allow students to develop an armature of strategies to cater for 'actual needs' in tandem with their own personal development. Could typically lecture-based professional studies courses in architecture school become more embedded in the design studio, with increasing complexity through the years? Could students be involved in more live community-based projects?

Further, demonstrated by the work of Assemble, students could engage more with the people who will make what they design. Not to serve the building industry, but instead to engage with and subvert it. To combat the inevitable dilettantism that afflicts every young architect, disconnected from making things and thrust on to a building site in practice surrounded by those who do, and improve the quality of what is created.

UNDERSTANDING THE NEEDS OF CITIES AND CITIZENS

Angdong Hospital Project. Hunan Province, China. 2011.
Rural Urban Framework.

MAKING THINGS

Tangassi Funeral House. San Luis Potosí, Mexico. 2012.
Tatiana Bilbao ESTUDIO.

Paradoxically, there is a need to expand our frames of reference. Studying buildings is not enough if we wish to play a more meaningful role in society. A deeper understanding is required of politics, sociology, philosophy, as well as the emotive power of music, literature, and art – and not always filtered through an architectural lens. Armed with greater practical powers and wider knowledge, we can fulfil the potential of our role as coordinators. To shift our focus to collaborative engagement. As Kengo Kuma notes, "Architectural design is teamwork". Learning to effectively communicate and collaborate with others will prepare students for this inevitability.

Architecture practice needs to change. This begins with employing staff to the best of their abilities, not simply to the practice's best economic advantage. Why hire talented young graduates to use them only as tools to get the work done? Good practices develop a "culture and an energy"[3] where a shared understanding of the decision-making process filters through the entire team, enabling the need for agency that every designer has and a greater depth in how the complexities and opportunities inherent in any project are understood and developed. Inquisitive, engaged minds aid and amplify the process.

Practices must allow more space for experimentation and reflection. This is not always easy in the rush and reality of practice; however, if not encouraged it will only breed repetition, sterility, and disengage talented young staff more used to the experimentation and reflection of architecture school. As Spela Videcnik of OFIS notes, a practice should "always try to explore something in each project".

EXPERIMENTATION IN PRACTICE

Guggenheim Helsinki. 2014–2015. Moreau Kusunoki.

Practice also has an obligation to develop you as a professional. This means encouraging the development of your skill set, beyond its current confines, as well as your mindset. Providing a supportive framework of continued education, guaranteed incremental responsibility, allowing agency, and providing mentors.

Finally, the primary reason talented people leave the profession is their pay and conditions. This requires action from across the profession, not least our professional bodies. If change is not forthcoming – form new ones. Change has been promised for at least 50 years![4] Like Assemble's Jane Hall says, "start from scratch". To fulfil your demanding role, you need to be freed from the strains and stresses that long hours, stunted career development, and relatively low pay can bring.

There are fundamental changes on the horizon. The democratisation of algorithmic design could dissociate the architect from the design process altogether, "clients able to tell an app what kind of building they want, describe the budget, location, size and other preferences and get a range of options in seconds …".[5] The increased use of virtual reality technology, more immersive than any graphic aid, creates walkable worlds unencumbered from the usual artistic licences architects often indulge in. Even the instructive role of the architectural drawing could disappear with the development of augmented reality headsets for construction workers which project holographic data via CAD renderings and laser projections onto the building site at a 1:1 scale, allowing contractors to accurately install walls and level floors, bypassing the need for cumbersome, perishable blueprints.[6]

It is vital we participate in these emerging technologies. However, two means of architectural communication will never die – the sketch and speech. Sketching is pictorial speech. It shares its ambiguity and brevity. Everything else takes time. In speaking and sketching instant dialogues emerge. A sketch opens lines of communication, inviting interaction just as words do. I see this assisting a student in unlocking a design problem; explaining a design concept to a client; or resolving complex technical challenges on-site with contractors. Sketching, like speech, is a direct manifestation of thought. Whatever means of architectural design or communication emerge or are extinguished, the core role of the architect will remain – in sketch and speech – to communicate future conditions. It is within these two means of communication that our core value as architects lies: to connect.

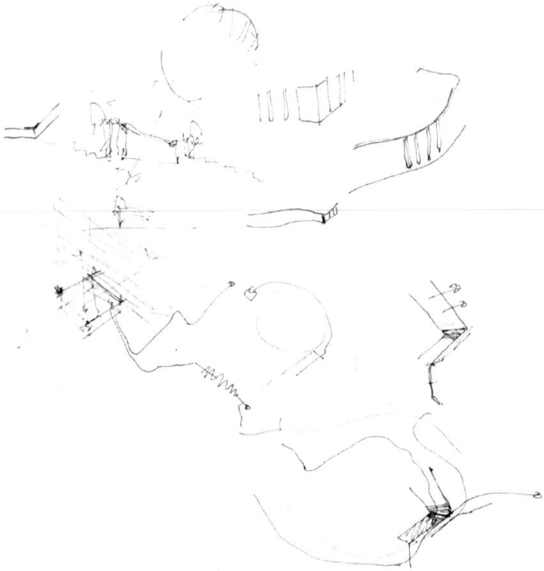

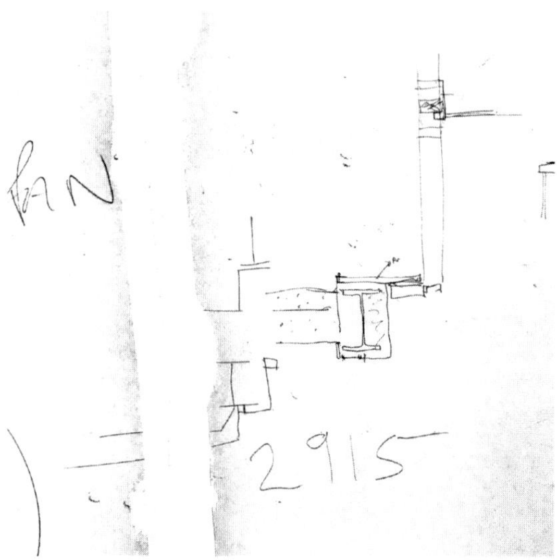

SKETCHING AS COMMUNICATION

© MOREAU KUSUNOKI

COMMUNICATING FUTURE CONDITIONS

Powerhouse Parramatta. Sydney, Australia. 2019. Moreau Kusunoki.

Only connect! ... Only connect the prose and the passion, and both will be exalted ...
(E.M. Forster, *Howards End*)

Architecture depends on the connection between what we create and how we create it, as much as it does on how we connect with the needs of society on "common ground".[7] Architects are collaborators by necessity. Through what we create – its site responsiveness, contextuality, layout, soundness of construction – we can connect with the immediate needs of others. Then using this as a platform to connect with their emotional needs through the provision of space, form, detail, materiality, and a considered connection with nature – sun, rain, wind, snow – to create an architecture which "reaches the soul".[8] To fuse the pragmatic dimension of architecture dominant in practice with the poetic dimension dominant in architecture school. This is the dual value of the architect.

This dual connective value must be harnessed with alacrity, if we are to respond to the key challenges that will define our future: climate change and the destruction of nature, inequality, and pandemics. Despite the many challenges it faces, the profession you are entering retains the unique ability to furnish and nourish human existence. To connect the experiences of those of the past to those of the future. This is not a role we can allow to diminish or vanish. The tapestry of the human condition would be missing a vital thread. It is now up to you and those around you to realise the full potential of your profession.

ONLY CONNECT!

MK Gallery. Milton Keynes, United Kingdom. 2019. 6a Architects.

ONLY CONNECT!

La Maison du Savoir. Esch-sur-Alzette, Luxembourg. 2015.
Baumschlager Eberle Architekten + Christian Bauer & Associés.
Photographer: Eduard Hueber.

ONLY CONNECT!

"Architects imagine new possibilities. How we communicate that is the most valuable skill we have. There's an opportunity for architects to synthesise new possibilities and make them tangible. To communicate them so people can see what a potential future could be. That is the strength of the profession – it is where its value lies. As long as you understand the needs of others, then with your own sense of agency you can bring new kinds of possibilities. New ways that we can shape how the built environment evolves." John Choi, CHROFI[9]

Lune de Sang Pavilion. Northern Rivers, Australia. 2011–2018. CHROFI.

Notes

1 Aeschylus. *Prometheus Bound*, translated by E.H. Plumptre. Vol. VIII, Part 4. The Harvard Classics. New York: P.F. Collier & Son, 1909–14, line 344.
2 Gropius, W., 1937. Architecture at Harvard University. *Architectural Record*, May, p. 11.
3 Choi, J., 2020. *Interview with J. Tait* [Interview] (17 June 2020).
4 Pearman, H., 2020. *Fantasy future – a New Year wish for architecture.* [Online] Available at: https://www.ribaj.com/culture/hugh-pearman-dreams-of-a-better-future-for-architecture [Accessed 1 July 2020].
5 Fairs, M., 2019. *Rise of artificial intelligence means architects are "doomed" says Sebastian Errazuriz.* [Online] Available at: https://www.dezeen.com/2019/10/22/artificial-intelligence-ai-architects-jobs-sebastian-errazuriz/ [Accessed 1 May 2020].
6 Bucknell, A., 2019. Real to Real. *Icon Magazine*, 190 (April), pp. 90–96.
7 Sennett, R., 2009. *The Craftsman.* London: Penguin Books. p. 269.
8 Märkli, P., 2018. *My Profession, The Art of Building.* Cambridge, MA: Harvard Graduate Design School.
9 Choi, J., *Interview with J. Tait.*

Index

Page locators in italic refer to captions.

U

V

W

Y

Z